peripateticus no ut ph, pe
cxxiiij.

Marsilius ficinus Lauretio medici · V· magnanimo·

Oliuerium ardouinum, insigne peripateticum comendare
t̃ no mediocrit̃, ñ aristoteles suus eu t̃ plurimu
comendaret·. Si aristoteles q pecunia felicitaté
necessariam iudicauit, libros suos absq̃ nu̅mis
coponere potuisset, & aristotelicus iste aristo
telica sine nu̅mis posset i̅nterpretari· Intelli
gis g̃ o q̃d uelit· Oliuerius peripateticus e̅, no
cynicus· At no e̅ i̅gres ph̃i hec appetere·
Sit ita sane· Verũ no ut ph̃s e̅, hec postu
lat, sz ut homo· Vtrum u ph̃s sit, pecunia petere, postq̃, cofesseris disputabimus· Vale
Salutat te Laurẽtius boni cotrus minimeselsis,
poeta astronomicus, astronomusq̃ poeticus·:

neq̃ amor sine religoe, neq̃ religio sine amore lau

Marsilius ficinus philippo cotronio lucensi· Mitto
ad te amorẽ quẽ pmisera· Mitto & religonem·
vt agnoscas, & amore meu religosu̅ esse,
& religone amatoria· Sane ita u̅a coparā
tu est, ut neq̃ amor honestus sit, ñ religio
suus· neq̃ religio uera ñ amore suscepta·
Salutat te Angelus manettus, Jã̅nnocij oratoris
filius, paterne uirtutis heres ·:

THE LETTERS OF MARSILIO FICINO

Volume 4

(Liber V)

Cosimo de' Medici, attributed to Verrocchio, Palazzo Medici-Riccardi, Florence (Photo: Fratelli Alinari, Florence). According to Ficino, Cosimo was 'the father of my soul'.

The Letters of
MARSILIO FICINO

Translated from the Latin by members of the Language
Department of the School of Economic Science, London

VOLUME 4

being a translation of
Liber V

SHEPHEARD-WALWYN

© 1988 Fellowship of the School of Economic Science, London
All rights reserved
This translation first published 1988 by
Shepheard-Walwyn (Publishers) Ltd
26 Charing Cross Road (Suite 34)
London WC2 0DH

ISBN 0 85683 070 4

Publisher's Note:

The beehive motif shown on the title page and also on
the book-jacket appears on a number of Ficino manuscripts
which were illuminated for Lorenzo de' Medici's library.
For a possible explanation see Letter 15.
The endpapers show two pages in Ficino's own hand
from a manuscript containing Book 1 of his *Letters*. This
is now in the Biblioteca Nazionale Centrale, Florence
(Cod. Naz. II IX 2).

British Library Cataloguing in Publication Data

Ficino, Marsilio
[Epistolae, *English*]. The letters of
Marsilio Ficino.
Vol.4
1. Ficino, Marsilio
I. Title   II. The Letters of Marsilio
Ficino
195   B785.F4

ISBN 0-85683-070-4

Typeset by Photo·graphics, Honiton, Devon
Printed in Great Britain by
St Edmundsbury Press, Suffolk

Contents

	Page
Acknowledgements	vi
Letter Titles	vii
List of Illustrations	xii
Introduction	xiii
Translators' Note	xix
The Letters	I
Appendix Letters	68
The Pazzi Conspiracy and Ficino	73
Notes on the Letters	93
Notes on the Latin Text	113
Notes on Ficino's Correspondents	161
Bibliography	172
Index	176

Acknowledgements

THE translators wish to acknowledge the help of Dr. Sebastiano Gentile who has given valuable advice on difficult and deleted passages in the manuscripts, especially the main manuscript Magl. VIII 1441 (M9). He also very kindly supplied a copy of the Sarzana manuscript (Cod. XXVI). They similarly wish to acknowledge the generosity of the Principessa Bona Borromeo-Arese, who allowed them to make use of the Archivio Borromeo, and of Dr. Pier Giacomo Pisoni who carefully assisted them in their research at the Archive. The translators also thank Sir Harold Acton for resolving points of difficulty in Letter 33. They are indebted to Dr. Antonietta Morandini of the Laurenziana Library in Florence for her advice and help in the supply of copies of manuscripts, including the colour photograph used on the front cover.

The following have also kindly supplied copies of their manuscripts: the Riccardiana and Nazionale Centrale libraries in Florence; Wolfenbüttel, Landesbibliothek; Berlin, Staatsbibliothek Preussischer Kulturbesitz.

Other libraries which have assisted the translators by allowing them to study the manuscripts in their libraries are the Biblioteca Communale Ariostea, Ferrara; the Bodleian Library, Oxford; the Biblioteca Nazionale Marciana, Venice; the Universiteitsbibliotheek, Leiden.

The translators are extremely grateful to Phaidon Press of Oxford for their generous help with the illustrations.

Letter Titles

1 Legis divinae fides scientia confirmatur
   Faith in divine law is confirmed by knowledge

2 Nihil potest esse proprium ubi communis est animus
   Nothing can be called personal where there is one common soul

3 Breviter loquendum: sed non breviter vel cogitandum vel
   amandum
   Let us be brief in speech, but not in deliberation or loving

4 Sacerdotes et philosophi pie loquantur et sentiant
   Priests and philosophers should speak and think rightly

5 Nullum in malis refugium est nisi ad summum bonum
   *In the midst of evils there is no refuge, unless it be with the highest
   good*

6 Non creavit ad parva quaedam deus homines, sed ad magna
   It was not for small things but for great that God created men

7 Nullus incontinens potest sapiens esse
   No one who lacks self-restraint can be wise

8 Philosophi saepe dum discunt curiosius disputare, interim consultare dediscunt
   *While philosophers learn to argue intricate points, they often forget to
   ask for advice*

9 Solitudo philosophis non remissio mentis sed intentio esse solet et debet
To philosophers solitude should be, and usually is, not a relaxation but an application of the mind

10 Profanis sapientia non conceditur
Wisdom is not granted to the ungodly

11 Omne tulit punctum, qui miscuit utile dulci
He who has blended the serious with the pleasing has satisfied everyone

12 Nullum commodius in malis remedium quam patientia
There is no remedy for evils more fitting than patience

13 Solum minervae templum contra fortunae procellas homines protegit
The temple of Minerva alone protects men against the storms of fortune

14 Amicitia vera externis non eget officiis
True friendship needs no outer formalities

15 Qui musis abutuntur, non mel, sed fel ab earum fonte reportant
They who abuse the Muses bring back from their fountain not honey but gall

16 Nunquam adversa revera patimur, nisi cum patimur et perverse
We never really suffer adversity, except when we suffer it perversely

17 Amicitia perfecta verbis litterisque non indiget
Perfect friendship does not need words or letters

18 Merito invitus omni caret bono, qui sponte caret deo, qui est omne bonum
He who by his own will cuts himself off from God, who is all good, inevitably cuts himself off, even against his will, from every good

19 Cum deus sit ipse amor, quicunque absque deo aliquid studet amare, hic absque amore temptat amare

*Since God is Himself love, whoever tries to love anything without
God tries to love without love*

20 Solus feliciter dominatur, qui volentibus dominatur
Only he rules happily who rules men willing to be ruled

21 Egregios grex improbat, deus probat, apud quem solum gratitudo
est et libertas
*The crowd disapproves of outstanding men, but God approves them;
in Him alone are bounty and freedom*

22 Quod philosophia non docet, imo vetat cum principibus vivere
Philosophy does not teach us to live with princes; indeed she forbids it

23 Solus in amando laudandoque nunquam fallitur, cui amandi
laudandique lex deus est
*In loving and praising, he alone is never mistaken whose law for love
and praise is God*

24 Fides gignit spem, spes charitatem, charitatis ardor affert
intelligentiae claritatem
*Faith gives birth to hope; hope gives birth to love. The flame of love
brings clarity of intellect*

25 Amore humano nihil infirmius. Divino nihil firmius
Nothing is frailer than human love, nothing stronger than divine love

26 Nemo vere servit, nisi qui servit volens. Nemo dominatur vere,
nisi qui volentibus dominatur
*No one serves truly who does not serve willingly; no one is truly
master except he be master of the willing*

27 Veritas de institutione principis ad Raphaelem riarium cardinalem
Truth addresses Cardinal Riario on the education of a ruler

28 Tunc solum viro dignitatem nacto congratulari debemus, cum
dignitate dignus apparet
*We should congratulate a man on attaining high office only if he seems
to be worthy of that office*

29 Veritas virum reddit, dignitate dignum
Truth makes a man worthy of office

30 Omne tulit punctum, qui miscuit utile dulci
He who has blended the serious with the pleasing has satisfied everyone

31 Malo meis litteris mente responderi, quam manu
I prefer my letters to be answered by mind rather than by hand

32 Maiorem charitatem nemo habet, quam ut animam suam ponat
quis pro amicis suis
*Greater love hath no man than this, that a man lay down his life for
his friends*

33 Felix est, qui habet omnia quae vult. Habet autem omnia quae
vult, qui omnia vult, quae habet
*Happy is the man who has all he desires; only he has all he desires
who desires all he has*

34 Prosperis perversius utimur, quam adversis
Our use of prosperity is even more perverse than our use of adversity

35 Nunquam deest amantibus scribendi materia
Lovers are never at a loss for something to write

36 Praestat dare superflua quam debita denegare
*It is better to give things which are superfluous than to refuse what is
owed*

37 Gratia naturalis plus persuadet quam acquisita eloquentia.
Humanitas plures vincit quam violentia
*Natural grace is more persuasive than acquired eloquence; love of
mankind conquers more men than force*

38 Excusatio de libro astronomiae serius reddito
Excusing the rather late return of a book on Astronomy

39 Excusatio diuturni silentii
An apology for a long silence

40 Patientia sine religione habere non potest
One cannot have patience without religion

41 Sola malorum medicina est patientia
Patience is the sole remedy for evils

42 Nihil magis vel necessarium vel voluntarium est quam amor
Nothing is more of a necessity, yet nothing is more freely willed than love

43 Excusatio ubi serius respondemus
An excuse for a late reply

44 Non ex humanis divina, sed ex divinis humana sunt iudicanda
The divine is not to be judged by human standards, but the human by divine

45 Non cortex nutrit, sed medulla
It is not the outer covering which nourishes, but what lies within

46 Prospera in fato fortuna. Vera in virtute felicitas
Good fortune is in fate; true happiness in virtue

47 Caelum pollicetur bona. Virtus praestat
Heaven promises good things, but virtue presents them

48 De salute philosophorum ante christi adventum
Concerning the salvation of Philosophers before the coming of Christ

49 Exhortatio ad respondendum
A plea for an answer

50 Felix est, qui vere gaudet. Solus gaudet vere, qui sola veritate gaudet
He is happy who is truly joyful; he alone is truly joyful who rejoices in truth alone

51 Pictura pulchri corporis et pulchrae mentis
A picture of a beautiful body and a beautiful mind

List of Illustrations

Frontispiece

Cosimo de' Medici, attributed to Verrocchio.

Between pages xvi and xvii

1. Portrait of four humanists, a detail from the fresco *Zacharias in the Temple* by Domenico Ghirlandaio.

2. Medallion portrait of Lorenzo di Pierfrancesco by Niccolò Fiorentino, c. 1480–1485.

3. Venus, from the *Primavera* by Botticelli.

Between pages 24 and 25

4. Bust of Lorenzo de' Medici by Verrocchio.

5. View of Florence, c. 1480.

6. Medal commemorating the Pazzi conspiracy, by Bertoldo di Giovanni.

Between pages 56 and 57 .

7. *The Resurrection* by Verrocchio.

8. *Pope Sixtus IV and his Court* by Melozzo da Forlì.

Between pages 88 and 89

9. Portrait of Giuliano de' Medici by Botticelli.

10. Portrait of Lorenzo de' Medici with three members of the Sassetti family, by Domenico Ghirlandaio.

Introduction

MARSILIO FICINO (1433–99) directed the Platonic Academy in Florence and it was the work of this Academy that gave the Renaissance in the 15th century its impulse and direction. Ficino, who was the son of Cosimo de' Medici's doctor, says that when he was still young[1] he was selected by Cosimo for an education in the humanities rather than medicine and was later directed by Cosimo first to learn Greek, and then translate all Plato's dialogues into Latin, which had never previously been done. This enormous task of translation he accomplished, according to his early biographer Corsi, in the astonishingly short period of five years.[2] He then wrote two important books, *The Platonic Theology* and *The Christian Religion*, showing how the Christian religion and Platonic philosophy were proclaiming the same message to humanity. As he put it in Letter 123 of Volume I to Bernardo Bembo, 'Lawful philosophy is no different from true religion and lawful religion exactly the same as true philosophy.' Later he wrote commentaries on the works of Plato, translations and commentaries on the works of the neo-platonic philosophers and *The Book of Life* (concerning health).

The extraordinary influence the Platonic Academy came to exercise over the age (which is discussed briefly in the introduction to Volume I) arose from the fact that its leading spirits were already seeking fresh inspiration from the ideals of the civilizations of Greece and Rome and especially from the literary and philosophic sources of those ideals.

Thus it was in Florence, already the cultural and artistic centre of Europe, that the leading men in so many different fields were drawn to the Academy: Lorenzo de' Medici (Florence's ruler), Alberti (the architect), Poliziano (the poet), Landino (the historian and poet) to name only a few.[3] Furthermore, Ficino bound together an enormous circle of correspondents throughout Italy and in Europe as a whole; from the Pope in Rome to John Colet in London, from Reuchlin in Germany to de Ganay in France. (The last was Chancellor of the Parlement in Paris).

Ficino's correspondence is extraordinary because the same letters combine the most sublime teaching for mankind with eminently practical advice for individuals. Nowhere is this more clear than in the present volume, which covers the period September, 1477 to April, 1478, months which gave rise to tragic events for the whole of Florence and in particular for a number of leading citizens who were also Ficino's correspondents. These events were the outcome of the Pazzi Conspiracy (discussed on pp. 73–91) in which Giuliano de' Medici was assassinated in Florence Cathedral, and from which his brother Lorenzo only just escaped. Immediately afterwards a large number of the Pazzi dependants, some quite innocent, were brutally executed or murdered. The real causes of this event were selfishness, greed and materialism in those places from where spiritual leadership should have come. It was symptomatic that those most involved in the conspiracy included a pope, a cardinal, an archbishop and two priests. A further cause was the breakdown of the respect for law and tradition and an absence of restraint: features usually found in times of gross materialism.

It was therefore to reawaken spirituality and, with that, respect for both divine and human law, that was Ficino's work. To a generation which had become largely disillusioned with the leadership of the higher ranks of the church the teaching of Plato, with its emphasis on the divinity of the individual soul, was the ideal means.

The theme of this volume of letters is that the truth is the unity and that only by the acknowledgement of this truth can man be freed from misery. In a letter to Michaeli (18) Ficino writes: 'He who simply pursues the One itself, in that One soon attains everything.' In fact it is not even necessary to pursue that which is everywhere, as he reminds us in Letter 5: 'Then let us not be moved or distracted by many things, but let us remain in unity as much as we are able, since we find eternal unity and the one eternity, not through movement or multiplicity, but through being still and being one.' He reminds us again and again that when we love any individual good thing it is the One Good itself, namely God, which we really love in that thing. 'Without the love of that One we seem to love something,' he writes in Letter 19, 'but, since we try to love outside love itself, instead of loving we are bound to hate.'

Love seems to spring from these pages of Ficino's letters and it was by this love that he bound his academy and his correspondents to himself. The whole creation is a product of love and it is through love that creation returns to that One,[4] (which, as Ficino has explained, it has never really left). He refers to this in Letter 19 when he writes, 'Just as beauty follows the light of the good as its splendour, so the ardour of love follows the rays of beauty as the reflection (or return) of those rays.' The end of love is therefore union. Friends are thus united to each other through their love of God.[5] This union between Ficino and his friends is frequently referred to in these letters and such references should certainly not be thought of as a stylistic flourish. The love of one friend for another is 'poured in its entirety' into the other's 'very self'. After that the lover has nothing left to give, because he has long ago given himself, and with himself all that he has.[6]

Such love expands to love of humanity as a whole. Indeed it is the Latin form of this word (*humanitas*) which Ficino uses to mean 'the love of mankind'.[7] Our use of the word *humanities* simply to convey studies based on Latin and Greek and a *humanist* as one who is versed in these studies, shows a descent in the power and meaning of language. Ficino commends Bernardo Bembo more than any of his correspondents for his humanity and speaks of its enormous power. He says that if the Venetians really wanted to conquer distant or rebellious peoples, they would not send a Pompey or a Caesar but Bembo, since he would conquer more people more effectively with his humanity than they would with their arms. The Venetians may even have taken him at his word.[8] Love is the principal means by which Man may discover his own nature. Another aspect of the word *humanity* is that it is human beings alone who have this power. In Letter 6 he writes to Cavalcanti words which seem to express the whole spirit of the Renaissance: 'Men are the only beings on earth to have rediscovered their infinite nature'.

Because the love of divine beauty could be kindled by beautiful sights and sounds,[9] Ficino regarded the creation of works of art and music as of great spiritual importance. In particular in Letters

46 and 51 he makes it clear that there is a precise correspondence between beauty in specific parts of the body and specific mental qualities. Such qualities could be inspired by the contemplation of their physical counterpart. The description of Venus in Ficino's letter to the young Lorenzo di Pierfrancesco de' Medici may have inspired Botticelli's Venus in the *Primavera* (See Letter 46 and notes). However that may be, the descriptions of beautiful physical beings in both Letters 46 and 51 are clearly given to inspire the appropriate qualities in Ficino's correspondents, who were intended to reflect on such forms. Ficino himself played the lyre to charm his listeners away from the concerns of the physical world. For instance, when members of his Academy were discussing in melancholy mood the Turkish threat to Europe, Ficino took up his lyre and by his playing dispelled their depression.[10]

The penalty for man is that if he does not set out to realise his 'infinite nature', his lot is far worse than that of beasts.[11] 'Why should we be surprised', he writes in Letter 18 to Michaeli, 'if all evils pursue us, when we ourselves, abandoning the first good, namely God, wrongly pursue individual things as good'. The first step is to stop pursuing the objects of sense as though they were good in themselves. In Letter 7 he speaks of 'the worried life of the man who serves the senses as though they were many mad masters.'

Above all, we should practise the virtue of *patientia*, which has been translated as *patience*. The word in Latin includes the meaning of sufferance, as well as suffering and is connected with the word *passion*, as in the passion of Christ. It also includes forbearance in the sense of forbearance to react in response to injury.[12] But Ficino means more than this. The wise man realises that his own will cannot in reason be different from God's, so he makes those things 'which fate has decreed to be inevitable . . . agreeable to his own will'.[13] The argument with which Ficino puts this advice forward in Letter 33 is a model of clarity and logic. The letter is addressed to Francesco Sassetti, the General Manager of the Medici bank, which as Lorenzo's rule continued became involved in increasing difficulties.

The first letter in the volume is a very strongly worded letter on the need to trust in divine law. As the main troubles that took place over the period when these letters were written arose from the setting aside of the law for reasons that may have seemed eminently

1. *Portrait of four humanists, a detail from the fresco 'Zacharias in the Temple'*
by Domenico Ghirlandaio, Santa Maria Novella, Florence (Photo: Fratelli
Alinari, Florence). From left to right the portraits are of Marsilio Ficino, the
scholar Cristoforo Landino and the poet Angelo Poliziano. The identity of the
fourth figure is not certain but may be Gentile Becchi, Bishop of Arezzo.

2. *Medallion portrait (37 mm. diam-*
eter) of Lorenzo di Pierfrancesco by
Niccolò Fiorentino, c. 1480–1485,
Florence (Photo: Phaidon Archive,
Oxford). Lorenzo di Pierfrancesco was
the cousin of Lorenzo the Magnificent,
and the recipient of Letter 46 which
describes the qualities of Venus, 'which
is human nature.'

3. Venus, from the 'Primavera' by Botticelli, Uffizi Gallery, Florence (Photo: Fratelli Alinari). 'Her eyes are majesty and magnanimity; her hands are liberality and greatness in action; her feet, gentleness and restraint ... her whole is harmony and integrity, honour and radiance.' Letter 46. The model for Venus is generally considered to be Simonetta Vespucci.

justifiable, this letter is very significant. The edition of the letters printed in Venice in 1495 adds the words 'most reverend' to the word 'friends' to whom the existing manuscripts have the letter addressed. If the letter was originally addressed to his 'most reverend' friends, these were probably Cardinal Raffaele Riario and Archbishop Francesco Salviati, who were involved in the Pazzi Conspiracy and for whom the letter would have been particularly appropriate.

Another quality on which Ficino lays particular emphasis in this volume is that of temperance. Ficino gives the Latin *temperantia* for the Greek word σωφροσύνη. Socrates in the *Republic*[14] says a state or man is temperate when that part of the soul 'which is better by nature has the worse under its control' and where there is no internal conflict between the ruling element and its subjects. *Temperantia* is perhaps best expressed in modern English by the word *restraint*. Ficino ends his letter to Sebastiano Foresi (11) with the application of this virtue to music when he writes: 'May the well-tempered lyre always be our salvation when we apply ourselves to it rightly.' More specifically he writes to the young Cardinal Riario (Letter 27), shortly to come so near to execution for implication in the Pazzi Conspiracy: 'Temper both the desires of the mind and all your actions lest, when all external things are in harmony for you, the mind alone be in discord.'

His warnings to Riario and Salviati are often sharp and specific, as though he could see the nature of the schemes that were fermenting in the minds of the conspirators (it is difficult to believe the accepted view that Riario was entirely innocent. See p. 86). Again, in Letter 27 Ficino urges Riario 'not to make a start on anything' unless he can see that 'the end is both good and well-assured.' His letter (34) to both Riario and Salviati is even more pointed. One must remember that they had both recently had strokes of good fortune. Riario had been appointed Cardinal in December, 1477 and the year before Salviati had been allowed to take up his position as Archbishop of Pisa, having been previously excluded for two years by Lorenzo de' Medici (see p. 76). Ficino writes to them, with numerous examples to prove his case: 'By some foolish, or rather unhappy, fate . . . most mortals make more perverse use of prosperity than adversity'. He then explains the reason: 'Let us remember that the nature of evil is to offer itself to us daily under the guise of good'. It is then 'very easily taken in . . . and given lodging as if it were the good; but soon after, it secretly strikes down its unwary host with a sword, as he deserves.'

In conclusion, these letters arouse our interest in a number of ways. They shed a new light on what was going on in Florence at this time, including for instance the relationship between the government of Lorenzo de' Medici and the Florentine clergy (see p. 100). They show how a non-political philosopher with no worldly ambitions yet found himself advising the two main factions struggling for political power in Florence. Finally, they show through Ficino the noble countenance of Plato, expanding men's view of their own nature, raising their ideals and aspirations and setting in the arts, literature, education and society as a whole new standards that were to last for many centuries.

NOTES

1 *Opera*, p. 1537.
2 *Letters*, **3**, G. Corsi, *The Life of Marsilio Ficino*, VI, p. 138.
3 Names of other members of the Academy are given in a letter, *Opera*, p. 936.
4 Ficino, *De Amore*, II, 2.
5 *Letters*, **3**, 32.
6 Letter 20 *et passim*.
7 *Letters*, **1**, 55.
8 Letter 37.
9 *Letters*, **1**, 7.
10 Della Torre, *Storia*, p. 807.
11 *Letters*, **1**, 83.
12 *Letters*, **1**, 49.
13 Letter 40.
14 Plato, *Republic*, IV, 430 and 441.

Translators' Note

THIS volume covers Ficino's fifth book of letters. Most of the letters fall within a period from September, 1477 to April, 1478, a period of a little over six months, but Ficino has included a number of later date. Some of these have been dated; for instance 44, 48 and 42, which were written in November 1478, February 1480 (new style) and November 1479 respectively.

Textual Sources

The following are the manuscripts which contain Book V of the letters, with the sigla of each as given in Kristeller's *Supplementum Ficinianum* I, v–lv:

Name of MS and shelf mark		Sigla	Contains Books	Library
Magl. VIII,	1441	M9	V & VI	Nazionale Centrale, Florence
Riccardianus	797	R10	I–VII	Riccardiana, Florence
Berolinensis	Lat. fol. 374	Be	I–VII	Berlin, Staatsbibliothek Preussischer Kulturbesitz
Guelferbytanus	73 Aug. fol.	G1	I–VIII	Wolfenbüttel, Herzog August
Laurentianus	90 Sup 43	L28	I–VIII	Laurenziana, Florence

Some individual letters are also contained in the manuscripts enumerated below, and for these Kristeller's *Supplementum* has again been consulted and also the Census of Manuscripts given in Appendix III of Kristeller, 'Marsilio Ficino and his work after five hundred years' in *Marsilio Ficino e il Ritorno di Platone, Studi e documenti*, ed. G. Garfagnini, Vol. I, p. 81 seq.:

Name of MS and shelf mark	Sigla	Contains Letter(s)	Library
Cod. XXVI F.175	S	1,3, 48	Biblioteca Communale, Sarzana
Lat. misc. d. 85	O3★	33	Bodleian, Oxford
Class II 162	F	5,9	Biblioteca Communale Ariostea, Ferrara
Magl. VII, 1135	M4	24	Biblioteca Nazionale Centrale, Florence
Incun. Magl. A7.8	M35	44	
Fondo Autografi F.10	Bo★	32	Archivio Borromeo, Isola Bella
Cod. Latinus Bibliothecae Publicae 160.a	Le	24	Universiteits-bibliotheek, Leiden.
Harleianus 5335	Lo4	27	British Library, London
Cod. XIII G 40	N3	42	Biblioteca Nazionale, Naples
Marc. Lat. XIV 266 (=4502)	Ve3	12,33, 40,41	Biblioteca Nazionale Marciana, Venice

★ See infra, p. xxii.

For Books V and VI there is extant a unique working copy-book, Magl. VIII, 1441 (M9), in which the handwriting of two scribes (as well as Ficino's own hand) has been established, and that of a third suggested. The names of the two scribes were Sebastiano Salvini and Luca Fabiani. M9 is a unique example of a working copy-book because it shows the manner in which both Ficino and his scribes worked on his letters, making subsequent additions and corrections. An example is Letter 27, which in its original form was a quarter to a third shorter than its final length; many of these additions are of a paragraph's length or more, added in the margin, and the majority of these amendments are in Ficino's hand.

In M9 there are letters, intact or in fragmentary form, which were crossed out, in some places so as to conceal the original words, before publication. Most of these letters were addressed to individuals who were implicated in the Pazzi conspiracy; they have survived in whole or in part because they were written on a page of M9 which had on the reverse letters intended for publication. These letters appear in the present volume as Appendix letters. However, other letters have been removed completely from the manuscript.

There are some letters in M9 where the names of some of the correspondents have been deleted in such a way as to render them almost illegible. These include three of those involved in the Pazzi conspiracy (Raffaele Riario, Salviati and Bracciolini), as well as the names of the Medici. In two letters the first name of the recipient, Francesco, has been retained but the second name, Salviati, has been deleted and 'the Cardinal of Siena' substituted.

Letter 21 is an example of a letter of which there are two versions. The original contained personal references to Ficino himself, but in the second version these references have been changed into the third person.

All these apparently political amendments are discussed in the Note on the Pazzi Conspiracy and Ficino, pp. 87–91. The translators have followed the original wording in these cases, but have in all other instances given the version they consider Ficino intended for publication.

In his *Life of Ficino* (which appears in Volume 3 of the present work) Giovanni Corsi stated that the titles of many of the letters were spurious. A study of M9 indicates that in many instances Ficino has added the titles of the letters in his own hand. In some cases a space has been left for this purpose.

The MS Ricc. 797 (R10) is a fair copy of M9 (perhaps prepared for printing). This is inferred from the fact that certain amendments in R10 have clearly arisen from idiosyncrasies in the marginal additions of M9. An important example in this connection is Letter 12. In comparing this letter in the two manuscripts it is clear that additions in the margin of substantial passages (set out in a possibly confusing manner) caused the scribe of R10 to make an error in the paragraph order, which leaves us in very little doubt that he was actually copying from the page of M9 itself.

Of the other manuscripts, L28 was copied by Luca Fabiani in 1490, and so it is a relatively late copy.

Except for Lo4, which is a calligraphed copy of the version of letter 33 in the Venice edition, all the manuscripts containing individual letters (see table on p. xx) are important. Detailed comments on these manuscripts are given in the Notes on the Latin Text within the notes for the respective letters. We have referred to the Bodleian manuscript Lat. misc. d. 85 as O3, since Professor Kristeller in his *Supplementum Ficinianum* has already given the sigla O1 to one manuscript in the Bodleian and the sigla O2 to a second manuscript there. The original letter 32 in the Archivio Borromeo we have referred to as Bo. The Sarzana manuscript (sigla S) contains letters to Antonio Ivani of Sarzana and his replies to them. The manuscript is valuable as it gives an example of questions put to Ficino in correspondence.

The first printed edition (*editio princeps*) of the letters was published in Venice by Mattheus Capcasa in 1495. The editions of Basle (1576) and Paris (1641) are the other main editions. These editions of Venice, Basle and Paris are mentioned in the Notes on the Latin Text and are referred to as V, B and P respectively. There was also an edition published in Nuremberg (1497, ed. Koberger). The editions of Florence (1494), Basle (1497), Strasbourg (1497) and Florence (1497) are 'ghost editions' (non-existent books which appear only in library catalogues). A record exists of a Prague edition (c. 1500) which only contains two letters and these in a Czech translation.

Where there are discrepancies in the text, M9 has been mainly followed as generally the most reliable source. For the manuscripts which contain Book V we have consulted copies in each instance. For the manuscripts which contain individual letters we have consulted the original in each instance, except for N3. We have also consulted M9 in the original. Discrepancies of any importance in the text are set out very fully in the Notes on the Latin Text. In these, the comparison is given between the manuscripts and the three most important printed editions. It is proposed that a full critical edition should follow. This critical edition is intended to be presented in the form of a parallel text.

In Book V there are very few instances of a manuscript giving a date for a letter. However there is one date given in M9 and that for the longest letter in the volume, Letter 27. The date is 27th January, 1477 (1478 in modern dating). Where there are dates in the manuscripts containing individual letters these are given at the foot of the particular letter and are mentioned in the Notes on the Latin Text for the letter concerned.

As regards paragraphs, there are some marked in M9 and R10 in the longer letters. Also some paragraphs are marked in the manuscripts which contain individual letters. These have mostly been followed and others have been added by the translators where the sense requires.

THE TRANSLATORS

The
Letters

Preface[a] to Book V

Marsilio Ficino of Florence[b] to Bernardo Bembo, the illustrious Venetian nobleman: greetings.

THE fifth book of our letters, beginning with a letter on divine law, seems, by that law, to require the name of the distinguished Bembo as its head, whom divine law and the law of the heavens have joined to us, as we show[c] elsewhere.[1] Therefore, it should, in justice, be dedicated to you above all.
May you read it with pleasure.

I

Legis divinae[a] fides scientia confirmatur[b]

Faith in divine law is confirmed by knowledge[1]

Marsilio Ficino of Florence to his most reverend friends:[c] greetings.

HUMAN laws are accepted from the outset or, once accepted, are kept in being in these ways only: through arguments[d] from common custom based on human and natural principles; through some dictatorial authority or the force of arms; or through ease and convenience of living and the allurements of pleasure. Not even the disposition of the stars[2] can ever establish laws among men by any means other than these. For this reason, if we see that any law has at any time arisen among reasonable men and been widely disseminated, even though the convincing arguments of many men are opposed to it, even though the force of the powerful rages against it, and even though it is clear that all[e] anticipation and enjoyment of human pleasure are completely removed by it,[f] we are forced to conclude that such a law is not a human law nor does it depend on heavenly fate, but is wholly divine and has its origin in some power higher than heaven.[3]

Now what is concluded from inescapable proof is understood with certain knowledge. Therefore[g] whoever trusts in such a law for such a reason will have[h] both knowledge as the mother of his faith, and faith made sure by knowledge. He who does not take account of this cannot take account of himself. He who does take some account of this but does not trust in it, trusts nothing. What others choose, I do not know. For myself, I would rather trust with divine faith than know with human knowledge. Since divine faith is far more certain than human wisdom, such trust is always confirmed by true knowledge, while human knowledge sometimes wavers through lack of trust.

Therefore, so that we can trust something[i] somewhere that is true, let us now trust truth itself, which, since it admits no ignorance or deception, certainly keeps no one in ignorance and deceives nobody. Furthermore, so that we can place our hope[j] in something somewhere that is good, let us place our hope in the good itself, which, since it does no evil and suffers no injustice, never disappoints those who hope[k] for it and never abandons those who love it. It has given them light that they may hope and set them afire that they may love; for the movement towards the good can depend on no other source than the good itself, and can return[4] there by no other means than that by which it came forth.[l]

2

Nihil potest esse proprium ubi communis est animus

Nothing can be called personal where there is one common soul

Marsilio Ficino to the poet Naldo Naldi:[a] greetings.

I RETURNED recently to my Celle, Naldo, or rather our Celle;[1] for nothing can be called personal where there is one common soul. On my second day in the country, I composed a very brief summary[2] of our book *On Religion*. As I was dedicating it to my friends, the first to come to mind was Naldo, the one whom I loved first of all. My steadfast love for the others is due wholly to him. For in first loving him I learned to love them. So I am sending you the summary. I have written what I have done, Naldo; you too write what you are doing and how you are.

Why do I say, 'I have written',[b] and why have I asked you to write? Let those whose love is ordinary be content merely with letters; but an exchange of letters will satisfy neither Naldo nor Marsilio; of that I am sure.[c]

3

Breviter loquendum: sed non breviter vel cogitandum vel amandum

Let us be brief in speech, but not in deliberation or loving

Marsilio Ficino to Antonio Ivani: greetings.

Do you see, Antonio, how acute an intellect I consider you to have? Whenever you ask for complete books, I send you summaries. First you asked for the book *On the Highest Good*,[1] and I sent a summary;[2] then you requested our *Platonic Theology*, and again I gave you a summary, which I had received a little earlier. Now, to sharpen[3] your intellect[a] three times over, accept a third summary; that of our book[b] *On Religion*,[4] which you have read.

You expressed a strong desire for the symposium *On Love*;[5] on this one occasion Ivani has received from us not just a summary but the whole work, since it is not a small part of Marsilio's love which is bestowed,[c] but that love in its entirety, which is poured into Ivani's very self. I have learned to discourse briefly,[6] but not to love briefly; where speech is restricted, love is abundant.[d] When the flame is less diffused,[e] the heat is more intense.[f]

Farewell.

Celle,
15th September, 1477.

4

Sacerdotes et philosophi pie loquantur.et sentiant

Priests and philosophers should speak and think rightly

Marsilio Ficino to Giovanni Cavalcanti, his unique friend:[a] greetings.

You will, I think, demand from us, my Giovanni, the first-fruits of our stay in the country, since whatever is first is quite rightly owed to him who is first. Today I have written to my friends, or rather to myself, a kind of short exhortation[1] on love and duty to God. I never seek to persuade others of anything of which I am not already persuaded myself. It is the duty of a priest[2] to say nothing which does not evidently lead towards love and duty to God. It is also the profession of the philosopher to act exactly as he speaks, to speak exactly as he thinks, but not to confuse the functions of mind and senses. Finally, that my efforts in writing such an exhortation may not have been in vain, read it carefully, my Giovanni, I beseech you. For if you do not read it, I shall wish that I had not written to my friends and I shall have failed to write to myself.

Farewell.[b]

5

Nullum in malis refugium est nisi ad summum bonum[a]

In the midst of evils there is no refuge, unless it be with the highest good[1]

Marsilio Ficino to his friends: greetings.

TRAGEDIES truly lament the wretched fate of mortals; but fate also brings about their truest tragedy. A tragedy is an imaginary life of men; but the life of men seems to be their truest tragedy. Leaving aside for the moment those utterances of orators, poets and philosophers in which every single evil and trouble of mankind is enumerated, let me now briefly express the full misery of our human race[b] with a single instance: those[c] who are commonly regarded as the happiest of men are usually the most miserable.

According to philosophers there are three[d] kinds of life:[2] the first is dedicated to study, the second to action and the third to pleasure. Those who in any one of these lives[e] are thought to be at the height of happiness are generally[f] in the depth of misery. Certainly those who in the eyes of the world appear to excel in the study of truth are often[g] more than anyone else locked in an insoluble dilemma of uncertainty. For while they have been inquisitively eager to learn every single thing and to make bold public statements on each, they have quite rightly learned[h] to have doubts about all this; and since they believe they have no one superior or equal to them, they have no one left whom they may trust or consult. O foolish wisdom,[i] O knowledge more confusing than all ignorance! Solomon, the wisest of all men according to divine authority, says that such knowledge brings toil and disappointment.[3] Paul the Apostle asserts that God holds this wisdom to be unwisdom.[4] The prophet Isaiah declares that the thinking based on this wisdom is judged by God to be vanity.[5] This seems properly to apply to those who hope to see true things in something other than the light of truth itself, like someone who, captivated by the light of the mind, believes he sees the colours of things not in the splendour of the sun but by the light of the eye alone.[6]

Next,[j] those who are considered to have reached the highest rank in active life really hold that position in suffering, and when they are said to have most power, then are they most in servitude. Finally,[k] those who too readily yield to pleasures often fall into torments, and when they seem to be gorging themselves as much as they can, they are desperately hungry and thirsty.[1] O miserable fate of mortals, fate more miserable than misery itself! Where[m] shall we wretches flee, if we are ever to escape from our misery? To the philosophy of the Sophists,[7] ever eager for new knowledge? Or to power? Or pleasure?[n] Alas, we already fly far too often to these, but in vain. The proud philosophy of the Sophists entangles us in most troublesome questions. Power casts us into the most acute and perilous bondage. Lastly pleasure, which is brief and false,[o] afflicts us with suffering, which is long and real.

Perhaps[p] it would be worthwhile, if we wish to attain what we are seeking, to flee only to that which does not flee anywhere.[q] But that alone cannot flee anywhere which cannot be moved anywhere,[r] since it fills the universe. However, is there any need even to be moved to that which is not moved anywhere, which is present everywhere in every single thing?[s] Then let us not be moved or distracted by many things, but let us remain in unity[t] as much as we are able, since we find eternal unity and the one eternity, not through movement or multiplicity, but through being still and being one. But[u] what is that one, friends? Come on,[v] then, say what it is. Is it not that[w] self-same good which fills the universe?[x] For nothing can be found which is not good in the presence of the good itself. It is the good itself, do you not see? It is the good itself which all things seek, since all things are from that good. And for this reason every single thing is perfected through that good to the extent that each strives to hold to it.[y] But we can hold fast to the good, it seems to me, only through love of the good, since it is the very nature of the good to be sought after; and the reason[z] for its being sought after is that it is good. Moreover, as soon as we love what is wholly good for us, we cleave to it, since love itself is something good, nearest of all to the highest good, as it is the flame of the good; and wherever the flame of the good burns most fiercely, there its light shines most clearly.

What[aa] more?[bb] If God is the good itself, and the light of the good, and the love of the light of the good, I beg you, friends, let us love, let us love before all else the good which is light and the light which is good. For thus we shall not merely love our God: we shall delight in loving Him, for God[cc] Himself is love, love itself is God. Therefore first and foremost let us burn with that love, without whose heat nothing has heat, that we may reflect, according to our desire, the blessed light of Him without whose splendour nothing has light! Come, friends! Let us rest in that which never recedes and there we shall ever remain. Let us serve the one Master of all, who serves no one, so that we are not enslaved by anything, but are the masters of everything. Let us delight in God if we can, and we can if we will, for through the will is the delight and the delight is in the will. Let us delight, I say, in that which alone fills the infinite; thus alone shall we be completely filled, thus alone shall we rejoice fully and truly. For where the good abounds without defect, there delight is experienced without pain, and everywhere joy to the full.[8]

6

Non creavit ad parva quaedam deus homines, sed ad magna

It was not for small things but for great that God created men

Marsilio Ficino to Giovanni Cavalcanti, his unique friend: greetings.

LOGICIANS say[a] it is the nature of a contradiction that someone who is disposed to one point of view cannot at the same time be disposed to its opposite.[1] Yet this autumn my thoughts have been so divided that I wish neither to speak nor yet to remain silent; I can neither act nor yet refrain from acting. Perhaps this is because I am in some sense two, though I seem to be one. But let me be two, as in *Phaedrus*[2] Plato would have us, or even three, as he argues in the *Timaeus*,[3] as long as that within me which draws me to honourable labour always overcomes that which draws me back to indolence and torpor. See, that which stirs me to action and speech is now dominant, and so I am speaking and acting as best I can. But somehow we are now faced with another[b] problem. For I would like to joke for a while in my usual way and to write something humorous at least to my Cavalcanti. I took up my pen chiefly with this intention, yet I am writing rather seriously; while attempting the lyrical or comic, I am producing elegy or tragedy.[c]

Would you[d] have me say, my friend,[e] that in these times Saturn has chosen me alone on whom to test all his stern powers? No. I see you would not want that,[4] my Giovanni, and neither would I. Then what shall we say, my friend?[f] We shall say that God wishes His priests to be the most serious of men and that He requires a serious rather than humorous attitude to sacred matters. This was perhaps what Pythagoras meant when he gave his disciples the symbolic instruction not to cut their finger-nails at a sacrifice.[5]

It was not for small things but for great that God created men, who, knowing the great, are not satisfied[g] with small things. Indeed, it was for the limitless alone that He created men, who are the only beings on earth to have re-discovered their infinite nature and who are not fully satisfied by anything limited, however great that thing may be.[6]

7

Nullus incontinens potest sapiens[a] esse

No one who lacks self-restraint can be wise

Marsilio Ficino to philosophers and teachers of sophistry: greetings.

OF all the powers of the soul which are concerned with knowing, the highest are intellect and reason, and the lowest are taste and touch. The last two for the most part lead down to bodily nature, while the first two lead up to divine substance, which is not of the body. Therefore, not surprisingly, whoever strives to serve all the

powers of the soul at once, strives in vain. For whoever completely
submerges himself in the darkness of the lower world will not be
illumined by the rays from the higher. Similarly, a man does not
heed the ridiculous attractions of the lower world once he has tasted
the true goodness and joy of the higher. The mind will not rise to
the truest causes of things, which are separate from bodies, unless
it has separated itself from the body, first by cleansing itself of its
habits and then by the effort of contemplation. He who already
possesses heaven and appraises eternity itself, so to speak, will
reckon as nothing those things which are subject to time on earth.
I need not say how people suffering from a bloody inflammation
of the eye[1] see everything as red, and those with a bitter taste on
the tongue taste everything as bitter. In the same way the mind,
which from a long-standing desire and indulgence in physical things
has become physical, so to speak, will believe the divine to be
completely non-existent, or will regard it as physical.[2] I shall not
discuss the peace, freedom or length of time necessary to investigate
the hidden causes of things. Nothing can be conceived as more
enslaving, giving rise to more agitation and anxiety, than the
worried life of the man who serves the senses as though they were
many mad masters. And while he is in bondage to foolish tyrants,
he is professing allegiance to wisdom as well.

So[b] if you catch anyone foolishly serving[c] the body you will
know he is not wise. But you will find those whom you know to
be wise are not slaves but masters of the body, which is their
servant. Troubled indeed are they who live only to serve the desires
of the body. But in much greater trouble are those who mistakenly
try[d] to couple the pleasures of the lower world with those of the
higher. For since they labour so hard in contrary directions, they
can enjoy the pleasures neither of the mind nor of the body. God
condemns none more than those who expect to drink nectar and
ambrosia out of the filthy vessels of vice. As Aristotle says,[3] God
values and loves none more than those who cultivate above all a
mind in the very likeness of God and who set it apart from this
body of decay, so unlike Him. These men take care not to obscure
the divine light with clouds of vice but to perceive it in pure peace
of mind.

This[e] principle, we think, led Socrates to offer men primarily a
moral training,[4] and Pythagoras to drive the ungodly far from his

sacred schools.[5] For if you pour liquid into a tainted vessel, the vessel will turn even the finest liquid foul by its contact. In the same way, an evil mind[f] on receiving knowledge produces not wisdom, but evil. Furthermore, as the sky is to the light of the sun, so is the mind to the light of truth and wisdom. Neither the sky nor the intellect ever receive rays of light while they are clouded, but once they are pure and clear they both receive them immediately. Plato's letter to the Syracusans refers to this.[6] It says that the divine cannot be spoken[g] or learned as other things are. However, from continued application and a matching of one's life to the divine, suddenly, as if from a leaping spark, a light is kindled in the mind and thereafter nourishes itself.

Why[h] therefore do you burden yourselves with so much night study, O philosophers?[i] What need for such long, tortuous arguments, O[j] sophists? Do you not see the one way? The one way to that light for us is serenity. Alas, to attain the pure, you often vainly put your trust in the impure. This Socrates condemns.[7] Learn from Galen the Platonist that it is impossible for a soul stifled by blood and fat to contemplate anything heavenly.[8] Learn from Pythagoras and Plato that wisdom of mind is nothing but the light of the highest good, diffused everywhere through minds which are truly good, like mirrors of spotless purity. Therefore, as soon as you have become wholly good, you will shine forth with the splendour of the highest good, that is, with wisdom.

The sun in the heavens gives birth to the eyes in creatures and the colours in objects, and the same sun shows those colours to eyes which are open and pure.[9] The sun which is above the heavens, that is truth itself, is the father both of minds and of true things. That same sun reveals true things to minds which are pure and turned towards it. Cleanse the eye of reason of all the dirt from this noxious body. Turn the keen edge of the mind away from the shadow of base matter. Turn the gaze of the inner intelligence to the light of the supernal form. From here substance, when it is fully ready, is instantly given bodily forms. From here the mind, when it is ready, is instantly impressed with incorporeal forms. And as the mind is illumined with the brilliant rays of truth, so does it overflow with true joy without limit.[10]

8

Philosophi saepe dum discunt curiosius disputare, interim
consultare dediscunt

*While philosophers learn to argue intricate points, they
often forget to ask for advice*

Marsilio Ficino to Giovanni Cavalcanti, his unique friend: greetings.[a]

My hero, what is it that you are saying so politely about our correspondence? Have I overwhelmed you recently? Are you complaining about the number of my letters? What is this all about, Giovanni? Bear[b] these light matters calmly, if you can, since I am bearing much heavier ones. Why does the number of my letters disturb you? Clearly because I myself am disturbed[c] by the tumult of my thoughts. This is what usually happens to very busy people who are given too much leisure. Nevertheless, it is better to be busy when idleness oppresses than to be idle when business presses. Please advise your fellow philosopher what he had best do in his case. My friend, forgive philosophers, for[d] while they learn to argue intricate points, they often forget to ask for advice.

9

Solitudo philosophis non remissio mentis sed intentio esse
solet et debet[a]

To philosophers solitude should be, and usually is, not a relaxation but an application of the mind

Marsilio Ficino of Florence[b] to Bernardo Bembo of Venice:
greetings.

On the fifth of September[c] I withdrew to our Monte Celle,[1] far
from the city, not to relax my mind, but to apply it. For to those
practising philosophy, solitude should be,[d] and usually is, not so
much a relaxation as an application of the mind. Here, Bernardo,
on the very day your eagerly awaited[e] letter arrived, I had just
written to my friends something which was perhaps more tragic
than philosophic.[2] But whatever it was, it would have been written
to my friends in vain, had it not been sent first of all to my Bembo.
Of course, we assume that whatever is said to Bembo is also said
to Febo Capella and Marco Aurelio. When I return to the city,
where I left the volume containing those ten summaries[f] of ours[3]
which Febo desires, I shall see that copies are made for him.

If I now commend myself to you, my Bernardo, understand that
it is that renowned hero of ours, Giovanni Cavalcanti, who is
commended under the name of Marsilio. Or if[g] I say farewell,
understand that in Marsilio's words our hero greatly desires you to
fare well.[h] So be mindful of your welfare. But I see that my Bembo
neither can nor will be well without the well-being of his loved
ones. Landino and Bracciolini are well for your sake, Bernardo:
therefore, fare well.

21st September, 1477.

10

Profanis sapientia non conceditur

Wisdom is not granted to the ungodly

Marsilio Ficino to Lorenzo Buonincontri, astronomer and poet: greetings.[a]

YOU often say, Lorenzo, that wicked men are never able to become true astrologers. This seems to me to be very true. For if the heavens are the temple of God Himself, it follows that ungodly men are far removed from the heavens and their mysteries. In addition, our Plato and other wise Greeks clearly acknowledge that not only astronomy but also all wisdom has come down from other races,[1] and we have learned that among these races only the priests were concerned with the sciences: physical, mathematical and metaphysical.[2] For they knew that wisdom, being the special gift of God,[3] should not and indeed could not be granted except to minds utterly devoted to God and in nature like his own. It is, I think, chiefly for this reason that Christ, the Master of Life, declares that sacred mysteries are given to the common people in veiled form, but are fully revealed[b] to chosen disciples.[4]

But why do I now go into this matter again? Read, if you will, what we have previously written, following the same argument, to philosophers and sophists.[5] Find someone to read it with you, my friend, if you can find anyone in whom integrity and learning are united to an exceptional degree.

Tell me, please, Lorenzo: whom do you now think it would be best to ask to read these things with you? Angelo Manetti? You are thinking of this very man, I see. I thought of him myself a moment ago, before I thought of anyone else.

II

Omne tulit punctum, qui miscuit utile dulci[1]

He who has blended the serious with the pleasing has
satisfied everyone

Marsilio Ficino to Sebastiano Foresi, his dear fellow priest: greetings.

THERE is no one amongst all my friends with whom I converse
more profoundly and more enjoyably than with you, my sweet
Foresi. For I address others with only the tongue or the pen, but
you I often address with lute and lyre.[a] In fact, without you my
lutes are silent, my lyres mute.[b] Come, I beseech you, my Foresi,
whenever you sing to the lyre, sing in harmony with me. But I
see that while you are so intent upon constructing one lyre, you
are forgetting the music of the other. Amongst the heavenly beings,
Sebastiano, even Phoebus does not both play[c] the lyre and make
it, while Mercury makes the lyre but does not play it.[2] Therefore,
let no-one on earth presume to exercise equally the skills of making
and of playing the lyre.

Should anyone object that those obsessed by matters lyrical are
driven delirious,[3] I know that you would reply[d] in turn that we
play the lyre precisely to avoid becoming unstrung,[e] so to speak.
It is no wonder that those who always deal with grave matters are
bowed by the sheer weight of gravity, while those forever occupied
with light matters are justly blown hither and thither by every light
breath of air. But we need to mix gravity with levity, just as nature
teaches us, so that gravity may be lightened and lifted, if I may put
it thus, with a measure of levity, and levity held steady by the
stability of gravity.

But what am I doing? Am I alleging that our music is a light
matter? As you know, I have already revealed in a long letter the
dignity, or rather the divinity, of music.[4] But lest we seem to be
indulging in music too much, we shall conclude briefly as follows:
nothing can be conceived which is graver than grave music, lighter
than light music or in better proportion than music which is well-
tempered.[5] So may the well-tempered lyre always be our salvation

when we apply ourselves to it rightly.[6] Blessings upon you, provided that you always remember to bless our two eyes: Giovanni Cavalcanti and Pietro Nero.

I,[f] Luca, Marsilio's scribe, having penned this letter, commend myself to you.[7] And if I seem to you worthy of so great a gift, I beg you to love me as much as I see you are loved by Marsilio himself. My master loves you, Foresi, as much as you yourself love to be loved.

12

Nullum commodius in malis remedium quam patientia

There is no remedy for evils more fitting than patience

Marsilio Ficino to Sebastiano Salvini, his nephew:[a] greetings.[b]

THE common saying has it, Sebastiano, that nothing is more difficult than patience. But we think the opposite: it is not at all difficult, because it involves no trouble; no trouble, because there is no toil; how can there be toil where there is no need for activity? What need is there of activity when it is a matter of not acting rather than acting? Patience, indeed, leads you not to act but to suffer[c] things to be. Just as it is more difficult to act than to suffer things to be, so is it more difficult to act well than to suffer well. All the other virtues hinge on acting well, while patience alone consists in suffering well. What is suffering well, other than not adding to the suffering occasioned[d] by evils? But what do we mean by this? Nothing but a willingness to suffer what you have to suffer, even if you do not wish to.[e] Unless you suffer willingly, you will certainly suffer unwillingly;[f] and unless you allow yourself to be led, you will be seized and violently dragged away.

O, the marvellous power of patience![g] The other virtues certainly battle against fate in one way or another, but it is patience alone, or patience more than all the others, that conquers fate; for patience, being in accord with the will of divine providence, changes what fate has decreed to be immutable[h] and unavoidable, so that it makes the unavoidable voluntary. Just as[i] he who acts badly turns what is good for him into evil, so he who suffers well turns what is bad for him into good. Certainly, in suffering ills, such a man ultimately becomes good. He is tested and made bright by adversity, as gold is tried by fire; and as a veteran[j] soldier is made wily and dauntless by frequent experience of danger, so he who has first tasted bitterness appreciates sweet experiences all the more keenly, puts them to wiser use, and enjoys them with greater pleasure. The man who has not experienced evil cannot rightly appraise the magnitude of goodness, while he who has never learned to make use of evil will never know how to enjoy the good.

There is no prosperity more frail than that of the man whom everything seems to have touched with prosperity.[k] The prudent man looks out for rain[l] in a clear sky and for a clear sky[l] in rain, or rather, he regards nothing as clear in this dark life unless it is beneath a clear mind. The unabating storm batters us from without, and it is only within that peace is to be sought.

Clarity comes from the same source as heat, and heat from the same source as light. Light, however, does not proceed from the shadow of matter, but from the light of the mind.

They speak falsely,[m] my friend, who say that the numerous sufferings in the life of mankind arise from its numerous evils. It would be much more accurate to say that life itself is a form of suffering which presses on the wretched without respite.[n] The cures to be applied to chronic diseases are not those which have temporary effect but those which bring permanent benefit.

We are not always strong enough to deliberate, fight and put up resistance, but we are always able to suffer well. We always suffer[o] and, by suffering, are taught how to suffer. Certainly we can always do something when the power to do it lies within the will itself. As soon as we have the will to suffer well, we do suffer well, since suffering well is nothing other than having the will to suffer. If we do ill, we shall undoubtedly suffer ills and suffer them ill. If we suffer well, we act well. If, perversely, we fight, my friend, we shall grow weary and be utterly defeated, if not by the weariness then by our own selves. If we yield, as we should, we shall undoubtedly conquer.

Air, being totally fluid, yields to the blows of hard bodies and immediately returns to itself just as it was before. But hard bodies in direct collision are broken. All that is softest and most pliant endures unbroken and can bind the hardest things; because the hardest[p] do not know how to yield, they are forced to be hewn, shattered and bound.[q]

Therefore,[r] my Salvini, overcome fortune by bearing it, and that you may overcome all else, overcome yourself, as you have already begun to do. Remember that in this malign region of the universe nothing escapes the touch of evil, but that under a just judge, or rather under justice as judge,[s] nothing good can be without just reward, nothing evil without due punishment. Remember, too, that patience is so perfectly good that without it none of the other good works of men can be perfected; for whatever arises from other virtues is perfected by patience.

Farewell,[t] most beloved brother, and, so that others may bear with you, bear with others. Indeed,[u] whenever I see in a man those things which offend me, I remember that I too am a man and therefore possess some attribute which may offend others. For this reason I bear with many every day, that many may bear with me. Even bear[v] patiently the severity and length of this letter of mine, since otherwise I shall have spoken of patience fruitlessly or else you will seem to have heard these things in vain, although through your own sound judgement you began to affirm[w] and practise them long ago.

13

Solum minervae templum contra fortunae procellas homines protegit

The temple of Minerva alone protects men against the storms of fortune

Marsilio Ficino to Giovanni Cavalcanti, his unique friend: greetings.

THAT friend of ours[1] has now written to me twice complaining of his fortune, or rather his fate. I have written to him just once, advising him to flee for refuge to the temple of Minerva,[a] where alone we are protected from the storms and thunderbolts of fortune. I do not know of anyone by whom a letter could better ascend the mountains of Mugello[2] than you. Read it if you wish; take it if you can. Farewell.

What did you think just now, when you read the words 'Read it if you wish'? Surely not that you were going to let our friend rather than you read what is yours? Well, do whatever you please; I, for my part, would not wish our thoughts to please anyone else until they had first pleased the man who pleases me more than anyone.

14

Amicitia vera externis non eget officiis

True friendship needs no outer formalities[a]

Marsilio Ficino to Giovanni Cavalcanti, his unique friend: greetings.[b]

TELL me, I beg you, Giovanni, if it is fair to ask, why do you now not reply to so many of my letters?[c] Do you not know that the flavour of your words imparts a most delightful seasoning to our feasts?[d] For what is it in the more bitter dishes that tastes sweet to me?[c] It is Giovanni. Again, what tastes bitter in the sweeter morsels? It is Giovanni. Perhaps you think that as soon as you have read our letters you have replied to them, especially since you always respond to my words with love and service. And often, before I say anything, you have done it all. Without question this is so. But I know that you have gone further than this, for at first you intended to reply and even considered what best to say.[f] Then you realised, as you have also seen before, that Marsilio is closer to your thoughts than are your tongue and hand.[g] That is why between your mind and mine the ministry of tongue and hand cannot intervene. You understand fully[h] and I understand too; for by your intention, Giovanni, you have written, and I by reflection have read while you were writing.

Nonetheless, that others also may read your reply to me, I myself shall now write it down: 'Giovanni to Marsilio: greetings.[i] A result of our long-standing friendship, Ficino, is that you are no longer able to impart to me anything new. I have long known your spirit, Marsilio; I understand your full intent and hold to your words. But I have just made a mistake. It is not so much the length of our friendship as its very beginning which has brought this about. Certainly, from the very inception of this divine love, you did not impart your mind to me by degrees, one part after another, my Marsilio, but you totally transfused the single whole into me all at once. And as this gift is poured out to others whom you love, so do I in the same measure pour it out to them.

'What more then are you trying to give us? You have nothing at all which one, who has you, does not already possess. Therefore, if the repeated courtesy of writing and replying, which amongst others is a sign of friendship approaching perfection, were to apply strictly to us, it would be an indication of an increasingly imperfect friendship.[j] Perhaps you yourself offend against our friendship far more by talking than I by remaining silent.[k] You still seem to imagine some sort of division between us, and an absence; but the simple unity and continuing presence,[l] which you so greatly desire to be confirmed, I do confirm: for thus it is.

'What then? Are letters never to be passed back and forth between us? Let it not be that from such brimming abundance of the inmost spring nothing should ever flow forth, nothing overflow to outside. God forbid that what burns within should never cast its radiance beyond. Indeed, the reason we have often written and shall continue to write to each other is so that others may understand through our letters those matters which our minds, or rather our mind, considers, and in considering speaks to itself.

'If[m] you wish me to fare well, which you certainly wish before all else, fare well yourself.'[n]

15

Qui musis abutuntur, non mel, sed fel ab earum fonte reportant

They who abuse the Muses bring back from their fountain not honey but gall

Marsilio Ficino to the distinguished citizen, Angelo Manetti: greetings.[a]

MY friend, there are[b] a number of writers, both Latin and Greek,[1] who compare to bees men who are totally devoted to study. For, like bees, they gather here and there from many authors, as from flowers, and store what they have gathered in the capacious hives of their memory. They then let it ripen by reflection, to bring forth the mellifluous liquid of learning and eloquence. If anyone should deny this comparison,[c] which is made by the best authors, he would seem to me to deserve to bring back gall rather than honey, even from the fount of the Muses. I shall therefore subtract nothing at all from this simile, but rather add to it.

You must have heard, my friend, that when bees suck from too many wormwood flowers they very often produce honey which, tasted on the lips, seems quite sweet but immediately afterwards, when swallowed, proves to be not sweet at all but bitter, almost like gall. We know full well that something very similar[d] often happens to gluttons for study and devourers of books,[e] who have neither measure nor discrimination. Indeed, the more greedily they

seem to drain the sweet liquor of the Muses, the more bitterly do
they take into their heart I know not what! Perhaps this is what
the Latin authors call bile,[f] the Greeks melancholy: a disease, as
Aristotle shows, peculiar to men absorbed by study.[2] For this reason
Solomon calls study a most onerous occupation; and he adds[g] that
the companion of knowledge is sorrow.[3]

What therefore shall we say of Aristotle's remark:[4] 'The tree of
knowledge indeed has bitter roots but the sweetest fruit'? We shall
certainly grant this to Aristotle, but add that such a fruit is perhaps
the peach, in which a bitter kernel lies within the sweetness.[5]

What then?[h] Should we denounce the Muses? Let us never think
that the fount of celestial nectar and ambrosia pours forth bitter
and deadly streams. Therefore, much as we praise the true use of
the Muses, so we condemn their abuse. Who then makes the greatest
abuse of the Muses? Surely one who heedlessly and importunately[i]
presses on their tracks; or one who impudently[j] involves them with
the common Venus;[6] or who separates them from their lord Apollo.
Ignorant[k] little men do not attain knowledge when they grasp
unwisely at wisdom herself. The Muses do not sing well when the
wanton son of Venus molests them; either they are silent or they
shriek. The chorus of the Muses does not dance becomingly, but
limps and falters, whenever its lord Apollo is far away.[7]

One[l] who believes that he will perceive the sun's light without
the sun's aid deservedly falls into darkness; he is not raised into
light. So one who pursues this truth and that truth, separated from
the highest truth, without doubt does not light upon truth but
upon falsehood. No wonder that whoever searches for the nectar
of heaven in the Stygian marsh deservedly drinks[m] the genuine gall
of opinion beneath the illusory honey of knowledge.

16

Nunquam adversa revera patimur,[a] nisi cum patimur et perverse

We never really suffer adversity, except when we suffer it perversely

Marsilio Ficino to Giovanni Cavalcanti, his unique friend: greetings.

ONCE more our dear nephew writes to us a long list of the many adversities he suffers from day to day.[1] But since I have for a long time found[b] in myself that I have never really suffered adversity more than when I suffered it perversely, I am writing to him, or rather to myself, a letter about the facility and felicity of patience. Perhaps in reading this letter there may be need of patience on the part of the reader and the hearer. Read it with patience, my dearest Giovanni, and if you deem it worthy to be sent, perhaps you will send it yourself.

17

Amicitia perfecta verbis litterisque non indiget

Perfect friendship does not need words or letters

Marsilio Ficino to Francesco Salviati,[1] Archbishop of Pisa: greetings.[a]

EVERY day, Reverend Father,[b] I try to take up my pen to write something to my own lord, by whose favour, or rather through whose efforts, I have obtained the leisure to write many things every day. But as often as I take up my pen, my lord stops me with these most welcome words: 'I, whom you seek, am here before your eyes.[2] So, Ficino, lay down your pen. For what need is there of any letter when it is given[c] to us to hear and reply to

4.   *Bust of Lorenzo de'Medici by Verrocchio (Photo: Fratelli Alinari, Florence).*

5. *View of Florence, c. 1480, Museo di Firenze com'era (Photo: Fratelli Alinari). It is possible to see in this painting many buildings that were new in 1480 and still stand today. Dominating the city then as now is the Duomo, or Cathedral, of Florence. It was under Brunelleschi's dome, the pride of the city, that Giuliano de' Medici met his death in the Pazzi conspiracy.*

6. *Medal commemorating the Pazzi conspiracy, by Bertoldo di Giovanni, British Museum (Photo: Phaidon Archive). On the left is the scene of Giuliano falling under the knives of the assassins; on the right, we see Lorenzo fighting off his attackers.*

one another at any time?[3] Let letters bring together occasionally those[d] who seem to one another to be apart. But letters would prove to be apart those who are always present to each other. Do not separate me from yourself with a pen, when you are always joined to me in heart.' What am I to do, my lord?[e] I do not know. For you are doing two opposite things[f] to me at the same time, so at the same time I suffer two opposite reactions. You often urge me on with spurs to run, and at the same time you restrain me with the bit to be still. If I am not moved I seem lazy and unwilling; if I am, unrestrained and foolish. You draw my mind in opposite directions, and I am torn apart. Meanwhile,[g] somehow, this letter springs from my hands, clearly for this purpose: that it should speak not to you, with whom I speak as I wish without any letter, but to the people, so that all may perceive how entirely a lord and his servant are at one.

This letter would now have commended our Cavalcanti to you, as though he were absent, but I see that as soon as it greeted you it saw Giovanni standing by your side.

18

Merito invitus omni caret bono, qui sponte caret deo, qui est omne bonum

He who by his own will cuts himself off from God, who is all good, inevitably cuts himself off, even against his will, from every good

Marsilio Ficino to Leone Michaeli, the Venetian Nobleman:[a] greetings.

WERE one of us to love the good itself, which is wholly good, as eagerly as we all habitually love one good thing after another, though none of these is good without the good itself, such a man would undoubtedly always experience at least as much good and joy as we now constantly all experience evil and pain. In fact, his joy would be far stronger than this real anguish of ours and sweeter than our unreal pleasure; just as the substance of the good itself is more powerful than evil and truer than the image of goodness, and as the pure mind is more clear-sighted than the impure.

Now why should we be surprised if all evils pursue us, when we ourselves, abandoning the first good, namely God, wrongly pursue individual things as good, when all these things, without the first good, are evil? We deservedly fall into every evil, albeit against our will, every time we wilfully fall from that which is wholly good. Why do we mindlessly and miserably stray hither and thither for so long? Certainly, all the time that we are pursuing merely one thing after another, we are running away from the One itself, which is everything. But he who simply pursues the One itself, in that One soon attains everything.[1] Without a doubt the mind, which depends solely upon that which is above all things, can attain all things. Thus man alone among living beings has received the power to achieve whatever he wishes, provided that he desires above all to pursue in whatever he wishes that which alone is good.

Therefore, lion-hearted Leone, I have a high regard for you because you are no longer troubled about many things; but, as our most trustworthy witness Carlo Valguli testifies, you have long since chosen that good part,[2] which, since it not only flows forth from the fullness of its own fountain but also flows back into the same, satisfies the whole thirst of those who taste it and will never be taken away from that mind which has once experienced it.

19

Cum deus sit ipse amor, quicunque absque deo aliquid
studet amare, hic absque amore temptat amare

Since God is Himself love,[1] *whoever tries to love
anything without God tries to love without love*

Marsilio Ficino to Lotterio Neroni: greetings.

MY dearest Lotterio, last summer I wrote a letter to my friends
about true friendship,[2] which perhaps had been written in vain were
it not being read by true friends, friends in that One without whose
warmth nobody can love anything, without whose splendour
nothing can be loved. Without the love of that One[a] we seem to
love something, but, since we try to love outside love itself, instead
of loving we are bound to hate. Without the friendship of that
One, the more friendly[b] things seem to be, the more harmful they
are. O how wonderful is the bond of goodness, of beauty and of
love! For where the goodness of things shines,[c] the beauty of the
beautiful sheds its splendour, and there too the love of loves is
aflame. Just as beauty follows the light of the good as its splendour,
so the ardour of love follows the rays of beauty as the reflection of
those rays.[3]

20

Solus feliciter dominatur, qui volentibus dominatur

Only he rules happily who rules men willing to be ruled

Marsilio Ficino to Francesco Salviati,[1] Lord Archbishop of Pisa.[a]

PLEASE tell me, my most generous patron, in what special terms I should now address you. Certainly that great office in which you have been installed seems to demand that I begin 'Reverend Father in Christ', but your great forbearance, and your even greater humanity, lead me to address you, almost too intimately, as follows: 'Greetings, my dearest Salviati.'[b] And lest the proper name of my patron, so pleasant on the lips of his dependant, be omitted,[c] greetings once again, my Francesco, sweeter than sweetness itself.

As I am now troubled by uncertainty of this kind, what am I to do? Certainly, where the status of a man's office exceeds his love of humanity we are accustomed to call him by proud official titles, but where exceptional humanity[d] transcends the power of the office, we ought to begin with human and familiar names. We especially[e] ought to do so, who are not aliens and strangers in your house but rather, by virtue of your generosity, members of your family.

My dearest Francesco,[f] dependants usually grieve most when it appears that their patrons are not going to give them anything. I, on the contrary, rejoice greatly that my patron is going to give me nothing further, because nothing of his own has been left to him; for a long time ago he gave us his very self, and with himself all that is his.

Be happy, most beloved patron. Your friends cannot but be happy[g] if you, who live wholly for your friends, are happy. All your friends serve you most punctiliously for this reason: that they serve quite freely.[h] No service is more punctilious or more joyful than that which is willing, no dominion safer and easier than that which is loving.

21

Egregios grex improbat, deus probat, apud quem solum[a]
gratitudo est et libertas

The crowd disapproves of outstanding men, but God
approves them; in Him alone are bounty and freedom[1]

Marsilio Ficino to Giovanni Cavalcanti, his unique friend: greetings.

PLEASE accept, Giovanni, copies of two letters[2] which I thought
out at dawn this morning[b] and gave today to those priests whom
you know: with what fortune I do not know, and that indeed is
not my concern, but I wish at least I knew their Muse.[3] I am not
mercenary. I know that the reward of being mercenary is to receive
the fruits thereof: but the end of a liberal art is to have done the
work well.[c]
Whatever happens, at least I[d] will be remembered. Perhaps you
will say that it is better to seek to be forgotten than remembered,
and to be hidden well than viewed badly. Let others forget me,[e] if
forgetting is what they want, but I cannot, I ought not, I will not
forget my own.[4,f] We know very well that no great man was ever
recognised[g] in his own age.[5] What is remarkable about that?
Outstanding men do not suit the crowd.[h] Opposites are not loved
by opposites. Envy takes the place of reverence.[6] Weak eyes are
blinded[i] by too much splendour. Those who are filled with small
things cannot receive the great.[7]
But you may perhaps grieve with me over one thing, my
Giovanni, that I am overlooked by my country, not perhaps because
I am so very great[j] but because I am so very small.[8] Let us not
grieve, my friend, provided that we please Him[k] who sees the
smallest as He sees the greatest and comprehends the greatest as He
does the least.
Whoever[l] is approved by Him will not be the least. Compared
to His magnitude, the greatest things are all infinitely less than the
least. Whoever shines in Him will never be hidden; for He shines
in all things, and all things shine in Him.
Yet nothing[m] is easier than to please Him, whom simply to wish
to please is to please. So you see, and this is astonishing, that even

the smallest good things are much dearer than the infinite good, since those small things are not obtained except with much effort and at great price. That infinite good, however, if it is bought, is bought by mere will. Why is that, my friend? Perhaps because it abounds without limit and because its price is in itself. Even though we buy everything else, the infinite good in fact buys us of its own accord. It buys us, I say, both by the goodness of its will and by our will for goodness. Therefore, since all this is brought about by goodness on both sides, and goodness itself is God Himself, God on both sides is the price." Nor are we ever completely free, except when we have sold ourselves freely° to infinite freedom. As soon as we are His who alone is His own, only then are we also our own. Children are nowhere more free and imperious than in their father's house. Parents yield to no one more freely than to their own children. But lest I seem to anyone to move further from where I began, I will make an end in Him, from whom to depart is only to return.ᴾ

22

Quod philosophia non docet, imo vetat cum principibus viveraᵃ

Philosophy does not teach us to live with princes; indeed she forbids it

Marsilio Ficino to Giovanni Cavalcanti,ᵇ his unique friend.

Iɴ the book in praise of Philosophy,¹ which I wrote this year for Bernardo Bembo, the Venetian ambassador, I tried with many arguments to showᶜ that Philosophy teaches all things. I ought to have made the one exception, that she does not teach us how to live with princes.ᵈ For if she forbids this altogether, as indeed she does, clearly she cannot teach us how. She altogether forbids it, it seems to me, since she commands the opposite; for in discovering[c] the love of truth she surely requires a tranquil mind and a free life. However, truth does not dwell in the company of princes; only lies, spiteful criticism and fawning flattery, men pretending to be what they are not and pretending not to be what they are. There is no tranquillity of mind, but cares, anxiety, envy and, in short, every kind of disturbance; not a freedom more precious than all gold, but a servitude so wretched that it spares neither subject nor[f] prince and ends either in slavery or in destruction.

Let no one confront me with Aristippus of Cyrene,[2] a lover not of wisdom but of slavery[g] and the body,[3] who was once so comfortably placed with Dionysius, the tyrant[h] of Syracuse. For if Aristippus ever put on the mantle[4] of Philosophy while with Socrates, he took it off as soon as he took on Dionysius. But the time came when he regretted this entanglement; for he realised that Dionysius was living under the shadow of the sword and that he himself was not only under the same threat but also in danger from Dionysius.

Much more prudent and certainly more fortunate were Democritus, Heraclitus, Socrates, Antisthenes, Diogenes, Crates, Xenocrates, Apollonius of Tyana, Plotinus[i] and many others who placed free and precious poverty far above the worthless and enslaving riches of kings, and sweet temperance far above the bitter pleasures of tyrants.[5]

It is worth considering those great philosophers whose memory we cherish who would have been far more successful than others in living with princes and kings if only Philosophy were able to teach men that.[j] I shall not describe how the young Octavian, being ungrateful for the services of his friend, the distinguished philosopher Cicero, handed him over for no good reason to his unscrupulous enemy for execution.[6] Nero condemned to death without cause his own teacher, the venerable philosopher Seneca.[7]

Alexander, king of Macedon, is said to have thrown his teacher, the philosopher Callisthenes, to the lions,[k] simply because he was often torn to shreds by him in argument.[8] But who would not marvel that those gods among philosophers, our Plato and Aristotle, the greatest authorities of all, who knew[l] all things that are, that had been and were soon to come, had the misfortune, not to say[m] the imprudence, to associate with tyrants, so that for the slightest reason their lives were quite often brought into great danger?" Nevertheless, although they adopted the prince, they did not discard the philosopher, as Xenophon, a follower of Socrates, was perhaps compelled to do at the court of King Cyrus of Persia.[9]

How wretched is the lot of philosophers who keep company with potentates! Twice was the divine Plato most shamefully sold! Three times he went in danger of death from both the elder and the younger Dionysius. This was partly because Plato virtually repudiated a certain book on theology[o] written by Dionysius which purported to represent Plato's thoughts;[10] but more particularly because he instructed them[p] daily as a master, urging them to govern more justly.

Alexander of Macedon ignominiously drove away that great and wise man, Aristotle, his teacher and instructor, and then cruelly persecuted him. This was either on account of Callisthenes, who was a follower of Aristotle, or on the grounds that Aristotle, having first taught the secrets of nature to Alexander, subsequently made them public.[11] The most trifling cause destroyed the divine teacher Pythagoras, mingling as he did with the aristocratic party in the republic,[q] or rather tyranny, of Croton.[12] It was a trivial cause that destroyed Zeno[r] of Elia,[13] that remarkable philosopher, under Hiero,[s] and the same was true of Anaxarchus under Nicocreon.[14]

But not wishing to turn my attention from philosophers to poets, I shall pass over the unjust exile[t] of Ovid;[15] Nero's longstanding hatred of his own Lucan, which was the result of a musical contest and which ended in his putting Lucan to death;[16] and Domitian's game of flies in which, under the compulsion of some strange desire, he killed his friend Statius.[17]

But allow me to return now to philosophers to conclude my discourse. Let no one be so ignorant of man's capacity as to believe that he can play the part of philosopher fitly and freely, and at the same time live with safety and serenity in the company of princes.[u]

However,[18] if anyone, ignorant of our affairs, raises our long-standing friendship with the Medici, I shall reply that they should not properly be called princes, but something greater and more sacred. For their singular virtues and great merit deserve more than any human title. They are fathers of their country in a free state.

23

Solus in amando laudandoque nunquam fallitur, cui amandi
laudandique lex deus est

In loving and praising, he alone is never mistaken whose law for love and praise is God

Marsilio Ficino to Giorgio Ciprio, a true physician: greetings.

Who is the lowest of all servants? He who is enslaved to his own servant.[a] Who is the most miserable? He for whom the wages of service are punishment. It therefore follows that the lowest and most miserable wretch is he who is enslaved to his body.

Now what sort of man is he who is slave to popular opinion? Empty; restless; unhappy. And what sort of man is he who binds himself to the idols of popular opinion? Hardly wise. Men may, of course, be exalted, but not idolized. Even then, they should be tested over a long period, fifteen years at least, and chosen with greatest care[b] before you exalt them. Otherwise love deceives judgement, and the outcome disappoints love. Moreover, very few men are fit to be praised, and then only when they are fully come to manhood, indeed when they are well advanced in years; and even then given only very moderate praise. Otherwise, in praising we are to blame and often regret our praises.

He alone is never mistaken for whom God is the law for both love and praise. For the sake of his own self, in order that he may worship God alone, let him love men in God, and in men praise God. To what purpose is all this? Simply to discuss with a man[c] who is firmly based in moral principles the principal bases of moral conduct.

24

Fides gignit spem, spes charitatem, charitatis ardor affert intelligentiae claritatem[a]

Faith gives birth to hope; hope gives birth to love. The flame of love brings clarity of intellect

Marsilio Ficino of Florence[b] to Bernardo Bembo, Venetian noble-man, doctor of law and illustrious knight: greetings.

THE Apostle Paul, the chosen vessel of divine wisdom,[1] was snatched up into the third heaven[2] from where heavenly love is kindled in the minds of earthly men. There, he suddenly saw that invisible sun[3] to whose splendour no man can raise his eyes until he has first been set on fire with divine love by its flames. A man is fully fired by these flames only if he always puts true faith in the rays of that sun, which illuminate everything, and if he firmly places all his hope in its heat, which warms all things with its love.

Now illustrious Bernardo, since I could not see clearly how much the light from this sun has recently illumined for me, I turned to Giovanni Cavalcanti.[c] But as, like me, he seems to be in darkness,[d] we decided with one accord that our Bernardo Bembo, who is endowed with the eyes of a lynx, should be the judge.

25

Amore humano nihil infirmius. Divino nihil firmius

Nothing is frailer than human love, nothing stronger than divine love

Marsilio Ficino to Girolamo Amazzi: greetings.

How different is the nature of love from that of almost everything else, my most loving and best loved[a] Amazzi.[1] For the bigger other things are, the stronger they are thought to be; but the more extreme love and friendship appear, the frailer they seem to be. For often extreme love is injured by a succession of little things,[b] more so than moderate love. Either the heat of the desire[c] itself arouses fiery choler which, fanned by something trivial, sometimes floods out in a great surge of anger;[2] or preoccupation with one fixed idea begets melancholy, which is full of groundless fears.[3] More precisely, when a man thinks that he has given everything to another and therefore demands everything in return from his beloved, his avarice[d] never obtains what it was seeking with the whole force of his mind.[4]

But the desire of the erring mind, essentially weak or self-seeking,[e] suffers these frustrations deservedly. Since this desire feeds on the winds of the world, just when it seems to be growing most it is not so much growing as swelling;[f] thus the stronger it appears, the weaker it is. Therefore human love is a thing full of anxious fear.[5]

Divine love, however, kindled by the flames of the virtues and growing strong from celestial rays, seeks to return to the sublime heights of heaven[g] which no fear of earthly ills can ever trouble. Of such a kind is our mutual love, Amazzi. Therefore, as you are sure of your love towards me, so be just as sure of my love towards you. Far be it from us that one human heart should fail to respond to another that is always calling. Even strings seem to respond to strings that are similarly tuned,[h] and one lyre resounds[i] in answer to another;[6] indeed a solid wall[j] may echo[k] to one who calls.

26

Nemo vere servit, nisi qui servit volens.[a] Nemo dominatur
vere, nisi qui volentibus dominatur

*No one serves truly who does not serve willingly; no
one is truly master except he be master of the willing*

Marsilio Ficino humbly commends himself to the Reverend Lord
Cardinal Raffaele Riario.[b]

AFTER we left you yesterday, I could not contain my keen envy of
your household for having your companionship, which is sweeter
than ambrosia[c] and nectar.

Therefore today, lest I perish from envy, I am swiftly returning
to those who are privileged to recline at the feast of the gods[1] (if
it is lawful[d] to say such a thing). And lest I be compelled to depart
from that feast once more and be tortured again by jealousy, I am
coming back to you now, guided by one who never strays far from
you and from whom I never stray; one who commands me and
obeys you. 'Now who is this?' you ask. Who this is you will
shortly hear, if you wish. On yesterday's journey my guide[e]
was the beautiful Venus in Taurus, attended by the moon and
commanding the middle of the heavens.[2] Pier Leone, the excellent
scientist and mathematician, will confirm this, I think. But our
guide on today's journey will be the offspring of heavenly Venus,
most gracious Love.

Therefore be pleased to receive with loving affection your lover
Marsilio; for I hear that by virtue of your remarkably benign nature
you love even the unloving. See, Reverend Father, with what
freedom, or rather licence, I address you. I have just called myself
your lover;[f] perhaps I should rather have said your slave. Alas, I
am at fault![g] But you yourself, my Lord, are the cause of this. For
you present yourself to all men everywhere in such a way that
whoever does not[h] show complete freedom and trust in your
presence will undoubtedly appear the most servile and untrusting
of all men.

Perhaps, after all, I am not at fault. For I have sufficiently
confessed myself a slave in professing myself a lover. No one serves

truly who does not serve willingly. No one is truly master except
he be master of the willing. Oh how wonderful is the dominion
of Venus and of Love! For, as the poets say, ferocious Mars cannot
tame Venus, neither can omnipotent Jupiter himself tame Cupid.
According to the poets[i] all divine beings are fired by Love's flames,[3]
or at least they shine in his rays and reflect his splendour.[j]

Fare well and prosper, most gentle Lord.[4] But why have I omitted
that name most dear to me, that of my Salviati, Archbishop of
Pisa? Clearly because in naming Riario I considered that I had also
spoken the name of Salviati. I would commend to you the
magnanimous Bracciolini if I thought that faithful Achates[5] were
in need of any commendation to Aeneas.

But now go forth, my letter; may your journey be fruitful.
Swiftly seek the hills of Montughi[6] and, lest you set out with too
little distinction, take with you for the journey the name of Cosimo
himself, the most distinguished of men. Give the poet Cosmico[7]
my greetings.

27

Veritas de institutione principis ad Raphaelem riarium
cardinalem

*Truth addresses Cardinal Riario[1] on the education of a
ruler[2]*

I BEG you, fortunate Cardinal, not to be surprised because you do
not read any man's name inscribed as the author of this letter. How
miraculous that at this moment no human mind is addressing you,
but Truth herself! Truth comes to you now, not merely defenceless
but naked,[3] as you may see, not protected by the barbs and subtleties
of disputation, not decked in the ornaments of fine words, for she
knows[a] that of all things she is the most powerful and beautiful.
She knows that just as[b] anything from outside which approaches a
light does not illumine that light but obscures it, so Truth herself[c]

is weakened, so to speak, and deformed by additions from anywhere else.

Let her now earnestly entreat you to hear her awhile with a generous mind, as she speaks out for your benefit, for she may not know that you always hear her willingly; to hear anything in any other way is erroneous and unprofitable.

To Cardinal Riario, her most beloved son, Truth gives many greetings and promises true salvation.

The Sceptic philosophers and many others falsely slander me as being[d] most obscure and nowhere to be found. This is far from being so; for what shines more clearly, than my light, whereby the very Sun and the world are lit? Again, what can be more widely and clearly visible than Truth, through whom[e] alone lies revealed all that is revealed anywhere, and outside whom whatever is said to be visible is nothing but darkness, in which all things are hidden? I am[f] not in any way mean or of ill will;[g] of my own accord I run to meet everything everywhere, and very willingly.

But many people grasp for me with clouded minds, whereas I am apprehended only by a mind which is clear. Most people think that I abide in the high palaces of princes. On the contrary, I am more often compelled to seek out cottages and to dwell in humble homes.[4] Leaking roofs and cracked walls are no obstacle whatever to me;[h] here the doors[i] are open and a bare house receives me. But I am driven back from the thick roofs and walls of rich houses; and if these doors are ever opened, a tumult of countless falsehoods immediately streams out to meet me. Not thinking to stay among enemies, I instantly take flight. I leave that house which is full of gold and lies but impoverished and empty of truth. Today, however, I come to you willingly, fortunate cardinal, to dwell with you always, if you but wish it. I have come in haste at the very outset of your appointment before your hearth is beset by my enemies, the pernicious lies of flatterers and slanderers.

You[j] should attribute your high rank of office to your ancestry and not to your own merits which, to speak truly,[k] could not have achieved so much in your few tender years. You should not attribute it to fate and fortune either, for sacred mysteries and holy orders do not arise from the caprice of fortune but from the eternal wisdom of God. For divine providence has ordained that in our times she should nurture at her breast the perfect shepherd of the Christian flock, feeding him from his very birth on spiritual food alone. And before he is caught up in childish games and applies his mind to harmful or trivial things, she should lead him to conduct becoming a man and instruct him in the greatest and finest duties. Thus, as you have heard, it is God Himself who has recently brought you forth as a new man.[5] For your part, therefore, when you have put the world aside, by your godly conduct embrace your Heavenly Father, who embraces everything. Believe me, you will stand fast so long as you hold fast to Him who is not moved. Do not in any way trust in the high position and power of men.[l] The highest positions are very often shaken by wind and lightning, and mighty edifices fall most heavily and are only with much difficulty reconstructed.[6] Arise, act in Him who cannot fall and you yourself will never fall. For men abandon themselves with unfortunate consequences whenever they foolishly and ungratefully abandon Him, without whom they can in no way exist. Alas, whoever attempts to desert such a protector[m] hardly leaves Him at all, for he instantly encounters him again as an avenger. Anyone who wickedly disregards the merciful Father's light discovers in this same Father a fiery judge.

Hence[n] you know that lawful cardinals are really vicars of the Apostles and pivots[7] of the Christian Church. For that reason, they ought not to consider any particular advantage, either for themselves or for another, but only the common good[o] of the Church. Furthermore, they should do, think and speak nothing which is unworthy of apostolic sanctity. Those who do the contrary are not cardinals, but robbers of the Church. They are not vicars of the Apostles, but their enemies. May I say this?[p] May I with your permission say this one thing above all else? Of course, I may say it even without your permission, for who will ever be allowed to speak the truth, if not Truth herself? Understand that nothing should be more foreign to apostolic men than pride, pomp and luxury.

Just as[q] it pleases you to control your servants outside, take as much care to serve divine laws and to control your servants inside:[r] the senses. Remember that your servants are men, equal to you in origin, and that the human species, which is by nature free, ought not to be, indeed cannot be, united by any fear,[s] but only by love.

Just as almost all men of power delight in their several possessions, neatly disposed and displayed in their homes, so will you delight in a mind that is ordered by fine language and conduct. It will be your art to temper both the desires of the mind and all your actions lest, when all external things are in harmony for you, the mind alone be in discord.[8] It will also be your schooling to make frequent study of the most select writers lest the mind alone be impoverished in the midst of such great riches.

Let the hunters[t] and fowlers around you be completely trustworthy and wise, men who by prudence and exceptional love[u] of mankind[9] obtain for you the favour and good will of all. Love of mankind alone is the food by which men are won, and only by the favour of men do human affairs prosper.[10] Nothing is more dangerous for a prince than that a great many men should feel contempt for him or hate him or envy him too much. Contempt is avoided by knowledge, worth and integrity. Hatred is softened by innocence and humanity, and envy is allayed by generosity, liberality and greatness of action. Since all men are of the same kind and possessed of free will, no wonder they bear servitude with a most unwilling spirit, unless those who rule are equal to them in humility, even as they surpass them in rank, and clearly excel them far more through wisdom than through good fortune.

Nature[v] has given to those parts of the body below the head only the power of touch, but she has furnished the head alone with the powers of all the senses. By doing this she seems to have warned men that those who, like the head, strive to rule others, should surpass the rest in wisdom, just as the head surpasses all members of the body in its range of sense.[11]

No great man[w] ought to believe that his conduct can in any way be hidden. For the greatest things, whatever they be, are most fully exposed to view and are the envy of all[x] who forgive little and disparage much. Since it is very difficult for a prince to conceal himself from others, let him see that nothing at all lies hidden either in private or in public life. Let him first be Argus; then let him raise a lynx in his house; Oedipus, too, should be there were that possible.[12] It is dangerous to despise little things[y] in great matters, for often a contemptible little spark kindles a great conflagration.[13] It is neither proper[z] nor safe that one who should be watching over many men, and who is being watched by still more men, should ever go completely to sleep, or that the leader of many, by serving greed and lust, should become slave to a beast.

The best[aa] and safest thing is never[bb] to be roused to anger. For does not a ferment of anger end in intoxication and madness? However, if anger shakes off restraint and rage is boiling up, the tongue must be curbed. And as is customary with madmen, hands and feet should be bound so that nothing may be said or done in a frenzy. The disciples[cc] of Pythagoras were never able to detect in him any sign of anger.[14] Nor had the close friends of Socrates any indication of his anger, except silence.[15] Once Plato, father of philosophers, angered by a boy who had done wrong, said to Xenocrates: 'Beat this boy, for I cannot while I am angry.'[16]

Let[dd] your mind be at once humble and exalted, a blend of dignity and courtesy;[ee] may you live temperately and speak truthfully, but sparingly. May you be generous in giving but not rash in promising. May you be firm in faith, your vision wide. May your judgements stand the test of time, following carefully the words of the wise. Lest many men should find it easy to deceive you every day, do not trust many and do not trust easily. Let not smooth persuasion or vain speculation move you, but nothing less than sure reason. Do not make a start on anything unless you have first seen that the end is both good and well-assured. Avoid servants who are evil or of ill repute, lest you yourself be reputed an evil master.

But why have we just passed with our eyes closed what is most important of all? The poets depict love as blind because the lover is very often deceived when he makes a judgement either about himself or about the beloved.[17] Since men love themselves more than anyone else, they are deceived by no one more than themselves. Therefore, do not trust your own convictions in anything. Again, do not entrust yourself entirely to a single counsellor but have many; and these should be elders whom long experience has taught and whose fine characters have been commended to you by the most reliable report, which is clearly proved in practice. Whenever you are discussing a serious matter with your counsellors, take care that they understand your will, lest in their counsel they follow your pleasure rather than what is useful and honourable.

Furthermore, daily declare to your counsellors that the gift of truth, from wherever it may be offered, will be as pleasing to you as the [gg] most costly gifts are to the greedy tyrants who often receive them. I pray you to listen to those who would warn you, lest you be compelled to lay bare your very heart to the darts of fortune. Stop your ears totally to those who praise you, as you would to the evil songs of the Sirens. Remember that you are human and consequently you always have within you some things which can be shown to be false. For this reason those in your household who praise you indiscriminately are either blind themselves or wish you to be. If the laws punish with the greatest severity as sorcerers those who hypnotise with the eye or captivate the ear with incantations, or poison the body, what do we think[hh] should be done to those who, by always agreeing and pleasing, deprive the mind's eye of light or rob its ear of hearing? So if you wish to see, if you wish to hear, if you wish to live, banish far away all flatterers and ministers of pleasure as you would your enemies.

But[ii] what shall we say of those men who sometimes make accusations against members of your household? Perhaps it may sometimes seem that they should be heard for a while, yet you should never heed them. If you ever do listen to them, let them lead you to caution rather than to punishment. But if you do show[jj] the power of punishment, be content with this one sort: that you drive far from your[kk] doors slanderers, evil speakers and envious men as if they were rabid dogs.

Finally,[ll] let your house be a temple of God. Let it be the eye of prudence, the scales of justice, the seat of fortitude.[mm] Let it be an example of moderation, a standard of integrity, the splendour of love, the source of the Graces and the chorus of the Muses. Let it be a school for orators and poets, a shrine for philosophers and theologians and a council chamber for the wise. Let it be a nursery of genius,[nn] a reward for the learned, a table for the poor, the hope of the good, a refuge for the innocent and a stronghold for the oppressed. If with all your strength you heed these things and others like them, you will at last hear those blessed words: 'Upon this rock I will build my church.'[18]

I commend to you Marsilio Ficino of Florence, through whose mouth I have spoken these things.[oo]

27th January, 1478.
Florence.

28

Tunc solum viro dignitatem nacto congratulari debemus,
cum dignitate dignus apparet

*We should congratulate a man on attaining high office
only if he seems to be worthy of that office*

Marsilio Ficino humbly commends himself to Cardinal Riario.

IF Truth herself had not recently instructed you to be deaf to those
who praise you,[1] I would not follow up your appointment with
the greatest praises. Almighty God, what a great appointment! But
listen! I seem to hear our modest Riario interrupting my song of
praise at its very start, even though Truth herself does not object.

You do not wish to be praised to your face, Reverend Father.[a]
So be it; but at least permit me to praise in my inward judgement
what you would prevent me from praising in your presence. Or
perhaps you would forbid that too, lest the sharp point of fame
which has pierced you from the front should strike you from
behind? Of course, I shall submit to my master.

But will you nevertheless grant me something very small?[b] That
if I may not congratulate you I may at least congratulate the office
itself,[c] because it has at last decided to honour the man by whom
it is now likewise seen to be honoured. Grant furthermore that I
may rejoice in my good fortune, because as a lover of Truth I have
newly acquired a patron whose own patron is Truth herself.[d]

I shall also congratulate Truth on her good fortune, for although
she went forth defenceless and naked she has found not enemies
but friends. But Truth frequently reproaches me these days,
Reverend Father, not because I have sent her out defenceless but
because she is unattended. Who would deny that she has gone forth
from our door unattended? Not even Religion herself, who sustains
the whole care of Truth, has accompanied her. Therefore, lest Truth
should further complain of me, whether to me or to you, I am
sending you this *Religion*[2] as the handmaiden[e] of Truth, similarly
naked and defenceless. I do not think, however, that either Truth
or her companion, Religion, will be in any way unattended in the
house of our Cardinal, who cares attentively for both.

29

Veritas virum reddit^a dignitate dignum

Truth makes a man worthy of office

Marsilio Ficino to Francesco Soderini, expert in civil law:^b greetings.

SWEETEST Soderini, Truth herself, moved by our prayers, has recently sent greetings to our friend Cardinal Riario.[1] However, it will seem that she has not satisfied my prayers unless she has also greeted my true friend, Soderini.^c If anyone thinks that Truth has come to you later than to Riario, he is wrong. For Truth came^d to Riario after his appointment, but is setting out to you before yours, with the intention of either making you worthy or at least declaring^e you to be already worthy, of such an appointment.[2]

30

Omne tulit punctum, qui miscuit utile dulci

He who has blended the serious with the pleasing has satisfied everyone[1]

Marsilio Ficino to Bernardo Bembo of Venice: greetings.^a

WHEN I consider the letters of my Aeneas, illustrious Bembo, I seem to be looking up at his mother Venus, joined with Jupiter. For at one moment our Aeneas pronounces weighty laws with Jupiter and at another he sings songs of love with Venus. Yet everywhere he appears full of light and everywhere benign. Should you enquire what connection there is between light and heavy qualities,^b the very nature of creation will directly reply: Beneath heaven, light and heavy elements are mixed, and flowers and leaves mingle with fruit. In the heavens, the swift are tempered by the slow and the fixed by the moving; also there is the greatest concord[c] among the qualities when Mercury is in conjunction with Saturn, and Venus with Jupiter.[2] He, then, who has blended the serious with the pleasing has satisfied everyone. Farewell and good fortune, my profitable and pleasing Aeneas!

31

Malo[a] meis litteris mente responderi, quam manu

I prefer my letters to be answered by mind rather than by hand

Marsilio Ficino to Giovanni Pietro Apollinare, the distinguished Aristotelian.[b]

WHETHER the same cause is able to bring about opposite effects in the same subject is a great controversy among philosophers.[1] Recently our Amazzi[2] has settled this issue for us, showing, not in words as the dialecticians do, but in action itself, that this can be achieved; for he has led us simultaneously into opposing states of mind. He highly praises Giovanni Pietro, the distinguished philosopher, and loves him deeply. Now when I hear him praising thus, I am immediately impelled to write something; however, when I see him loving so deeply I recognise the beloved[c] philosopher present with us in the lover, and so am restrained from writing, realising that friends present have no need of letters.

What shall I do? Shall I write? I certainly shall, and I too shall divide your mind into opposing states, so that at the same time you both do and do not respond. O remarkable man, believe me, my love is as strong and deep as my writing is weak. To my unworthy writing, therefore, pen no response at all; but to my worthy love please respond with love. And if you love us, take the greatest care of your health, for if you do not yourself[d] fare well, neither in these times can philosophy.

32

Maiorem charitatem nemo habet, quam ut animam suam
ponat quis pro amicis suis[a]

*Greater love hath no man than this, that a man lay
down his life for his friends*[1]

Marsilio Ficino to the magnanimous Lorenzo de' Medici: greetings.

GREETINGS, magnanimous Medici, our very best doctor. You alone
have truly performed the office of the heavenly physician, since He
sent His eternal son from heaven to earth as the healer of human
ills, and yesterday you too, of your own accord, sent your beloved
son[2] to us to bring sick souls to full health. For the salvation of
mankind He did not spare His son,[3] while for our consolation you,
too, did not spare your son. For this widespread fear of the plague
did not restrain you from consoling your sorrowing friends with
the presence of your noble son, so that you have directly fulfilled
those divine words: 'Greater love hath no man than this, that a
man lay down his life for his friends.'[b]

Lorenzo, while you exercise such careful watch[c] over our safety
on all sides, you draw to yourself all that is ours, so that we now
live in you, rather than in ourselves. It follows that we cannot
repay you in turn.[d] We would certainly offer ourselves and our[e]
souls for your sake, if we had them. But you yourself have them,
Medici. So lay them down whenever you please. Farewell, once
my sole patron, now my sole father.[4]

33

Felix est, qui habet omnia quae vult. Habet autem omnia
quae vult, qui omnia[a] vult, quae habet

*Happy is the man who has all he desires; only he has
all he desires who desires all he has*[1]

Marsilio Ficino speaks of happiness to Francesco Sassetti.

THE wise, Sassetti, judge that man alone to be happy for whom all
things come to pass according to his intent. All things come to pass
according to his intent[b] for him alone who has all he desires.[c] Only
he has all he desires who desires all he has.[2] That man alone desires
everything he has (that is, whatever happens to him, either because
of his nature[d] or by chance) who first of all understands that there
is nothing good that he should not desire.[e] Secondly, he considers
that He who from the beginning made all things good[f] daily
disposes everything everywhere for the good. Finally, since nothing[g]
anywhere is at variance with him, he is at one with the creator of
all. So we judge him alone to be happy who has committed himself
wholeheartedly to God, the helmsman. Whatever happens he either
approves as something coming from God, or at least praises as
something to be brought to its place in the good by God.

  Perhaps you will ask[h] by what reasoning I may best demonstrate
this? By just this for the moment, because a letter delights in
brevity:[i] if the light of the sun were infinite or the heat of fire
without limit, no place would admit of darkness, nor the least cold
be felt anywhere. We know that the one ruler of the whole universe,
who directs and moves such a great body so well over so great a
span of time[j] without ever wearying, is good and without limit. If
He is indisputably without limit and reproduces Himself infinitely
throughout space and surpasses everything infinitely in degree of
virtue, where then does evil dwell, if it cannot exist with the good,
and the good itself fills the universe? Evil therefore has no true
place anywhere, only an imaginary one. It is certainly not in nature
herself, but rather in that mind which deceives itself to such an
extent about divine goodness that it thinks things[k] could be disposed

other than well under the infinite good. By contrast, nothing other than good happens to the man who realises that there is nothing other than good.[1] To be able[m] to consider all things thus, and therefore live happily, only devotion to God can be of use to us. Moreover, it will always be twice as useful to you as to anyone else, my Francesco, if you surpass others in devotion to the same degree that that[n] spacious mansion of yours surpasses the rest. Your home, Sassetti, is twice as fit for devotion as other homes. It is rare for other homes to have even one chapel. But yours contains two;[3] and very beautiful ones at that. Be[o] twice as devoted as the rest, my Francesco. Be twice as happy.

34

Prosperis perversius utimur, quam adversis

Our use of prosperity is even more perverse than our use of adversity

Marsilio Ficino to Cardinal Raffaele Riario[a] and Francesco Salviati, Archbishop of Pisa[b]

ARISTOTLE writes[c] in his book on Ethics[1] that it is more difficult to endure pain than to abstain from pleasure. Indeed,[d] this seems provable by reason, since pain is more potent in destroying nature than pleasure is in preserving or restoring it. For this reason,[e] a man of sound mind will choose, if the choice be given,[f] to abstain from pleasure rather than to accept or suffer pain.

In spite of this, by some foolish, or rather unhappy, fate it happens[g] that most mortals make more perverse use of prosperity than of adversity, and that those who have not yielded to the threat of pain may yet succumb to the allurements of pleasure. I could mention Achilles, Hannibal,[2] Mark Antony and many others who had indeed stood firm while the north wind raged, yet collapsed when caressed by a gentle breeze; and although they freed themselves from a sea of gall, the merest drop of honey[3] overwhelmed them instantly. And if, like Homer, I were allowed to compare flies with heroes,[4] I would add that flies are never drowned in sour wine, but often in sweet.

Is there anyone who, upon due reflection, is not truly astonished[h] at how wisely Solomon, the wisest of the Hebrews, persevered with his labour, and how unwisely he succumbed to his lust?[5] Or how bravely Hercules, the bravest of the Gentiles, overcame every danger, no matter how great; yet how weakly he placed[i] his neck under the yoke of pleasure?

Should you enquire[j] why good fortune rather than adversity softens and breaks men's spirits, Philosophy's brief reply would be that prosperity fills men's spirits with the breeze of abundance and that this abundance makes them unrestrained and neglectful; licence renders such men weaker, that is more inclined to evil, than all other men.[k]

The truth is that by nature every appetite chooses and pursues the good, while it shuns and drives away evil.[6] Now pleasure appears to carry before it an image of the good, but pain an image of evil. Therefore, when pleasure comes to us, not only do we not shun it, we wantonly pursue[l] it as if it were a mistress, yielding and giving ourselves up to it. And so, as Plato says,[7] we are caught, as if on a fish-hook,[m] and then unwittingly we are destroyed by enemies, that is by those evils which lurk beneath the pleasure. But when the hideous face of pain shows itself, the whole strength of our nature is instantly armed within us, as against an enemy; and so we often fight vigorously, overcoming this open foe more easily than the hidden traitor.

Therefore to prosper from prosperity, let us remember that the nature of evil is to offer itself to us daily under the guise of good, that is pleasure, a snare to deceive and destroy the wretched. As for evil itself, especially corruption of the mind, should it ever come to us undisguised,[n] being even[o] more ugly than ugliness itself, it would be promptly shunned. But when it comes to us covered by pleasure,[p,q] the image of the good itself, it is very easily taken in by anyone and given lodging as if it were the good; but soon after, it secretly strikes down its unwary host with a sword, as he deserves.[8]

Therefore let us flee from pleasure to escape from pain. Pleasure bought with pain brings destruction.[9]

35

Nunquam deest amantibus scribendi materia

Lovers are never at a loss for something to write

Marsilio Ficino of Florence to Bernardo Bembo of Venice, most illustrious lawyer and knight: greeetings.

FOR a long time I have been looking to you for an explanation for our long silence, and because I find no cause in particular to account for it I have been prolonging it still further. Nevertheless I am writing now because of this silence, good Bembo, and as I do not find anything better to write I am writing this: that I have nothing to write. Now what are we to do, dearest Bembo? Do you see what harm expectation does us? For so long as I am expecting your letter at any moment, and you mine, neither[a] of us gives what is so eagerly expected, and neither of us receives a letter! So from now on let us strive to anticipate each other with letters. In particular, we should not wait for the muse to dictate to us what to write, for those who must wait for the inspiration of the muse are those who are not inspired by love;[1] but for those whose hearts are continually fanned into flame by the breath of love, invention always shines, illuminated[b] by the same love.

36

Praestat dare superflua quam debita denegare

It is better to give things which are superfluous than to refuse what is owed

Marsilio Ficino of Florence[a] to Pier Leone of Spoleto, his fellow philosopher: greetings.

YOUR letter, fellow philosopher, asks us for the Platonic Mysteries,[1] and at the same time discusses them. So beautifully does it ask that I do not know how to refuse him who asks; so well does it discuss them that I cannot send anything, since I have absolutely nothing to send to him who already possesses all.[2]

What then am I to do? Shall I be ungenerous to one who demands so graciously? Or shall I needlessly bestow liberality on one who possesses all?

On the whole I prefer sometimes to give things which are superfluous rather than perhaps refuse what is owed.

37

Gratia naturalis plus persuadet quam acquisita eloquentia. Humanitas plures vincit quam violentia

Natural grace is more persuasive than acquired eloquence; love of mankind conquers more men than force

Marsilio Ficino of Florence to Marco Aurelio, the illustrious orator: greetings.

JUST as everything seems sombre at sunset but joyful at sunrise, so some time ago everyone[a] openly showed his grief at Bernardo Bembo's departure, but now gives thanks for his return.[1]

At this moment I should like to address a few words to the Venetian Senate: 'O divine Senate,[b] if ever you wish to stem the flow of rivers or to move rocks, you will not summon an Orpheus or an Amphion[2] but rather Bernardo. For through a marvellous grace he is as persuasive by his silence as they are by their music. If ever you need to subdue distant or rebellious nations you will not send a Caesar or a Pompey but rather Bernardo, for he captures more men more easily with his love of mankind than do generals with their armies.'

What relevance has this for you, excellent Marco? It is that you yourself may know and tell your friends how universally popular is this appointment of yours and theirs; and that you ask Bernardo, particularly on behalf of our men of letters, to make his way here with speed, and happily, with his coming, to restore to me my own self, which he carried off with such ease when he departed.[3]

38

Excusatio de libro astronomiae serius reddito

Excusing the rather late return of a book on Astronomy

Marsilio Ficino to Antonio Benivieni, a true physician: greetings.

THE book on the stars,[1] which you gave me at a propitious moment a long time ago, I am now at last sending back to you. Do not blame me that it is returning to you rather late, for I am usually swifter, but blame the stars themselves. For they have decreed that they should all complete their own courses, Antonio, before returning to their houses.

39

Excusatio diuturni silentii

An apology for a long silence[1]

Marsilio Ficino of Florence humbly commends himself to Raffaele Riario,[a] Cardinal of San Giorgio.[2]

WOULD you ever have thought, Reverend Father, that so long a silence could occur[b] between us? I think that you may cease to be surprised by this one particular thing if you just consider[c] carefully the general state of everything at this time. Do you not see what an extraordinary year this is?[d] So many new and unheard-of events occur every day that every day one finds oneself repeating such words as, 'I would not have believed it'.

But putting aside public affairs, let me come to my own. I had long desired to find and to follow a lord who would satisfy me completely and whom I myself might equally satisfy. Finally I found him. A thousand times I was summoned; I did not go. I would never have believed this possible; oh, how often might I have cursed that I could not go. At first, my Raffaele, when you implored me to follow your footsteps, you demanded the impossible. For not only the private business, which I mentioned, held me back, but also public affairs of the greatest importance, which I could not reveal. However, a few days after you had gone, weary of my own company and longing for yours, I too wanted the impossible: not just to have come to you, but to have got there first. Alas, for the same reasons I was again held back. But benevolent Venus and Jupiter, seeking to restore what Mars and Saturn in their cruelty had been trying to tear or pull[e] apart,[3] suddenly brought our Archbishop of Amalfi[f] back to Florence. He is a very close friend of mine, but above all is devoted to you.

I have been able to speak freely with him of my Raffaele; as often as ardent love has moved me to do so. He it is above all[g] with whom I could join in praising you. Thus he has been the chief physician in my illness. He has restored my Raffaele to me, since wherever two are gathered together in your name, there are you also.[4]

You remember how frequently and how highly I have praised the judgement and goodness of the Archbishop to you. If you ever came to know him[h] in person you would agree with me that I have indeed praised the man truly, but too sparingly. His brother, the excellent Pietro Niccolini, will commend the Archbishop's cause to you.[i] If your Marsilio had ever merited anything from you, he would commend Pietro to you on these merits.[j] Yet since there are no such merits, which he much regrets, it is solely through your kindness and Amalfi's virtue that he commends Pietro's cause to you again and again.

40

Patientia sine religione habere non potest

One cannot have patience without religion[1]

Marsilio Ficino to Antonio Cocci, the distinguished lawyer: greetings.

THREE things in particular patience teaches us, it seems to me: first, that you should be willing to bear cheerfully the ills which nature herself bids you bear unwillingly; second, that you should make those things which fate has decreed to be inevitable, agreeable to your own will; third, that you should turn[a] any evil whatsoever into good, which is the office of God alone. In the first of these, patience requires you to oppose nature, in the second to confound fate, and in the third to raise yourself to the level of God.

It was far easier for Hercules long ago to obey[b] the commands of Eurystheus[2] and to conquer those unconquerable monsters than it is for us to comply with the precepts of patience. And indeed the very great difficulty with which we strive to do this makes this point very clear to us; because in other matters, whatever we frequently put our hand to, in the end we usually accomplish in the best and easiest way. But I cannot see what progress[c] most people are making in the practice of patience. This is not surprising, since the whole of man's life in this region of the universe, which is malign and opposed to celestial minds, seems to be nothing other than sickness and perpetual sorrow. But, as I was saying, although we continually suffer evils, almost continuously we suffer them badly. Added to the other evils, which are countless, impatience comes to us as the culmination of them all. Impatience is so bad that without it nothing is bad for us, and with it nothing good.

For impatience alone causes adversities, which could relate merely to external things and to the body,[d] to pass right through to the soul as well. In addition, it allows us but scant enjoyment of the good things provided by nature or by fortune. Patience, on the other hand, both transforms evils into good by bearing them well and also finds the greatest delight in good things by using them well.

Assuredly,[e] just as we bear evils badly, that is with difficulty and unhappiness, when we are separated from the supreme good, so in equal measure do we bear them well, that is easily and happily, when we are united[f] with the supreme good. For where there is all good there alone is found the remedy for all evils. Moreover, we are united with the supreme good whenever we join wholeheartedly with the will of God, the governor of all. Finally, we join with that will if we love, especially if we acknowledge that in loving individual good things we are really loving nothing other than the supreme divine good itself. From this good, individual things have that whereby they are good and have to be loved and we[g] have that whereby we have to be loved and are able to love.

Let us therefore acknowledge,[h] O friend, I beseech you, let us finally acknowledge this: since nothing anywhere pleases except by its reflection of God, then it is God Himself who pleases us in things that please.[i] From Him[j] those individual things have precisely that which makes them please. Thus, in loving all things, we shall realise beyond doubt that it is God Himself who is being loved; in this way we shall join wholeheartedly with His will. Thus united with God, we shall successfully surmount fortune, nature and fate. We shall readily understand[k] that, just as individual particles of heat or light must return to absolute heat or light, so whatever has any part of the good, that is all things, so well and wisely[l] ordered in the one system of the universe, must clearly come home to that one absolute goodness and wisdom. Since no good is lacking from absolute goodness, fully present are eternal life, full knowledge of all things,[m] unlimited bounty, total service and perfect happiness. And since everything is thence disposed in the best possible way, we shall always accept whatever happens as the best.

The whole virtue of patience consists in this alone, that we fully accept as good whatever takes place under the governance of infinite goodness.

41

Sola malorum medicina est patientia[a]

Patience is the sole remedy for evils

Marsilio Ficino of Florence to the distinguished Bernardo Bembo, lawyer, knight and Venetian ambassador: greetings.

WHENEVER[b] I take up[c] my pen these days, which I do frequently, it comes to mind that I should write something about patience. These iron ages bring us nothing but evil. The Muses impart to us nothing but patience, the virtue required for bearing evils. There is now a need for this transforming alchemy, which turns iron into gold,[d] so that the worst ages, which come as iron because of suffering, may be transformed at least for us[e] into gold[1] through the exercise of patience.

Therefore,[f] O most patient of men, accept copies of three letters[2] which briefly discuss patience.

7. 'The Resurrection' by Verrocchio, National Museum, Florence (Photo: Phaidon Archive). This relief sculpture was made for the Villa de' Medici at Carreggi in 1478. It represents Christ rising from the tomb, but from the date it could also commemorate the death of Giuliano. On this interpretation the Roman soldiers represent the Medici in mourning. However, the risen Christ imparts to the work a message of supreme hope.

8. *Melozzo da Forlì: 'Pope Sixtus IV and his Court', Vatican Picture Gallery (Photo: Phaidon Archive). The man on his knees, receiving audience of the Pope, is the scholar Platina, the librarian of the Vatican Library, and possibly Ficino's tutor in Greek. Second from the left is Girolamo Riario, nephew of Sixtus and main architect of the Pazzi Conspiracy.*

42

Nihil magis vel necessarium vel voluntarium est quam amor

Nothing is more of a necessity, yet nothing is more freely willed than love

Marsilio Ficino of Florence to the most learned Antonio Vinciguerra, scribe to the Venetians: greetings.

MAY both you and Bembo enjoy reading our book on religion. May you always remember your Marsilio or, to be more accurate, your Bernardo Bembo. Long ago I was transformed into Bernardo by the god, or perhaps I should say magician,[1] who alone among the divine powers commands free wills. Only divine love,[a] most loving Antonio, often makes what is freely willed a necessity; then I love in such a way that I cannot help loving. On the other hand, divine love sometimes makes necessity freely willed, and then I love in such a way that I do not wish not to love, and I do not even wish to be able to wish not to love.

Should you therefore wish to use the name Marsilio Bembo or Bernardo Ficino, you would name both[b] quite correctly. On the same principle, you surely realise that you are also bound[2] with us. A triple cord, Antonio, is difficult[c] to break.[3] Yet, while in all things we ought to comply with our Bembo,[d] in one particular he ought perhaps for once not to be complied with. Shall I speak? Yes, certainly I shall, for where love overflows, there also forgiveness abounds. Bernardo seems in a way to be an Averroist rather than a Platonist, since he on his own, by remaining silent, is far more persuasive of the heresy of Averroes[4] than all the Averroists by their arguments. For by a marvellous grace and an inspiring love, he creates in the many a single will, thus implying with Averroes that mind in the many is one.

But let us not impute any impiety when we are discussing piety itself. Let our Bembo be a man of David, not of Averroes. Behold how good, and how pleasant it is, for brethren to dwell together in unity.[5]

43

Excusatio ubi serius respondemus

An excuse for a late reply

Marsilio Ficino to Lotterio Neroni: greetings.

Do not be surprised, my best Lotterio, if you receive rather late
our letters in reply to yours, for your letters reach us late, being
sent down, it seems, from heaven itself; and ours in turn are later
still, since they seek the realms of heaven from earth. But I have
recently discovered, I do not know how, the best way[a] to raise
myself from the ground[1] and for a little while to scale the very
heights of heaven. So I will seize,[b] as best I may, the rays from the
sun that reach down to earth. By these, as if by ropes,[2] I shall from
now on, with all my strength, ascend the ethereal realms,[3] and
there I shall embrace my Lotterio, who already embraces the
heavens. Thus I am sending you a copy of that little work on light[4]
which I composed long ago for Phoebus, the Venetian orator.[c] May
you find it profitable! But do not let my letter now be silent when[d]
my soul speaks. Were you not a second self to me, I would urge
you from now on not to steal away any more of my friends.[e]
Yesterday you bound my Giovanni Cavalcanti so fast to you, I
know not by what spells, that were you yourself not mine, he
would be mine no longer.

Farewell and good fortune.

But why do you stop here, foolish[f] pen? Why this ungrateful
delay? Proceed a little further,[g] and [h] gratefully write the names so
dear to us of those whose image love itself has long impressed upon
my soul:[5] greet Tomaso Valori and Giorgio Antonio Vespucci, men
remarkable for their learning and goodness. But please read the
work now, Lotterio.

44

Non ex humanis divina, sed ex divinis humana sunt iudicanda[a]

The divine is not to be judged by human standards, but the human by divine

Marsilio Ficino of Florence to Girolamo Rossi of Pistoia: many greetings.[b]

READ well our book on the holy faith,[1] O devout friend, more faithful than faith. If you should discover in it anything praiseworthy, praise God, without whose grace nothing is truly worthy of praise. If by chance anything should not please you,[c] take care that religion itself does not please you less on that account. Do not measure the stature of what is divine from the base level of humanity.[d] For the divine does not depend upon the human, but the human upon the divine. Dwell in happiness,[e] and be mindful of us, most loving brother.

29th October, 1478.
Florence.

45

Non cortex nutrit, sed medulla

It is not the outer covering which nourishes, but what lies within

Marsilio Ficino of Florence to his Lord, the Reverend Father in Christ, Giovanni Niccolini, Archbishop of Amalfi.[a]

WE should not read the works of philosophers and theologians with the same eye as we read those of poets and orators. In other writings, even though much may please us superficially, hardly anything is found to give nourishment. But in these it is not the outer covering which nourishes anyone but what lies within. It is one thing to smell the blossom, another to pick the fruit and suck the juice. That is why the fruits of wisdom should be carefully removed from their skins so that they may bring nourishment. It is not the man who just sees a wine who judges its strength correctly, but he who drinks it. It is not the man who just handles pepper who really knows how hot it is, but he who tastes it on his tongue. We do not observe the great splendour of the sun in the sky below the clouds, but beyond them; or rather when the clouds have been dispersed. 'The light shineth in darkness and the darkness comprehended it not.'[1] So you will remind your friends often that, according to the ancients, Minerva is veiled by a robe,[2] and that they should on no account skim through the extraordinary works of Wisdom with eyes[b] that are half asleep,[3] as they do other things, but they should study them with eyes more penetrating than even those of Lynceus.[c] However, enough of this.

I hear that you, Giovanni, as a close friend enjoy the sweet companionship of the Archbishop of Florence. You have made me happy of late, my Niccolini, you have indeed made me very happy. You have divined, I think, how much[d] I have long wanted to live my life with someone of a Jovial nature, so that something of a bitter and, as I might say, Saturnine element, which either my natal star has bestowed on me or which philosophy has added, might eventually be alleviated by the sweet fellowship of someone born under Jove. So in order to grant my wish, Niccolini, you have completely given yourself to Rinaldo Orsini, the foster child of Jove himself. You must have known that where the second self of Amalfi is, there surely am I. Do you wish me well?ᶜ Then greet Orsini often, and every time you greet him, commend Marsilio to him.

Farewell and prosper. But be so good as to tell me: did you think that our Quarquagli had now slipped from our memory? Anyone who thinks I have forgotten my Quarquagli would also think I have forgotten myself.ᶠ Therefore I am writing to him something philosophical drawn certainly from the same workshop,⁴ but it is, I hope, a good one!

46

Prospera in fato fortuna. Vera in virtute felicitas

Good fortune is in fate; true happiness in virtue[1]

Marsilio Ficino of Florenceᵃ to Lorenzo de' Medici, the Younger: greetings.ᵇ

My great love towards you, excellent Lorenzo, has long bidden me give you great gifts. Among all the things which he sees with the eyes, the observer of the heavens considers nothing to be great except the heavens. Therefore, if I were to give you the heavens themselves today, Lorenzo, what would be their price? But let me not bring price to mind just now, for love born of the Graces gives or receives all things freely, nor can anything under heaven itself be weighed in balance with the heavens.

Astrologers say that he is born most fortunate of all men, for whom fate has so apportioned the signs from the heavens that the Moon firstly has no unfavourable aspect with Mars or Saturn, and secondly has favourable aspects with the Sun and Jupiter, Mercury and Venus. Just as astrologers account him to be fortunate for whom fate has favourably disposed things celestial, so equally theologians count him to be blessed who has similarly disposed the same things for himself. But, you will say, surely this is far too much! Much certainly; nonetheless, approach the task with good hope, free-born Lorenzo; far greater than the heavens is He who made you; and you yourself will be greater than the heavens as soon as you resolve upon the task. For these celestial bodies are not to be sought by us outside in some other place; for the heavens in their entirety are within us, in whom the light of life and the origin of heaven dwell.[2]

First,[c] what else does the moon in us signify other than that continuous movement of our mind and body? Next Mars signifies swiftness, and Saturn tardiness; the Sun signifies God; Jupiter, law; Mercury, reason; Venus, human nature.[3] Come! Gird yourself now, noble youth, and together with me apportion the heavens for yourself in this way: let your Moon, that is the continuous movement of mind and body, avoid the excessive speed of Mars and the tardiness of Saturn; that is, let it deal with every single thing as it arises and as it requires, neither hastening more quickly than is meet nor postponing it till later. Furthermore, let this Moon within you continually turn towards the Sun, that is God Himself, from whom it always receives life-giving rays, so that in all places you may worship Him before all others; Him, from whom you have that Self by which you too are worthy of worship.

Also let your Moon observe Jupiter, that is laws divine and human, which it should never transgress, since to depart from the laws on which all things are established is surely to perish. Again,[d] let this Moon be directed to Mercury, that is to counsel and reason, knowledge and discernment. And let it not attempt anything without the counsel of the wise, nor do or say anything for which it could not render good reasons. Again, let it consider a man without knowledge and education as, in a way, blind and dumb.

Lastly, let this Moon fix its gaze on Venus herself, which is human nature, by whom it is, of course, warned to remember that nothing great can be possessed by us on earth, unless we men, for whose benefit all earthly things were created, possess ourselves; and to remember[e] that men can be taken by no other bait whatsoever than their own nature.[4] Beware that you never despise it, perhaps thinking that human nature is born of earth,[5] for human nature herself is a nymph with body surpassing.[f] She was born of an heavenly origin and was beloved above others by an ethereal god. For indeed, her soul and spirit are love and kinship; her eyes are majesty and magnanimity; her hands are liberality and greatness in action; her feet,[g] gentleness and restraint. Finally, her whole is harmony and integrity, honour and radiance.

O excellent form, O beautiful sight! My Lorenzo, a nymph so noble has been placed wholly in your power. If you yourself unite with this nymph in marriage and call her your own, she will bring sweetness to all your years and make you progenitor of beautiful offspring.[6]

Finally,[h] to sum up: if by this reasoning you prudently temper within yourself the heavenly signs and the heavenly gifts, you will flee far from all the menaces of the fates and without doubt will live a blessed life[i] under divine auspices.

47

Caelum pollicetur bona. Virtus praestat

Heaven promises good things, but virtue presents them

Marsilio Ficino[a] to his own Giorgio[b] Antonio Vespucci.[1]

I AM writing a letter[2] to the younger Lorenzo about the prosperity destined by fate, which for the most part we receive as our portion from the stars outside us; and also about the happiness freely available, which we obtain as we will from the stars within us. If necessary, you will expound the letter. You will also advise him to learn it[c] by heart and to keep it stored in the depths of his mind.[3] Those great things which we promise in that letter he will provide for himself, if only he will read it in the spirit in which we have written it.

48

De salute philosophorum ante christi adventum[a]

Concerning the salvation of Philosophers before the coming of Christ[1]

Marsilio Ficino to his Antonio Ivani of Sarzana:[b] greetings.

THE Mosaic precepts[c] are distinguished in the works of the theologians as being of two kinds.[2] Some pertain to natural and moral law,[d] others to rites and the administration of justice.[3] The first were given by God to Moses and the people; the second Moses himself ordained when divinely inspired. Again, the first are given to the whole human race to be kept for all time. The second bind the Jews alone; that is, until the coming of the Messiah himself. The first precepts which we have mentioned are so universal that they could be known to anyone, even of little education, simply through natural understanding. For what else is contained in them other than worship of the one God and the leading of a lawful life?[e]

Through either Mosaic or innate knowledge of this kind, Pythagoras, Socrates, Plato and other similar worshippers of the one God,[f] men established in the traditions of ancient law, avoided the company of the infernal regions. But they could not merit the heavenly regions without the grace of the heavenly Christ. For this reason they were carried into a middle region, that is Limbo,[4] where, through the prophets, who were also kept there, or through angels, they knew for certain of the coming of the Messiah. Hence Gentiles as well as Jews, first in the hope of Christ,[g] then in the presence of Christ, returned to those above.

You have read what we have recently written, during this war, to the Pope about peace.[5] Read again what we once wrote about war in the time of peace a few days before the war to a certain Pace[6] in Rome, secretary to the Archbishop of Florence. I am sending you a copy of that letter.

Farewell.

Florence,
26th January, 1479.[i]

49

Exhortatio ad respondendum

A plea for an answer

Marsilio Ficino to Phoebus[1] Capella of Venice, the illustrious orator.[a]

PHOEBUS, if you do not give me answers when I have asked for them again and again, perhaps we shall deny that you are Phoebus, whose chief function, men say, was to give answers.[2] Perhaps you will say, 'You are not such a great man, Marsilio, that Phoebus himself should answer you.' But, Phoebus, only answer, and I shall on the instant be a great man. If only I could say, 'Phoebus himself once answered me', how great a man would I be!

50

Felix est, qui vere gaudet. Solus[a] gaudet vere, qui sola veritate gaudet

He is happy who is truly joyful; he alone is truly joyful who rejoices in truth alone

Marsilio Ficino of Florence to Bernardo Capponi, son of Niccolo: greetings.

I HAVE composed a short address to mankind, dealing briefly with instructions for living.[1] I shall believe that I have dealt well with such an important subject only when it seems to you, who are so rightly instructed, that I have instructed mankind rightly. I have made a copy of this address for you; read it happily. But I have not said enough unless I add this: live happily too. What indeed is happiness but the true joy, for the sake of which everyone pursues everything? So to live happily, be truly joyful; to be truly joyful, be joyful in truth alone.

51

Pictura pulchri corporis et pulchrae mentis[a]

A picture of a beautiful body and a beautiful mind[1]

Marsilio Ficino of Florence[b] to his friends.[2]

PHILOSOPHERS debate, orators declaim and poets sing at great length to exhort men to the true love of virtue. I admire their works and praise them. Indeed, if I did not praise good things, I would not be a good man. But[c] I consider that if Virtue herself were ever to be brought into the open she would encourage everyone to take hold of her far more easily and effectively than would the words of men.

It is pointless for you to praise a maiden to the ears of a young man and describe her in words in order to inflict upon him pangs of love, when you can bring her beautiful form before his eyes. Point, if you can, to her beautiful form; then you have no further need of words.[3] For it is impossible to say how much[d] more easily and powerfully Beauty herself calls forth love than do words.

Therefore, if we bring into the view of men the marvellous sight of Virtue herself, there will be no further need for our persuading words: the vision itself will persuade more quickly than can be conceived.

Picture[e] a man endowed with the most vigorous and acute faculties, a strong body, good health, a handsome form, well-proportioned limbs and a noble stature.[4] Picture this man moving with alacrity and skill, speaking elegantly, singing sweetly, laughing graciously: you will love no one anywhere, you will admire no one, if you do not love and admire such a man as soon as you see him.

Now,[f] in order to reflect more easily upon the divine aspect of the mind from the corresponding likeness of the beautiful body, refer each aspect of the body to an aspect of mind. For the body is the shadow of the soul; the form of the body, as best it can, represents the form of the soul; thus liveliness and acuteness of perception in the body represent, in a measure, the wisdom and far-sightedness of the mind; strength of body represents strength[g] of mind; health of body, which consists in the tempering of the humours, signifies a temperate mind.[h] Beauty, which is determined by the proportions of the body and a becoming complexion, shows us the harmony and splendour of justice; also, size shows us liberality and nobility; and stature, magnanimity; in the same way dexterity indicates to us civility and courteousness; fine speaking, oratory; sweet singing, the power of poetry. Finally, gracious laughter represents serene happiness in life and perfect joy, which Virtue herself showers[i] upon us.

Now bring[j] into one whole each single part and attribute of Virtue, which we have mentioned; you will at once see clearly a spectacle to be admired and venerated. How worthy of love, how worthy of admiration, is this form of the soul, whose shadow is the form of the body so loved and admired by everyone. But just as Virtue, when she is seen, instantly draws each man to herself by her lovely form so, without doubt, will Vice, if clearly seen, immediately terrify by his deformity and drive everyone away.

Come,[k] friends. Let us always hold before our eyes the divine idea and form of Virtue. She will at once draw us to herself by the grace of her splendour, unceasingly delight us with the sweetness of her proportion and harmony, and completely fill us with an abundance of all that is good.

Appendix Letters

The following correspondence was not included in the printed editions. It comprises three complete letters and two fragments all of which are found only in Magl. VIII 1441 (M9). The Latin texts of these letters are printed in the *Supplementum Ficinianum* (I, pp.47 to 50) but the translators give their own reading of the text of M9 for these in the Notes on the Latin Text. For some of the 'under-readings' of passages deleted in M9 we have consulted the original manuscript of M9. The possible reasons for the deletions from the manuscript are discussed in the note on the Pazzi Conspiracy, pp. 87–91.

A

Fragment of a letter from Ficino probably intended for Lorenzo de' Medici[1]

. . . . . . you take your places at the feast. Greetings first of all to Medici, the sole saviour of our country. Remember those feasts held for many years, always in happier circumstances.

Medici: Who is so impudent as to disturb me now? Who is rudely disrupting this great feast?

Friend: I am a guest of Cosimo, Lorenzo. So perhaps I can in a way interrupt the sacred feast in his honour,[2] but I certainly cannot disrupt it. A man whom Cosimo himself from on high freely invited cannot upset the number of guests, which just before was one short of the right number.[3] For he sent him to you without warning, so that the sacred number of his own family should be complete. Therefore receive me gladly, Medici, I beg you receive me as your own.

Medici: How dare you come in here, peasant? Where is your wedding garment?

Friend: I am not such a sight. I have just seen myself in your mirror. Look within, Lorenzo, as you usually do. Beneath this peasant dress, unless I am mistaken, you will see a wedding garment. So I hope that no one will bind the hands and feet[4] of a man whose spirit lives at the very heart of your home, amongst your own household gods, a man who is always bound to you by true piety. I know that no one will cast into outer darkness this man who burns with an inward fire, who loves the light within.

Medici: Well done, good servant. Enter thou into the joy of thy Lord.[5]

B

Marsilio Ficino humbly commends himself to his most reverend Fathers and Lords, Cardinal Raffaele Riario and Francesco Salviati, Archbishop of Pisa.

At a recent gathering of old friends[1] a speech on morals[2] sprang to my lips. Though it was not well-suited to those delicate ears, yet it was perhaps well-suited to these times. Philosophers traditionally say that the nature of opposites is that they cannot exist together in the same place at the same time. But not long ago I considered whether the very opposite could be true. For I saw some of those listening laugh outwardly at my absurdities all the time I was speaking, but at the same time they were bewailing their inner misery upon which my words turned. I am not sorry to have appeared absurd to these people, as I pride myself that by joining opposites I have brought about miracles which nature herself does not perform. Lest anyone else should consider me a speaker to ridicule, I shall repeat a similar speech today to my Lords, my pious and eminent Fathers. For I know that men outstanding for their gravity and piety will never laugh at pious words, and am confident that if men of the greatest authority do not laugh at someone, no one else will ridicule him.

C

Non est dicenda veritas nisi auscultanti

Truth should not be spoken except to someone who is listening

Marsilio Ficino to Jacopo Bracciolini: greetings.

ENCOURAGING her with your arguments, magnanimous Bracciolini, I recently prevailed upon Truth to come to Pisa, if she were needed, for the installation of Riario as Cardinal.[1] Although at first she cheerfully accepted, a while later, in some strange way, she seemed a little less inclined to take this path. Even though she knew full well that all the Cardinal's servants are her friends, she feared that someone else would intervene and interpret her words maliciously. But then, when she remembered that Bracciolini, one of her keenest defenders, was now there, she immediately seized upon this path with the utmost confidence.

Now, my Hercules, if necessary, do not hesitate to summon the assistance of your Iolaus;[2] I mean Cosmico,[3] the vigorous soldier of Pallas. But why do we needlessly lack confidence, as if any of my interests were less than safe under the ample roof of my patron Salviati? Among friends all things have a happy issue.

Farewell, happy men.

D

Marsilio Ficino of Florence to Pietro Guglielmo Rocca, the Most Reverend Archbishop of Salerno.

IT is the mark of envy to be unwilling to praise something worthy of the highest praise. Equally it is presumptuous to try to express in ordinary words an extraordinary, indeed unique, virtue. Therefore, not to be envious, Reverend Father, I decided at the outset to praise Cardinal Raffaele Riario. But not to be thought presumptuous, I declined to take upon myself the role of eulogist. Let the dignity of Cardinal, which has made the man known and has now proved his goodness to all men, also proclaim his praise and goodness to the Pope. For Raffaele fulfils the office of Cardinal with such dignity that the dignity of this office alone seems worthy of the right to praise him. Therefore under the mantle of this dignity I am writing to the Pope a few words full of praise for Riario. I have chosen you before all others as a faithful Achates to the Pope, so that, knowing the easiest means of access and the most propitious times,[1] you may give him our letter.[2] Would you also explain that what he has read from my hand he may consider to have been written by everyone in Florence and Pisa. For everyone ardently loves our Raffaele both as a model of conduct and an embodiment of the Graces. Everyone gives him the most extraordinary praise, cherishing and revering him with great devotion. Those who praise princes are usually in their pay or are their servants; but gracious God has filled this man with such grace that all are prepared to love and serve him without reward. Indeed if I did not know . . .

E

De Libertate et Servitute

On Freedom and Bondage

Marsilio Ficino to Marchionne Donati, the 'Mercury' of the Council of Eight:[1] greetings.

You ask, my friend, why I am bound to no man; because I have no desire for power. But then why do I not want power? To avoid perpetual bondage. Most men buy a false power at the price of perpetual bondage, and when they seem to have most power then will they be most severely bound. But we have attained true freedom simply through the exercise of restraint. It is the mark of a great soul to value lightly what mean spirits prize highly. Only such a man lives in freedom. A man in bondage is not master of himself, and he who does not master himself is the master of nothing.

The Pazzi Conspiracy and Ficino

THE remarkable qualities of Ficino's letters are the more apparent
when one considers the times in which they were written. It is as
if the most violent and lawless times call forth the most sublime
statements of philosophy, and make them peculiarly appropriate.
The Pazzi Conspiracy (which was being hatched at the time these
letters were written) is an extreme example of ruthless violence and
utter contempt for the law, but the letters of Ficino written both
to the conspirators and to the Medici, the rulers of Florence, as
well as to others, remind their readers directly of the real and divine
nature of the soul. They also show the lengths to which Ficino, a
poor parish priest, went to try and turn the conspirators from their
course and at the same time to rekindle Lorenzo de' Medici's interest
in the practice of the philosophy of Plato.

The Conspiracy began in earnest in the first few weeks of 1477,
when three men, Girolamo Riario, 'nephew' of Pope Sixtus IV,
Francesco de' Pazzi, head of his family's bank in Rome, and
Francesco Salviati, the recently installed Archbishop of Pisa, met in
Rome to plot the downfall of Lorenzo de' Medici, absolute ruler
(in all but name) of the Florentine Republic, and of his younger
brother Giuliano.

For each of these men the Medici represented a major stumbling
block to their ambitions. Each nursed in differing degrees a sense
of grievance over past injustices that they wished to avenge.

Since the death of his father Piero in 1469, Lorenzo had ensured
that his family held the upper hand in the city's affairs. 'The
government of the Medici was a party government, usurped by the
party, preserved by tyranny, neither violent nor cruel, except in a
few cases in which they were constrained by necessity, but founded
upon the policy of favouring the lower classes, uniting the interests

of the stronger with their own interests, and suppressing all who seemed inclined to go their own way', wrote Bernardo del Nero.[1]

As the power passed from father to son, the memory of ancient rivalry and enmity lived on and despite or even because of Lorenzo's brilliant gifts, it was inevitable that those families who saw their power wane as Lorenzo's increased, became more and more restive. Among the most prominent of those families were the Pazzi.

The main instigator of the plot being hatched in Rome, however, was not a Florentine. Girolamo Riario, a 'nephew' of Sixtus, had his own peculiar set of grudges against Lorenzo. Since the death in 1474 of the infamous Pietro Riario, yet another 'nephew' of Sixtus, (which Ficino saw no reason to regret)[2] Girolamo had held first place in the Pope's affections.

Like Sixtus, Girolamo was jealous of the control Lorenzo had been able to gain over the Tuscan clergy since Pietro's death. As long as Lorenzo kept such control there was little chance that the Pope and his 'nephew' could undermine Lorenzo's position by appointing their own supporters in key clerical positions in the Republic. In the struggle between Rome and Florence, both sides viewed this area of influence as crucial. Sixtus could not rest until he had re-established the papal control that had existed up to the death of Pietro. He was also greatly angered by Lorenzo's attempts to foil his political ambitions in the sensitive states bordering the Republic. Sixtus was determined that his various 'nephews' should obtain title to the states over which he planned to gain control. Girolamo's ambition likewise knew no bounds. He clearly took as a personal affront Lorenzo's blocking of his uncle's plans to increase his own power and influence.

The disaffected members of the Florentine ruling classes were the obvious means by which the Medici stronghold could be undermined. One of the principal causes of resentment was the system of taxation, which arbitrarily penalised certain individuals who were not members of the Medici faction. They often had to surrender entire estates to meet the tax assessments made against them. Francesco de' Pazzi was the ideal ally for Sixtus and Girolamo, because of his direct contacts with this dissident faction.

It was probably in 1473 that Francesco's collaboration with Sixtus and Girolamo began. In that year, following a dispute between

Lorenzo and Sixtus, the Medici were replaced by the Pazzi as the papal bankers. The dispute inevitably involved an attempt by Sixtus to increase Girolamo's political power. He had decided that Imola (a small town between Bologna and Forlì which belonged to the Duke of Milan) was the perfect base from which Girolamo could build up larger estates in the Romagna. The asking price for Imola was 40,000 ducats and the Medici bank in Rome was asked to raise the necessary funds. But Lorenzo, who up to that time had seemed to have fairly good relations with Sixtus, was suspicious of this move which seemed to pose a threat to the security of Florence's frontiers. He therefore tried to prevent the Pope from raising the money he needed by using his influence with the other banking houses, including the Pazzi. The attempt failed, however, for Francesco de' Pazzi lent the funds required for the transaction, thus allying his family's interests with the papacy's more closely than ever before; a fact which was to prove crucial four years later, when he lent his wholehearted support to Girolamo's plans for Lorenzo's elimination.

The fact that the Pazzi now depended heavily on the papacy in their business dealings, which had suffered serious setbacks in Florence under the Medici, was undoubtedly an added incentive to follow the lead of Girolamo and Sixtus in the plot against Lorenzo.

The confrontation over Imola was undoubtedly a watershed in the relations between Sixtus and Lorenzo. On more and more issues these two powerful personalities were to find themselves at odds. Nowhere was the political dispute between Florence and Rome more bitterly fought than over the question of who should control the Tuscan clergy and its rich benefices. The appointment of Pietro Riario, brother of Girolamo, as Archbishop of Florence in 1473 exacerbated tensions on this issue, since in his short reign as Archbishop he had led a scandalous and profligate existence. When he died unexpectedly on January 5th, 1474, another man appointed by Sixtus, Francesco Salviati, was put forward as Pietro's successor. Salviati had close ties with the Pazzi, since he was first cousin to Jacopo, the head of the family, who had also supported him during his early days in the Church.[3]

Lorenzo would not agree to Salviati's appointment, insisting that his own brother-in-law, Rinaldo Orsini, should become Archbishop.

Sixtus relented, but when in the same year the Archbishop of Pisa, Filippo de' Medici, died he immediately appointed Francesco Salviati as his successor without consulting the Florentine government, as he should have done (Pisa being within the territories of the Republic). So angry was Lorenzo that for over two years he refused to allow Salviati to take up his post. Thus were sown in Salviati's heart the seeds of enmity which culminated in his agreement to form an unholy trinity with Girolamo Riario and Francesco de' Pazzi. There seemed to be some hope of settling the dispute involving Salviati in 1476, when Lorenzo put forward three conditions to be agreed upon before he would allow the new Archbishop to assume his duties: first, that a cardinalate be conferred on the Archbishopric of Florence; second, that no appointment be made to the office of Archbishop within the territories of the Republic without the consent of the Signoria (the governing body of Florence) and, finally that permission be granted for Lorenzo to levy a tax on the clergy for the upkeep of the new university of Pisa.[4] The last two requests were granted in a papal brief on the 12th January, 1476. Salviati was then allowed to take office. The first part of Lorenzo's agreement with the Pope, that a cardinalate be conferred on the Archbishopric of Florence, was never implemented while Lorenzo's brother-in-law, Orsini, was Archbishop, but the glittering prospect after the anticipated removal of Lorenzo must have made that event seem all the more desirable to Salviati, Orsini's likely successor. Quite possibly this consideration might have largely accounted for his taking part in the conspiracy.

It was, however, Jacopo de' Pazzi who was to play a more important role in the plot that was about to unfold. He had taken over as the head of the family in 1464 on the death of his elder brother Pietro. He was a proud man, proud particularly of his family's ancient lineage. The family fortune, like that of the Medici, had been based on banking. But with the Medici in the ascendant in Florence the Pazzi business was in some decline. Even though our main source of information on his character is Poliziano's one-sided account of the conspiracy, he was clearly not the most likeable of men: 'Their chief was Jacopo de' Pazzi, cavaliere, who spent night and day dicing, when if things went wrong, neither God nor man was safe . . . . he had two conflicting characteristics – sordid avarice and boundless ambition. The fine mansion his father left him he levelled to the ground, to build another on its foundations. He was not a good payer in his business operations and defrauded the poor, who had to eke out a bare existence with the work of their hands. Everybody hated him. He had no legitimate children and thus had the goodwill of his relatives, who were his greedy inheritors. He was careless in everything, especially domestic matters. With these "virtues" he set about bringing his nefarious plans to fruition. This insolent and ambitious man proposed to bring a common destruction upon himself and the Republic.'[5]

Jacopo, however, was perhaps more astute than Poliziano makes out. When Francesco first approached him, he refused to have anything to do with the plot being hatched in Rome. He was far more aware than the conspirators of the level of support that the Medici brothers commanded in Florence. It was only when he knew that the plot had the full support of the Pope that he began to change his mind.

Girolamo, meanwhile, who had never wasted any opportunity to stir up his 'uncle's' anger against Lorenzo, had begun to set his plans in motion. Force would clearly have to be used. It was only a question of how and where. Above all, it was important to ascertain how Sixtus would react to the plot, for without his consent it could not succeed.

Girolamo made a point of underplaying the role of violence in the undertaking, realising that however much Sixtus wanted the removal of Lorenzo and his brother he could not openly condone actions that might lead to the murder of two of Italy's most eminent citizens. On the other hand he would not be able to resist the opportunity of encouraging others to do the work that would enable him to further his ambitions in central and northern Italy.

An example of how political rulers could be successfully removed by force had been furnished in 1476 by the assassination of the tyrannical ruler of Milan, Duke Galeazzo Maria Sforza, who had also been accused of oppressing his people with burdensome taxes. The Pazzi conspirators, however, faced a more difficult task. They had to strike at the two brothers at the same time, if this were possible. But the initial plan concentrated on enticing Lorenzo to Rome and, in his absence, dealing with Giuliano in Florence. 'That my wish may be fulfilled', wrote Girolamo Riario to Lorenzo on 15th January, 1478, 'that the public and private affairs of your

Magnificence take a prosperous course, and it is known to me that various things have happened between his Holiness and the illustrious Signoria, in which your Magnificence, as the most distinguished citizen and head of state, have had occasion to share, and which have somewhat disturbed his Holiness, it would please me much for the state and on account of your personal position if your Magnificence would resolve to come to Rome to present yourself to the Pope for the removal of all misunderstandings and doubts. I do not in the least doubt that the Holy Father would receive you with joy; while I, with the affection which I owe you from our mutual friendly relations, would behave so as fully to satisfy your Magnificence, and all considerations of grievance which may have arisen from the afore-named events would vanish.'[6] Had Lorenzo come to Rome the last statement would, of course, have proved true!

Lorenzo may have been tempted to take the opportunity to heal his rift with Sixtus. However, the risks were too great and he gave Girolamo no definite response. Thus the conspirators were forced to carry out their plans in Lorenzo's territory.

Three problems had to be dealt with immediately: the recruitment of trustworthy allies in Florence itself, the appointment of an experienced soldier to deal with military preparations, and arrangements needing to be made on the frontiers of Florence so as to follow up the advantage if the coup succeeded, by advancing immediately with an armed force.

The man picked to handle the military side was Giovan Batista da Montesecco, a captain of Abruzzi in the service of Girolamo. When first approached by Salviati and Francesco de' Pazzi he displayed grave reservations about the whole affair. He was employed by Sixtus and Girolamo and could do nothing without their permission, he explained. Even when assured that Girolamo was a party to the plot and that the Pope had given his blessing to it, Montesecco was dubious.

Soon afterwards Montesecco was summoned to the Pope and, no doubt in awe of Sixtus, soon changed his view of the undertaking. According to his account, the various aspects of the plot were discussed with the Pope, who gave his consent to a revolution in Florence but insisted that there should be no bloodshed. Montesecco protested that it was highly difficult to execute such an intention without the death of Giuliano and Lorenzo. In reply the Pope repeated that he would not condone any bloodshed. 'It is not my office to cause the death of a man,' he said.[7] Not for the first time it was left to Girolamo to reassure the Pope that everything would be done to avoid bloodshed. But when he suggested to Sixtus that, if unavoidably, violence proved necessary, he should pardon those involved, the Pope grew angry. Girolamo thus reiterated that all would be done to avoid the necessity for violence. However, as he dismissed the conspirators, Sixtus gave his consent to the employment of arms!

The plot now gathered pace. Montesecco was sent to Florence on a pretext in order to familiarise himself with the city and to make the necessary military arrangements with Jacopo de' Pazzi. During the course of the visit he met Lorenzo on several occasions and was impressed by his qualities. This induced further doubts in his mind about the whole enterprise. However, he was much encouraged by the knowledge that it had Sixtus' backing and was finally won over to the cause by the enthusiasm of Francesco de' Pazzi.

It was decided that Salviati must come to Florence on some pretext in order take part in the execution of the plot. Montesecco would lead to the Romagna all the mercenaries of Girolamo who could be spared from Rome and hold himself ready.

Still no definite decision had been made as to how Lorenzo and Giuliano were going to be dealt with. There were inevitably various delays and all the time the likelihood of exposure increased as more and more people became involved.

It was in April, 1478 that Salviati finally came to Florence, supposedly on papal business. Soon he was busy discussing details of the plot in various houses of the Pazzi and in their country villa at Montughi. Surprisingly, despite all this activity, the plot either failed to come to the attention of the Medici or was not taken seriously by them.

At last a workable plan was agreed upon by the conspirators. This involved a nephew of Girolamo, Raffaele Riario, who had been sent to Pisa University to study Canon Law, before being made a cardinal by Sixtus on 10th December, 1477 at the tender age of 16. He had become a major pawn in the drama. Raffaele's nomination as cardinal would enable Girolamo to gain a foothold in the Sacred College of Cardinals and remedy the loss of influence there and regain the power that his brother Pietro had enjoyed in Tuscany. As part of the plot, Raffaele was now appointed papal legate, with full powers over Umbria. Presumably this would have opened the doors to Salviati taking the Archbishopric of Florence, once Lorenzo had been removed. His appointment would also enable the new cardinal to bring the two Medici brothers together in his presence.

Girolamo caused Raffaele to be summoned to Florence. Accompanying him was Jacopo Bracciolini, a member of Ficino's circle and the son of Poggio, who had been a distinguished historian and an old friend of the Medici. Since January, as part of the plot, Bracciolini had been given the nominal role of tutor to Raffaele. Bracciolini had reason to resent the Medici. He had been implicated in the Dietisalvi Neroni plot of 1466 against the Medici. He had been convicted of seditious behaviour for corresponding with Ferrante of Naples, since the Aragonese were the enemies of the Sforzas, who were in alliance with Florence, fined 1,000 florins and banished from Florence.[8] Probably, unlike the other conspirators, Bracciolini was also something of an idealist as well as an historian and may have been inspired by classical models as well as by the assassination of Duke Galeazzo.

Meanwhile, other major characters in the coming drama were also preparing themselves: Jacopo Salviati, brother of the Archbishop; Antonio Maffei of Volterra, who blamed Lorenzo for the way his town had been ravaged by Florentine forces six years previously; Bernardo Bandini, an adventurer who had dissipated a fortune and who was apparently deeply in debt to the Pazzi (his brother Francesco belonged to Ficino's Academy and had been sent to the court of King Matthias of Hungary in 1476);[9] the clerk, Stefano da Bagnone, who had served Jacopo de' Pazzi as a scribe and was tutor to his illegitimate daughter; all these, and several more who had reason to hate the Medici, hastened to the conspirators' cause.

When Riario came to Florence, he was lodged at the Pazzi villa in the Montughi hills. He invited the Medici brothers to his house. However, because of rumours of danger it may have been Lorenzo's policy at this time not to appear in public with Giuliano more than necessary for their mutual safety. Lorenzo thus went on his own, and the execution of the plot was therefore delayed. Lorenzo then invited the Cardinal to visit the Medici villa in Fiesole. This seemed at first to offer a perfect opportunity for the conspirators to strike at their targets, but because of the illness of Giuliano, whether genuine or not, this was cancelled at the last moment. Finally, however, it was decided that 26th April, the Sunday before Ascension Day, was to be the day of revenge. The Cardinal was made to announce his intention of visiting the Medici palace in the city in order to view their priceless art treasures. He would also be present at High Mass in the cathedral nearby.

The brothers prepared to meet the Cardinal royally and a distinguished company was invited. Giuliano was again unwell and sent a message to say that even if he did not appear at the banquet that was to be held in the Cardinal's honour, he would certainly not fail to appear at the cathedral. This meant the conspirators had to alter their plans yet again. The cathedral, not the banquet, would have to be the scene of the attack. The plan was now that, while the two priests carried out their murderous office on Lorenzo, Francesco de' Pazzi and Bernardo Bandini were to kill Giuliano. At the same time Salviati and Bracciolini with armed retainers were to seize the Signoria. Once this was accomplished, Jacopo de' Pazzi with his mercenaries was to proclaim the freedom of the city. At a prearranged signal from Salviati and Francesco de' Pazzi that they had done their part, the mercenary troops stationed outside Florence were to move on the city. Montesecco, who ever since his meeting with Lorenzo at the Medici villa at Cafaggiolo had begun to harbour severe doubts about the whole project, had been marked down as the man who would deal the fatal blow against Lorenzo. He now suddenly refused to carry out his task in the cathedral. His conscience would not allow him to 'add sacrilege to murder'. This single fact probably saved Lorenzo's life. For Stefano da Bagnone and Antonio Maffei, both priests who had not found it inconsistent with their profession to take Montesecco's place, were not at all experienced in the use of arms.

Arriving at the Medici palace in the middle of that Sunday morning, Raffaele changed into his Cardinal's vestments and proceeded to the cathedral with Lorenzo. Salviati accompanied them to the entrance of the building and then withdrew under the pretext of visiting his sick mother. All the others entered. Within the choir, which is beneath the dome of Brunelleschi, the Cardinal took his place opposite the altar, surrounded by his retinue.

The singing of the Mass had already begun when the conspirators anxiously noted that Giuliano had not appeared. Francesco de' Pazzi and Bandini rushed to the Medici palace and persuaded Giuliano to come with them. Taking him between them playfully, they ascertained that he wore no shirt of mail beneath his doublet. Giuliano, following his companions, made for the northern side of the choir. The sounding of the bell when it was rung at the elevation of the host, was the signal for the conspirators to go into action. At that very moment, Giuliano dutifully lowered his head and Bandini plunged a dagger into his breast. Giuliano made a few steps forward and then fell. Francesco de' Pazzi followed, stabbing him time and time again in such a blind fury that according to some accounts, he severely wounded his own thigh. Simultaneously the two priests had attacked Lorenzo from behind. Maffei's dagger, with which he had intended to pierce Lorenzo's throat, missed its aim and only grazed him. With great presence of mind Lorenzo whirled round, tore off his mantle, wrapped it around his left arm, and, after slashing at the priests with his sword, vaulted over Ghiberti's wooden choir screen and hurried past the altar to the new sacristy. Bandini was in hot pursuit, killing Francesco Nori, a former manager of the Medici bank in Lyons, and wounding Lorenzo Cavalcanti, as they tried to stop him from reaching Lorenzo. Fortunately, Lorenzo and some of his supporters had had time to reach the comparative safety of the sacristy, the bronze doors of which were closed by his supporters, including Angelo Poliziano (according to his own account),[10] in the face of the pursuers.

All this was the work of a moment. 'Nothing but noise', wrote Filippo Strozzi,[11] 'prevailed in the cathedral,' where in the confusion some were shouting that the dome was collapsing.

The conspirators now fled in all directions; Guglielmo de' Pazzi, brother-in-law of Lorenzo, cried out his innocence; Cardinal Raffaele stood dumbstruck by the altar. The friends of the Medici now gathered together and hastened, some to the choir, some to the sacristy. Lorenzo, learning of the tragic murder of his brother, emerged from his hiding place and was escorted back home by a large band of his followers. Giuliano's corpse, which had been lying in a pool of blood, was taken out of the cathedral by anguished friends and supporters.

As these events were unfolding, Archbishop Salviati and Jacopo

Bracciolini proceeded to the palace of the Signoria surrounded by a band of mercenaries, who were disaffected Perugians, disguised as the Archbishop's suite. The Gonfaloniere, Cesare Petrucci, was dining with the prior and on receiving the news that Salviati had arrived with an urgent message from the Pope, got up from the table to greet his unexpected guest. Salviati was shown into a reception chamber while his 'suite' were taken to a room adjoining. When Petrucci joined Salviati, the Archbishop began to mumble some lines about the purpose of his visit, but kept glancing nervously at the door. Petrucci's suspicions were aroused. He hastened out to call attendants and met Bracciolini in the corridor, barring his way. He grabbed Bracciolini by the hair and hurled him to the ground. Meanwhile Salviati began to call for his men; but in vain, because the door to their chamber could only be opened from the outside by a mechanism known to the guard alone. Petrucci, armed at first only with a cooking spit against Bracciolini and his companions, quickly organised the guard. At the same time Salviati's mercenaries outside the palace began to pour in. The fighting in the palace was sharp, and the tolling of the great bell, the 'Vacca', sounded the alarm to the people of Florence. Petrucci and his guard captured some of the assailants and put the rest to flight.

Meanwhile, the square of the Signoria was in commotion. Jacopo de' Pazzi, showing great determination, had hastened to the square with about a hundred armed men, summoning the populace to regain their liberty. 'Freedom! Freedom! The people and freedom! Down with the Medici!' was the cry. But to Jacopo's horror these exhortations for the most part fell on deaf ears. In reply the gathering crowd of Florence's citizens shouted back, 'Palle, Palle! Death to the traitors!' ('Palle' refers to the balls which were the emblems on the Medici coat of arms).[12] Within minutes it was clear to Jacopo that the show of force had utterly failed. Outnumbered and demoralised he and his supporters hastened off as the growing crowd showered them with stones and began to bay for the conspirators' blood. Sending part of his force to secure the Santa Croce gate, through which he intended to make his escape, Jacopo rushed to his house. There he found Francesco concealed in a bedroom, bleeding profusely from his self-inflicted wounds. Having attended as best he could to Francesco's needs, Jacopo rode off at high speed through the gate that had been secured, taking advantage of the chaos in the city to make good his escape.

As the news of Giuliano's death became known, the streets of Florence filled up with its now hysterical citizens. Bleeding heads were being carried around on pikes and everywhere the cry was one for vengeance. Mob rule predominated, leaving little room to differentiate between the guilty and the innocent. Back at the palace of the Signoria, the Perugians locked into their chamber were dragged out, slaughtered and hurled into the square. Francesco de' Pazzi had been dragged from his hiding place to the Signoria and hanged from a window. Salviati was thrown out with a rope round his neck to join him. As he hung he fixed his teeth in Francesco's body, perhaps in an effort to save himself. In this position he remained after death. On the following day Jacopo Bracciolini was hanged, with other members of Salviati's family and followers. More than 100 supporters of the Pazzi were hung and many others killed by the mob.

Jacopo de' Pazzi's escape was short-lived. On his way to the comparative safety of the Romagna he was recognised by peasants at the village of Castagno and detained by them. Returned to Florence, he faced torture and a trial. He also was hanged from the palace windows. Antonio Maffei and Stefano da Bagnone fared no better. Discovered hiding in the Benedictine Abbey, both were castrated and then hanged. Renato de' Pazzi, Jacopo's innocent brother, who was found in a house in the Mugello, was also executed for not denouncing the others. Most of the other prominent members of the family escaped with imprisonment in the dungeons of Volterra. Guglielmo de' Pazzi, Lorenzo's brother-in-law, was cleared of complicity in the plot but was banished to his country villa.

Montesecco was finally caught on 1st May. He revealed many details of the plot and particularly the Roman connection. Following a short trial he was beheaded in the courtyard of the Bargello. Girolamo Riario remained safe in Rome. But he, too, died a violent death ten years later when he was murdered by disaffected members of his own household.

Bernardo Bandini was probably the most wanted of all the plotters, but he escaped from Florentine territory, having originally concealed himself in the tower of the cathedral. He finally reached

Constantinople, but was given up by the Sultan Mohammed II and executed in 1479. His hanging body was drawn in meticulous detail by Leonardo da Vinci. The deliverance of Bandini was the final nail in the conspirators' coffin and confirmed, if confirmation were needed, that the Medici were now undisputed masters of Florence and that Lorenzo had become an almost god-like figure to the vast majority of its citizens. Botticelli was commissioned to paint the portraits of the conspirators on the walls of the Bargello and Lorenzo employed his poetic talent in writing their epitaphs.[13]

The problem for Lorenzo throughout this harrowing period was not that his adherents would do too little but rather that they would go too far. In a speech from a window of his palace to a vast crowd that had gathered to cheer him on the day of the tragedy, Lorenzo had made his position clear.[14] He complained of the envy and hatred of those who, instead of opposing him in an open fight, attacked him unawares. His own safety, he said, was nothing to him where it was a question of the dignity and security of the state, for which he would be willing to give up his position and submit to all. He was most sincerely grateful to those who had protected and saved him, but the avenging interposition of the people must now be restrained in order not to afford the enemies of the Republic a pretext for complaints and attacks. It was the voice of reason, but by the time the government had regained control the damage had already been done.

Meanwhile in Rome the fierce reprisals of the Florentines against the Pazzi had aroused the utmost fury. Girolamo Riario unlawfully arrested the Florentine Ambassador, Donato Acciaiuoli, and was only prevented from throwing him into the dungeons of Sant' Angelo by the protests of the Milanese and Venetian ambassadors. Sixtus meanwhile ordered the arrest of all the principal Florentine bankers and merchants in Rome, although he was compelled to release them a little later because of Cardinal Raffaele's sensitive position in Florence. However, he sequestrated the assets of the Medici bank and all the Medici property he could seize. He also repudiated the debts of the Papal Curia to the bank.

The Florentine Ambassador to Rome then wrote to the Signoria urging that Cardinal Riario be set at liberty without delay. The Signoria announced to the Pope that the Cardinal had been brought to a safe place to protect him from the mob's fury. In spite of further requests from the Florentine Ambassador and Venetian Senate for Riario's release, the Signoria hesitated. Riario still seemed a useful hostage.

The confession and execution of Montesecco as well as the continued imprisonment of the Cardinal only increased the anger of the Pope and Girolamo. Sixtus now declared that an interdict would be laid against the whole of Florence if the Cardinal was not immediately set at liberty. Lorenzo and the Signoria gave way; from the confessions of Montesecco the Cardinal did not seem to be implicated in the plot. Furthermore Lorenzo was concerned over the attitude of Venice and Milan to the continued detention of Raffaele Riario. A bull of excommunication had already been published against Lorenzo when on 5th June Raffaele left the safety of the Medici palace and repaired first to the Servite cloister by S. Annunziata, from where he addressed the Pope by letter in the following terms.[15]

'A few days ago I informed your Holiness that perfect freedom over my movements had been granted me. Besides this I said how much I was obliged to the Government here, and especially to Lorenzo de' Medici for their great kindness to me. Finally I begged your Holiness to grant the Florentines some favour in return for the benefits shown me in your name. My hope has, however, been bitterly disappointed on learning that Lorenzo and the Florentine people have been laid under an interdict; and I, unhappy man that I am, expected and wished that good might befall them, whereas the contrary has happened. But I cannot say, Holy Father, how much it grieves me that my requests have so little weight with your Holiness, and that I should appear ungrateful towards those to whom I owe so much, and it seems to me not fitting I should leave this city before such a sentence should be reprieved. Were the attachment of this people to the Medici fully known to your Holiness, you would not hate them as you do. As I rejoiced when your Holiness granted me the Cardinal's dignity, just so and even more will I rejoice if I hear that these men, who have deserved so much from us, have received grace for my sake. I shall then believe that I am in favour with your Holiness when this senate, and Lorenzo above all, have a share in your favour.'

Whether this was dictated to Raffaele or not, he had good reason to be thankful for his deliverance. By now he had been released by the Signoria. On 13th June the Cardinal reached Siena, the first stop on his return journey to Rome, 'more dead than alive from the terror he had undergone and still imagining he felt the rope about his neck'. It was an experience which apparently affected him for the rest of his life. His complexion is said to have turned permanently pale.

The bull of excommunication, issued a few days before the Cardinal's release against Lorenzo de' Medici (styled 'the son of iniquity and foster child of perdition') and the Signoria of Florence gave a lengthy catalogue of all the crimes and wrongs the Pope alleged had been perpetrated by them.[16] Lorenzo and the entire Signoria should be banished and delivered into the hands of the Pope together with all their possessions. The Pope then declared war on Florence and persuaded King Ferrante of Naples to follow suit. The war which followed, while being inconclusive, caused considerable difficulty and hardship to the people of Florence.

It remains to consider Ficino's relationship to these events and to the main actors in the drama. Originally Ficino had been one of Lorenzo de' Medici's tutors when he was a child. A very loving relationship had developed between them, as is clear from the frequent exchange of letters between the two while Lorenzo was setting up the new University of Pisa in 1475, (see Letter 23 in volume 1). There is not much correspondence after that time until the Pazzi Conspiracy, and such correspondence as there is has little of the original warmth. In a letter (*Letters,* **2**, 34) probably written about December, 1476 Ficino seems to imply that he is under attack from those now in Lorenzo's favour and is being ignored by Lorenzo himself. Ficino had probably never received from Lorenzo the financial support he had received from Lorenzo's father and grandfather. He had been ordained priest in 1473 and Lorenzo gave him a small benefice for which Ficino ironically thanks him in Letter 24 in volume 1 of the *Letters*. Ficino's income seems to have remained very low, and in Letter 21 of the present volume he may have been referring to attempts to gain exemption from the new tax on the clergy; if so these attempts were unsuccessful. The new tax, which Lorenzo had instituted for the upkeep of Pisa University, may have led Ficino to move closer to Salviati and away from Lorenzo, especially as Salviati seems to have given Ficino financial support during this period. Appendix A, whether it was actually sent to Lorenzo or not, shows the estrangement that had taken place between the statesman and the philosopher. In this Appendix letter Lorenzo is made to say to Ficino, who is pictured as trying to gain admittance to the feast of St. Cosmas: 'Who is rudely disrupting this great feast?' This Platonic *convivium* had been celebrated every year since the time of Cosimo, and Ficino had regularly been present. Appendix B emphasises Ficino's exclusion from Lorenzo's court and Letter 22 shows Ficino's disillusionment with court life in general. In this he writes to Cavalcanti: 'Truth does not dwell in the company of princes; only lies, spiteful criticism and fawning flattery, men pretending to be what they are not and pretending not to be what they are.' The harmony between the active and contemplative life which Lorenzo had advocated in his poetry had failed to develop in practice. However, although Ficino's relationship with Lorenzo had cooled, he did not desire to see him removed from power. He wrote to Lorenzo in Letter 32: 'While you exercise such careful watch over our safety, you draw to yourself all that is ours.' At the end of Letter 22 he excludes the Medici from his general censure of princes on the grounds 'that they should not properly be called princes, but something greater and more sacred. For their singular virtues and great merit deserve more than any human title. They are fathers of their country in a free state.' This statement was subsequently deleted in the manuscript M9 but possibly not by Ficino and in any case not until after the conspiracy. There is correspondence in volume 3 of the *Letters* which may also have been intended as a strong warning for Lorenzo. Letter 8 in that volume was written to Pace, Secretary to Rinaldo Orsini, Archbishop of Florence, who was Lorenzo's brother-in-law, a fortnight before Giuliano's assassination. Ficino begins: 'Marsilio Ficino desires peace for his Pace but fears war.' He continues, 'The evil spirits are in opposition to the blessed angels . . . , deprivation against possession, light against darkness, the white and clear against the black.' These words should be taken as strong advice to Lorenzo to look to his safety. He can hardly have been in much doubt as to the quarter from which danger threatened.

For some time Ficino had been in correspondence with Salviati, probably since before 1474–5 when Ficino writes to him apologising for his long silence. Ficino seems to have been fully aware of his

9.   *Portrait of Giuliano de' Medici by Botticelli, Kress Collection, Washington, after 1478 (Photo: Phaidon Archive). An epic poem by Angelo Poliziano recounting Giuliano's ascent into the realm of Venus, by way of his love of Simonetta Vespucci, was brought to an abrupt and premature end by Giuliano's death. The murder occurred on the second anniversary of Simonetta's own death.*

10. Portrait of Lorenzo de' Medici with three members of the Sassetti family,
by Domenico Ghirlandaio, Capella Sassetti, Santa Trinità, Florence (Photo:
Fratelli Alinari). Lorenzo is second from the left. Third from the left is Francesco
Sassetti, the manager of the Medici bank and recipient of Letter 33 (see Notes on
Correspondents).

ambitious and restless character as he warns him in 1476 or early 1477 that 'just as a man falls swiftly who is swiftly moved, so is he deceived easily who believes easily.'[17] At the time the new tax was levied on the Florentine clergy in 1476 Ficino's relations with Salviati became more intimate. Ficino refers to Salviati in Letter 20 as 'my patron' and in Letter 17 he thanks Salviati in these terms: 'My Lord, by whose favour, or rather through whose efforts, I have obtained the leisure to write many things every day'. It is these letters which indicate that Ficino was receiving financial assistance from Salviati; however, this assistance may have been coming to an end, since Ficino says he rejoices greatly that his patron is not going to give him anything further.

Ficino seems to have divined the character of Bracciolini at an early stage. A few years before the Conspiracy he was encouraging him to concentrate on writing history.[18] There are two letters to Bracciolini in Volume 2 which are so apposite to the situation immediately before the conspiracy that it is difficult to avoid the conclusion that they were written at this time but subsequently incorporated into the manuscript which was to form Volume 2.[19] In the first of these (Letter 36) Ficino quotes a letter purporting to be from Plutarch to Trajan in which he says, 'the further you are seen to be from the charge of ambition, the more worthy are you deemed. . . . public opinion usually flings the transgression of disciples back at their teachers. . . . I have represented to you the essence of political order and practice. If you are conforming to this, you have Plutarch as your authority... Otherwise I call upon the letter before us to witness that you are not pursuing the ruin of government on Plutarch's authority.' (For Plutarch read Ficino!) In the second of these letters (44) Ficino urges Bracciolini to beware of the violence and treachery in man (not least in himself, perhaps).

Ficino's friendship with Salviati naturally extended to Salviati's young companion, Raffaele Riario. Ficino seems to have fully understood the political reasons for the appointment of Riario as Cardinal in 1477. After receiving hospitality from Riario at the Pazzi Villa in Montughi shortly after his appointment[20] he wrote a thinly disguised warning to him, purporting to come from 'Truth herself' urging upon him restraint, moderation and caution. 'Anyone who wickedly disregards the merciful Father's light discovers in this same Father a fiery judge.'[21] He was clearly concerned that this

letter might fall into the wrong hands but, perhaps hoping that
Bracciolini would take the hint, he declared that Truth was reassured
by the fact that Bracciolini, as Riario's tutor, would have charge of
the letter and would see that Riario read it.[22]

Ficino seems to have found an ingenious way of giving the same
advice in the strongest terms about the dangers of the lust for power
to both sides at almost the same time. Appendix B tells Riario and
Salviati how Ficino had given an address to 'a recent gathering of
old friends' (presumably Lorenzo's circle). This address is in fact
Letter 5 (see Notes on the Latin Text p. 158) which Ficino then
sent to Riario and Salviati. Thus both groups of protagonists in
the coming drama would have been directed to the trenchant advice
it contains on the vanity of the lives in which power, action and
study are pursued for their own sake. The opening paragraph
(perhaps written after the event) contains a fitting epitaph on the
whole affair: 'Tragedies truly lament the wretched life of mortals;
but fate also brings about their truest tragedy.'

A number of the amendments on the earliest manuscript, M9,
appear to have been made as a direct consequence of the Pazzi
Conspiracy and the upheavals which followed. Some references to
Salviati have been deleted (e.g. in Letter 26), as have a few entire
letters to Salviati and Bracciolini; other letters appear to have been
completely removed from the manuscript. Those deleted have been
translated and published as an Appendix. In two letters (17 and 20)
the address to Francesco Salviati has been crossed out and the name
of Francesco, Cardinal of Siena, has been substituted. This was in
fact Francesco Piccolomini, one of Ficino's correspondents, who
subsequently became Pope Pius III. It was not necessarily Ficino
who deleted the references to Salviati and added the name of
Francesco, Cardinal of Siena, since this addition is not in his hand.
These changes may have been made for political reasons by Ficino's
cousin and scribe, Salvini, while Ficino was not resident for a while
in the city of Florence, immediately after the Pazzi Conspiracy.[23]
Possibly they were made in response to an urgent request for a
further copy of the letters.

There are two other occasions where alterations have been made
to the manuscript M9 for reasons other than philosophical ones. In
Letter 21 to Cavalcanti, which probably relates to the tax on
the clergy, Ficino has removed references to himself and made

substitutions in his own hand. In Letter 22 the eulogy on the Medici at the end of the letter has been deleted in a style the translators do not associate with Ficino.

This again may have been done by Salvini when the war against the Pope and the King of Naples was at its height, Lorenzo was absent on a secret peace mission to Naples and the political survival of the Medici was uncertain.[24]

In the 15th century published correspondence of a philosophical nature was a vehicle for instruction rather than a record of personal details. Alterations made to words and names before publication were an accepted part of the literary conventions of the time. To Ficino's contemporaries, as to us, it is the philosophical content of the letters which is important. Although these letters contain very specific advice to some of the leading political protagonists of the time, they speak also of principles which raise the human mind above the level of narrow materialism prevalent in that age as well as in our own. The most important of these principles are the essential unity of mankind and the infinite nature of the individual human soul.

NOTES

1 A. von Reumont, *Lorenzo de' Medici*, tr. R. Harrison, London, 1876, p. 244.

2 *Letters*, **1**, 117.

3 R. Fubini, Ficino e i Medici all' avvento di Lorenzo il Magnifico, *Rinascimento*, XXIV (1984), p. 39, footnote.

4 Fubini, *op. cit.*, p. 42.

5 Angelo Poliziano, *Della Congiura dei Pazzi,* ed. A. Perosa, Padova, 1958, p. 5 seq.

6 Quoted in Reumont, *op. cit.*, p. 318.

7 Reumont, *op. cit.*, p. 321.

8 See *Poggio Bracciolini nel VI Centenario della nascita. Mostra di codici e documenti fiorentini,* ed. R. Fubini and S. Caroti, Florence, Biblioteca Medicea Laurenziana, 1980, p. 57 seq. no. 103.

9 See P. O. Kristeller, 'An unpublished description of Naples by Francesco Bandini' in *Studies in Renaissance Thought and Letters,* p. 399, Rome, 1956.

10 Angelo Poliziano, *op. cit.*, p. 34.

11 Reumont, *op. cit.*, p. 328.

12 The Medici coat-of-arms was originally a number of red balls on a gold ground, sometimes 8, sometimes less. In the time of Cosimo this settled to 6. In 1465 Louis XI granted that the upper ball might bear the lilies of France. (See shield at bottom of book-jacket).

13 For a vivid and clear account of the whole conspiracy, particularly the events in the Signoria and immediately following, see Harold Acton, *The Pazzi Conspiracy*, Ch. 3. For this incident see p. 76.

14 Reumont, *op. cit.*, p. 333.

15 Reumont, *op. cit.*, p. 341–2.

16 Reumont, *op. cit.*, p. 342–3.

17 *Letters*, **2**, 52.

18 *Letters*, **1**, 107.

19 Perhaps the pages on which these letters were written in the manuscript M9 were among those which were deliberately torn out of that manuscript.

20 Letter 26.

21 Letter 27, page 38.

22 See Appendix Letter C.

23 See *Opera*, p. 825, 1.

24 See also S. Gentile, 'Un codice delle epistole di Marsilio Ficino', in *Interpres*, III (1980), pp. 149–150, for further changes on the manuscripts, Laurenziana 90 sup. 40 and Laurenziana Strozziana 101.

Notes on the Letters

ABBREVIATIONS

Cosenza—M. E. Cosenza, *Biographical Dictionary of Humanism and Classical Scholarship*, 5 vols., Boston, 1962.

Della Torre—A. Della Torre, *Storia dell' Accademia Platonica di Firenze*.

De Vita—M. Ficino, *De Vita Libri Tres.*

Diog. Laert.—Diogenes Laertius, *Lives of Eminent Philosophers.*

Diz. Biog. Ital.—*Dizionario Biografico degli Italiani*, Rome, 1960 onwards.

Gentile, *Un Codice*—S. Gentile, 'Un Codice Magliabecchiano delle Epistole di Marsilio Ficino' in *Interpres*, III, 1980, pp. 80–157.

Gior. Stor. della Lett. Ital.—*Giornale Storico della Letteratura Italiana.*

Iter Ital.—P. O. Kristeller, *Iter Italicum*, a finding list of uncatalogued or incompletely catalogued humanistic manuscripts of the Renaissance in Italian and other libraries, 3 vols., London and Leiden, 1963, 1967, 1983.

Kristeller, *Studies*—P. O. Kristeller, *Studies in Renaissance Thought and Letters.*

Letters—*The Letters of Marsilio Ficino*, Vol. 1, 1975; Vol. 2, 1978; Vol. 3, 1981.

Marcel—R. Marcel, *Marsile Ficin.*

Opera—Marsilius Ficinus, *Opera Omnia*, Basle, 1576.

Sabbadini—R. Sabbadini, *Le Scoperte dei Codici Latini e Greci ne' Secoli XIV e XV*, Florence, 1905.

Sermoni Morali—M. Ficino, *Sermoni Morali della Stultitia et Miseria degli Uomini.*

Sup. Fic.—P. O. Kristeller, *Supplementum Ficinianum.*

Vespasiano—Vespasiano da Bisticci, *Lives of illustrious Men of the XVth Century*, translated by W. George & E. Waters.

PREFACE

1 See the letter addressed to Bernardo Bembo in Book VI of the *Epistolae* (*Opera*, p. 821): *Votum, oraculum, miraculum*, dated 15th July, 1479, indicating that this dedication was written after that date.

I

1 This letter is given as a summary (*argumentum*) of Ficino's *De Christiana Religione* in the Sarzana MS (Cod. S). It was also translated into Italian by Ficino to make it available to a wider audience and included in the *Sermoni Morali della Stultitia et Miseria degli Uomini* dedicated to Jacopo Guicciardini (*Sermone decimo*, preserved in MS Riccardiana 2684).

2 Ficino discusses whether the laws of Christianity could be influenced by the stars in *De Christiana Religione*, especially Chapter IV, *Opera*, p. 12, entitled *Auctoritas Christi non ab astris sed a Deo* – 'The authority of Christ comes not from the stars but from God.' It was a commonly held belief among the astrologers of the Middle Ages, such as Alkindi and Albumasar, that major changes in religion were brought about by planetary conjunctions.

3 The first paragraph is almost identical with a passage in Ficino's *Praedicationes*, (Sermons) *Opera*, p. 479. The composition of the *Praedicationes* is of uncertain date (*Sup. Fic.*, I, LXXXii).

4 This idea is beautifully expressed in the words inscribed around the walls of Ficino's Academy mentioned in *Letters*, **I**, 5: 'All things are directed from goodness to goodness.'

2

1 Celle is a hamlet outside Florence. Cosimo de' Medici owned a small house there which he gave to Ficino's father.

2 Ficino refers to Letter 1.

3

1 Plato's dialogue on the highest good is the *Philebus*. The *argumentum* to the *Philebus* is found in *Opera*, p. 1206.

2 *Argumentum in Platonicam Theologiam*, *Opera*, pp. 706–16, which is in the second book of letters, is dedicated to Lorenzo de' Medici. The earliest version of this work is in MS Laur. LXXXIII, 12.

3 The Latin word for 'sharp' is *argutus* and for 'summary' *argumentum*, so that the original Latin is a play on words.

4 This summary is in fact Letter 1. See Note f in Notes on the Latin Text, p. 116.

5 Ficino refers to his commentary on the *Symposium* entitled *De Amore*, *Opera*, pp. 1320–63.

6 Ivani's writings were erudite but verbose, and Ficino is discreetly pointing this out. This letter is a good example of Ficino's method of giving specific advice which has a universal application.

4

1 *Exhortatiunculum*: this is a pun, for *ex-horto* = from the garden, which refers to the first-fruits mentioned earlier in the letter. This exhortation is Letter 5.
2 Ficino was ordained priest in 1473.

5

1 This letter was translated into Italian by Ficino and included in his *Sermoni Morali* (second sermon) in MS Ricc. 2684.
2 Ficino in the preface to his commentary on the *Philebus* explains that these three kinds of life exist because 'men choose three paths to happiness: wisdom, power and pleasure.' See M. Allen, *Marsilio Ficino: the Philebus Commentary*, Appendix III, p. 480.
3 Ecclesiastes 1: 18.
4 I Corinthians 1: 20–21.
5 Isaiah 44: 24–25.
6 This simile is taken from Plato, *Republic,* VI, 508, which Ficino also uses in *De Amore*, I, 3 and in a letter in praise of medicine (*Letters*, **3**, 14: *Opera*, p. 759): 'Just as the brilliance in the eyes discerns the brilliance of colour within the sun's very light, creator of both colour and eye, so the truthful mind comprehends the truth of anything within the highest truth, the begetter of every truth and of every mind.'
7 The Sophists represented a profession rather than a school of thought, though some taught definite philosophic views. They were itinerant teachers in ancient Greece who from around 500 BC went from city to city giving instruction for a fee on a variety of techniques related to advancement in society. Oratory and the art of disputation were perhaps the most important of such skills. Plato attacks the Sophists in several dialogues for their pseudo-reasoning, which he likens to a form of 'flattery' in the *Gorgias*. In the *Sophist* he calls the Sophist a 'magician and imitator of true being'.
Ficino, in his *Commentary on the Sophist of Plato,* (*Opera*, p. 1284) says that God alone is wise; the philosopher is a true imitator of God, but the Sophist is a pretentious and false imitator of the philosopher.
8 Kristeller quotes the passage from 'Come friends!' to the end to show how Ficino identifies an important doctrine of ancient ethics, that the highest good is always associated with happiness, with knowledge of God and the return journey of the soul to God. See Kristeller, *The Philosophy of Marsilio Ficino*, p. 291.

6

1 Aristotle, *Physics*, VIII, 7, 261b.
2 Plato, *Phaedrus,* 230A: 'Am I a monster more complicated and swollen with

passion than the serpent Typho, or a creature of a gentler and simpler sort, to whom Nature has given a diviner and lowlier destiny!'

3 Plato, *Timaeus*, 69C–72C; also, *Letters*, **3**, 27, where Ficino summarises this description of the soul in *Timaeus*, 89D–E.

4 Ficino is probably referring to a previous letter from Cavalcanti (*Letters*, **2**, 23) in which he commends the benefits which the planet Saturn brings.

5 Iamblichus, *Protrepticus*, 27. In Ficino's notes to *Protrepticus* in MS Vat. Lat. 5953, and *Sup. Fic.* II, 99–101, he gives the meaning of this metaphor: one should not be distracted by bodily concerns on a spiritual occasion, but should purge oneself of the superfluous before approaching the divine.

6 These last two sentences seem admirably to express the whole spirit of the Renaissance.

7

1 Translation of the Greek *ophthalmia*. It is mentioned in Plato, *Gorgias*, 495E, where Plato uses similar arguments to show that the good and the pleasant are incompatible.

2 See *Phaedo*, 81B.

3 Aristotle, *Nicomachean Ethics*, X, 8, 1179a.

4 See Augustine, *City of God*, VIII, ch. 3: 'He (Socrates) saw that man had been trying to discover the causes of the universe, and he believed that the universe had its first and supreme cause in nothing but the will of the one Supreme God; hence he thought that the causation of the universe could be grasped only by a purified intelligence. That is why he thought it essential to insist on the need to cleanse one's life by accepting a high moral standard, so that the soul should be relieved of the weight of the lust that held it down, and then by its natural vigour should rise up to the sphere of the eternal and behold, thanks to its pure intelligence, the essence of the immaterial and unchangeable light where dwell the causes of all created things in undisturbed stability.' tr. H. Bettenson, p. 301.

5 See Iamblichus, *Life of Pythagoras*, XXXII: 'Pythagoras showed favour to just and good men, whilst rejecting the company of the violent and malevolent.'

6 Plato, *Epistle VII*, 341C.

7 Plato, *Phaedo*, 67B.

8 Cf. Jerome, *Contra Jovinianum*, II, 11 (Pat. Lat. Vol. 23, p. 313). See Ficino, *De Vita*, I, 7, *Opera*, p. 499. See also John of Salisbury, *Policraticus*, VIII, 6, 256. These passages may have their origin in Plato, *Republic*, IX, 586.

9 Plato draws an analogy between the visible sun perceived by the eye and the Good perceived by the enlightened mind. See *Republic*, VI, 508E–509B; also Plotinus, *Enneads*, I, 6, 9.

10 See Kristeller, *Philosophy of Marsilio Ficino*, p. 301, for a translation of parts of this letter. Kristeller says: 'Philosophy is here conceived as an active and living force guiding men by means of knowledge toward their real goal. We must go back to antiquity to find such a sublime yet concrete conception of philosophy.'

9

1 This was a small country estate where Ficino periodically retired to study (see Letter 2). See Marcel, p. 242.
2 Ficino refers to Letter 5 of this volume.
3 Ficino is referring to the ten Platonic dialogues which he had translated by 1469 for Cosimo de' Medici with brief commentaries. See Marcel, p. 259 seq.; *Sup. Fic.* II, pp. 103–5.

10

1 See Plato, *Phaedrus*, 274C, where the Egyptian God Theuth is said to have been the inventor of many arts, including the alphabet and astronomy.
2 A similar idea is discussed in the *proem* to Ficino's *De Christiana Religione, Opera*, p. 1. See also *Letters*, I, 5.
3 See Plato, *Timaeus*, 47: ' . . . philosophy . . . no greater good ever was or will be given by the gods to mortal man.' See also *Republic*, VII, 518D.
4 Matthew 13: 10–17; 13:34.
5 See Letter 7 of this volume.

11

1 Horace, *Ars Poetica*, 343.
2 Mercury (Hermes) is said to have invented the lyre from the shell of a tortoise, bestowing it as a gift upon Phoebus (Apollo), who played it with consummate skill. See *Homeric Hymns* (to Hermes), 40–55, 470–503; Orpheus, *Argonautica*, 381.
3 *Lyrare ne deliremus*: A rhetorical figure of speech (paranomasia) which transfers into English.
4 See *Letters*, I, 92, to Antonio Canigiani.
5 The qualities of gravity and levity and the combination of the two (*temperatio*) were associated by Ficino with the music of Jupiter, Venus and Mercury respectively: *De Vita*, III, 2, *Opera*, p. 534. See also Quintilian, *Institutes* I, X, 24.
6 An allusion to Horace, *Odes*, Book I, xxxii, 15, *salve rite vocanti*, in which the poet invokes his lyre to grant him the song which he desires, if he invokes her rightly.
7 This last paragraph is a postscript written by Luca Fabiani, Ficino's scribe (Della Torre, p. 102).

12

1 Cf. Virgil, *Georgics*, I, 393.

13

1 This refers to Sebastiano Salvini. See *Letters*, **3**, 35.
2 A mountainous district east of Florence, where Salvini lived.

15

1 Latin and Greek authors, known to Ficino, who used this simile were Seneca, Plutarch, Isocrates, Basil, John Chrysostom, Macrobius, John of Salisbury and Petrarch.
2 Aristotle, *Problemata, XXX*, 1. See also Cicero, *Tusculan Disputations,* I, 33. In *De Vita Libri Tres*, I, 4, Ficino lists the three causes which produce melancholy in scholars.
The first cause is heavenly: 'Mercury, which invites us to pursue learning, and Saturn, which makes us persevere in the pursuit of learning, are said by the astronomers to be somewhat cold and dry . . . in the view of the doctors this is the melancholic nature, and this nature Mercury and Saturn impart to the students of letters.'
The second cause is natural: 'To pursue studies that are particularly difficult it is necessary for the mind to betake itself from the outer to the inner, as if from the circumference to the centre . . . . But to be established in the centre is principally the property of the earth itself, to which black bile has a very close resemblance . . . . Contemplation produces a nature very similar to black bile.'
The third cause is human: the brain turns dry and cold through excess of thought, and the man's spirits are depleted. The finer parts of the blood are utilized in the work of replenishment, leaving the blood thick, dark and cold. The powers of digestion are weakened, while lack of exercise leads to accumulation of poisons in the body.
To relieve the melancholic condition Ficino (*De Vita*, I, 10) recommends 'the frequent sight of shining water and of the colour green or red, the enjoyment of gardens and groves, walks by the riverside and delightful rides through pleasant meadows . . . gentle sailing . . . easy occupations and various harmless activities, and the constant companionship of agreeable men.' (See *Opera*, pp. 496–502).
3 Ecclesiastes 1: 18.
4 Diog. Laert., V, 18 (Life of Aristotle).
5 Pliny, *Natural History*, XV, 34 (110–11).
6 Ficino, following Plato, distinguishes two Venuses, a heavenly Venus and a 'common' or natural Venus. The heavenly Venus, Ἀφροδίτη οὐρανία (Venus Caelestis), daughter of Uranus, has no mother and dwells in the world of causes as a divine idea; she represents the intelligible beauty that cannot be seen by the eyes. The second Venus, Ἀφροδίτη πάνδημος, (Venus Vulgaris), the daughter of Jupiter and Dione (a sea nymph), gives life and shape to the things in nature and thereby makes the intelligible beauty accessible to our perception and imagination. The higher Venus draws the mind to the contemplation of

divine beauty, while the lower draws the mind to recreate that same beauty in bodies. See Ficino, *De Amore*, II, 7 and 8 (*Opera*, pp. 1326–7). The origin of the idea is in Plato, *Symposium*, 180 DE, and is elaborated in Plotinus, *Enneads*, III, 5, 2; see Panofsky, *Studies in Iconology*, Ch. 5, on 'The Neoplatonic Movement in Florence and Northern Italy.'

7 Ficino in his commentary to Plato's *Ion* writes, 'Jupiter is the mind of God from which come Apollo, the mind of the world-soul and the soul of the whole world, and the eight souls of the celestial spheres, which are called the nine Muses; because as they move the heavens harmoniously they produce musical melody which, distributed into nine sounds, namely the eight notes of the spheres together with the one harmony of them all, gives rise to the nine Sirens singing to God. Wherefore Apollo is led by Jupiter and the Muses by Apollo, that is, the chorus of Muses is led by the mind of the world-soul.' (*Opera*, p. 1283). See also *Letters*, **1**, 7.

16

1 See Letter 12 to Sebastiano Salvini.

17

1 This letter was originally addressed to Francesco Salviati, Archbishop of Pisa, but the reference to Salviati was deleted on the most important manuscript, Magl. VIII 1441 (M9), because of the part he played in the Pazzi conspiracy, and was replaced with the name of Francesco, Cardinal of Siena. This Francesco Piccolomini subsequently became Pope Pius III. The letter appeared in the amended version in the later manuscripts and in the printed editions. The translators have restored the original wording of the letter.

2 Virgil, *Aeneid*, I, 595; *coram quem quaeris adsum*. Aeneas in a godlike form has suddenly appeared from an encircling cloud to Dido.

3 Virgil, *Aeneid*, I, 409; VI, 689. *Audire et reddere voces*. Aeneas is communicating with beings separated from him, whom he loves. The first is his mother, Venus, and the second is his dead father, Anchises. Ficino, like Virgil, does not regard physical absence as a barrier to communication.

18

1 Cf. Matthew 6: 33: 'But seek ye first the Kingdom of God, and his righteousness; and all these things shall be added unto you.'

2 Luke 10: 41–2.

19

1 1 John 4: 16.
2 See *Letters*, **3**, 32, (*Opera*, p. 777. 3).
3 See *De Amore, Oratio*, II, 2. Ficino describes creation as a circular movement:
'And so one and the same circle from God to the World and from the World
to God is called by three names. Inasmuch as it begins in God and attracts to
Him, it is called Beauty; inasmuch as emanating to the World it captivates it,
it is called Love; inasmuch as returning to its author it joins His work to Him,
it is called Delight. Love, therefore, beginning from Beauty ends in Delight. . .
Love is the good circle; a perpetual revolution from the good to the good.'
(The last sentence is quoted from Dionysius, *The Divine Names*). Sears Jayne
has translated *De Amore*. See Bibliography.
The three qualities upon which this revolution turns are often represented in
Renaissance Art by the three graces (See Edgar Wind, *Pagan Mysteries in the
Renaissance*), Ch. 2, 'Seneca's Graces'.

20

1 This letter was originally addressed to Francesco Salviati, Archbishop of Pisa.
See Letter 17, note 1 and pp. 90, 129–130.

21

1 This letter shows major deletions on the main manuscript (M9) where Ficino
has removed references to himself, replacing them by references to 'a friend'.
The translators have followed the original version which is given in S. Gentile,
Un Codice delle epistole di M. Ficino, pp. 125–6. In later manuscripts and in the
printed editions the letter appeared in the version as amended by Ficino.
2 According to Gentile these letters may have expressed concern about the effect
of a tax which the Pope had given Lorenzo permission to levy on the Tuscan
clergy for the upkeep of the new University of Pisa. Ficino seems to be
indicating in this letter that he cannot collect the necessary money from his
benefice and that, being only a priest, he is not important enough to be granted
any special exemption from his tax.
3 This letter may possibly be linked with Appendix D which shows that Ficino
used Rocca to deliver letters to the Pope.
Their Muse might refer to the priest who would finally deliver the letters to
Rocca. On the other hand it may simply mean that Ficino was not used to
writing letters about money and had no idea whether an able muse had been
present to inspire him.
4 *Let others forget me* probably refers to Lorenzo becoming distant from Ficino
and would also perhaps indicate that he was not going to grant Ficino exemption
from the new tax.

I will not forget my own may refer to Ficino's determination not to pass the burden of the tax on to those in his care as priest.

5 Cf. Matthew 13:57.

6 Ovid, *Remedia Amoris*, 369.

7 Cf. Ovid, *The Art of Love*, I, 159. *Parva leves capiunt animos*: 'Frivolous minds are won by a trifle.'

8 This may be taken as a reference to Ficino's small physical stature and at the same time to his being little considered.

22

1 S. Gentile points out that this letter was written around 1476 because of the mention of the letter 'In praise of Philosophy', *Letters*, I, 123, written at the beginning of that year. See S. Gentile, *Un Codice. . .*, p. 146.

2 A cynic philosopher, Epicurean and flatterer of princes. See Diog. Laert., *Lives*, II, 65 seq.

3 Lover of slavery, philodoulos (φιλόδουλος): lover of the body, philosomatos (φιλόσωματος): Plato, *Phaedo*, 68B.

4 A possible allusion to the anecdote mentioned in Diogenes Laertius that Dionysius once commanded everyone to put on purple and dance. Plato declined on the grounds of modesty, but Aristippus put on the dress, claiming it did not offend modesty. Diog. Laert., II, 78 (Life of Aristippus).

5 Diog. Laert. II, 25, IV, 8–9, VI.

6 According to Plutarch it was Cicero's influence that originally induced Caesar to make his great nephew, Octavian, his heir. Afterwards Octavian became a member of the second triumvirate, which included Antony, who, with the reluctant consent of Octavian, ordered Cicero to be put to death: Plutarch, *Life of Cicero*, XLVI. This was the price paid by Octavian for the formation of the second triumvirate.

7 The conspiracy of Piso provided an excuse for Nero to accuse and execute his former tutor and minister. See Tacitus, *Annals*, XV, 60–4.

8 Callisthenes of Olynthus, kinsman of Aristotle, who was presented to Alexander by the philosopher, was later put to death on suspicion of complicity in a plot against the King's life: Diog. Laert., V, 5 (Life of Aristotle); Plutarch, *Life of Alexander*, LIII–LV; Arrian, *Anabasis*, IV, 11–14.

9 Xenophon describes the circumstances of his joining the expedition of Cyrus the Younger (who was not a King), apparently against the wishes of Socrates. On Socrates' advice, he had consulted the oracle at Delphi on this proposal, but had changed the nature of the question. Instead of asking whether he should go, he asked, 'To what god shall I sacrifice in order that I may best and most honourably go on the journey I have in mind?' Xenophon, *Anabasis*, III, i, 4–7.

10 See Plato, *Epistles*, VII, 341B, where this book is mentioned, which Plato repudiates on the grounds that his teaching cannot be transmitted by the written word.

11 Aristotle's lectures were divided into the *exoteric* (training in rhetoric, logic and statecraft meant for general dissemination) and the *acroatic*, a more profound philosophy relating to the study of the laws of nature meant only to be given orally to the initiated. Alexander said Aristotle was wrong to make public some of his acroatic teachings, since their previous exclusiveness had allowed Alexander, who was privy to the teaching, to excel all others in learning. Aristotle replied that, since his teachings could only be understood by those who had attended his lectures, they had not in fact been made public. Plutarch, *Life of Alexander*, VII, 3–5; Aulus Gellius, *Attic Nights*, XX, v,1–12. Diog. Laert., V,5 (Life of Aristotle).

12 According to Diogenes Laertius, the followers of Pythagoras were accused of being identified with the oligarchic party in Croton and exciting the enmity of the popular party. In the ensuing persecution of his school Pythagoras was either killed or forced into exile: Diog. Laert., VIII, 39 (Life of Pythagoras). See also Iamblichus, *Life of Pythagoras,* 255–9.

13 Zeno (not to be confused with the celebrated Stoic philosopher) was put to death for stirring up a revolt against Nearchus, the tyrant of Agrigentum. Valerius Maximus, III, 3, 2–3. Diog. Laert., IX, 5, 26–28.

14 Anaxarchus of Thrace bit off his own tongue rather than allow the tyrant Nicocreon to cut it off. See Diog. Laert., IX, 59; Valerius Maximus, III, 3, 4; Ficino, *Theologia Platonica*, XIII, 1 (*Opera*, p. 286); Cicero, *Tusculan Disputations*, II, xxii, 52.

15 The sole reason given for Ovid's banishment by the Emperor Augustus was his having published *The Art of Love*, but this may have been a pretext. The real reason is unknown.

16 According to one life of Lucan he incurred the hatred of Nero by defeating him in a poetic contest at the quinquennial games, after which he was prohibited from reciting in public. Lucan sought revenge against Nero by lending his support to a conspiracy and was put to death. Tacitus, *Annals*, XV, 70.

17 'At the beginning of his reign Domitian would spend hours alone every day catching flies. . . and stabbing them with a needle-sharp pen. Once, on being asked whether anyone was closeted with the emperor, Vivius Crispus answered wittily: "No, not even a fly."' See Suetonius, *Twelve Caesars* (Domitian, 3, tr. Robert Graves, p. 297). Domitian was thought in post-classical times to have killed his friend Statius with a similar implement in a fit of rage.

18 This paragraph was deleted from the main MS (M9) and does not appear in the printed editions or other manuscripts. See *Sup. Fic.*, I, p. 32. See also p. 135.

24

1 Acts 9: 15.

2 2 Corinthians 12:2. See Ficino, *De Raptu Pauli Ad Tertium Caelum, Opera*, p. 697. See also Notes on the Latin Text, note d, p. 136.

3 Dionysius, believed in the Middle Ages to be one of St. Paul's followers,

discusses the invisible Sun in the *Divine Names*, IV, 5–6. St. Paul's references to 'light' are in Acts 9:3 and Romans 1:20.

25

1 *Amantissime atque amatissime mi Amati*: Rhetorical figures which do not translate into English.
2 Virgil, *Aeneid*, IV, 532.
3 Virgil, *Aeneid*, IV, 298.
4 Virgil, *Aeneid*, IV, 100.
5 Horace, *Heroides*, I, 12. The word human (*humanus*) has been added by Ficino.
6 Ficino frequently uses this idea: see Ficino, *Letters*, **1**, 129, which may be derived from Plotinus, *Enneads,* IV, 4, 41.

26

1 Virgil, *Aeneid*, I, 79.
2 Ficino is saying that the outward journey was made at a time when Venus was at its highest point and therefore at its most influential; however, the return journey was guided by love, which Ficino knew to be above the influence of the planetary gods. See *De Amore,* V, 8 (*Opera*, p. 1339); also Plato, *Symposium,* 195–7.
3 See Plato, *Symposium,* 196C, where Agathon describes the power of love to overcome the god of war. See also *Symposium,* 178–180.
4 The last two paragraphs, referring to Salviati and Bracciolini, were deleted on the main manuscript (M9), before publication. See *Sup. Fic.,* I, p. 32.
5 Achates was the faithful standard-bearer of Aeneas, and Ficino is likening Bracciolini, who was Cardinal Riario's secretary, to Achates.
6 Ficino's *ugos colles* are the Montughi hills upon which the Pazzi had a villa. Dr. Gentile has pointed out this connection to the translators. See E. Repetti, *Dizionario Geografico, Fisico, Storico della Toscana,* Florence, 1833–43, Vol. III, pp. 604–5.
7 According to Kristeller, the poet referred to is Niccolo Lelio Cosmico of Padua, who acted as Riario's tutor. See *Sup. Fic.,* I, p. 122.

27

1 Raffaele Riario was made a cardinal at the age of 16 by Pope Sixtus IV on 10th December, 1477.
2 This letter was written on the 27th January, 1477 (1478 new style), according to the MS Magl. VIII 1441 (see p. 142). The letter was therefore written three months before the Pazzi conspiracy (26th April, 1478).

3 See Horace, *Odes,* I, xxiv, 7, for the image of naked truth.

4 Virgil, *Eclogues,* II, 29: *humilis habitare casas.*

5 *Colossians 3:10.* These words are used in the ordination ceremony.

6 Cf. Horace, *Odes,* II, x, 9–10: 'The wind most oft the highest pine tree grieves; the stately towers come down with greater fall; the highest hills the bolt of thunder cleaves' (tr. Sir Philip Sidney).

7 The Latin word *cardo* means a pivot. *Cardinalis* is the adjectival form.

8 Ficino gives a similar instruction to Giovanni Aurelio of Rimini in an earlier letter. See *Letters,* **3,** 7.

9 *Humanitas* is used by Ficino here to convey the love of mankind. He probably used this word as an equivalent for the Greek φιλανθρωπία (philanthropia). See Plato, *Euthyphro,* 3D.

10 See Plato, *Epistles,* IV, 321 B.

11 For this simile of the head and its members cf. John of Salisbury, *Policraticus,* IV, 1. (*The Statesman,* tr. J. Dickinson, p. 3).

12 Argus, called 'the all-seeing', had eyes in the whole of his body. Only two were closed at any one time. See Apollodorus, II, 1, 3; Hyginus, *Fabulae,* 145. Oedipus solved the riddle: 'What walks on four legs at sunrise, two legs at midday and three legs at sunset?' The answer is man. Apollodorus, III, 5, 8; Diodorus Siculus, IV, 64, 3; Hyginus, *Fabulae,* 67. This indicates that a prince should be always watching (like Argus); he should be able to see through the outer mask (like Lynceus) and understand the nature of man at all stages in his life (as Oedipus).

13 Quintus Curtius Rufus, *De Rebus Gestis Alexandri Magni, VI, 3.*

14 See Iamblichus, *Life of Pythagoras,* XXXI, 196–8.

15 Cf. Seneca, *De Ira,* III, 13, 3: 'In the case of Socrates it was a sign of anger if he lowered his voice and became sparing of speech.'

16 Diog. Laert., III, 39 (Life of Plato).

17 See Plato, *Laws,* V, 731 E: 'The lover is blinded about the beloved so that he judges wrongly of the just, the good and the honourable.' Horace, *Satires,* I, 3, 38: 'The lover in his blindness fails to see his lady's blemishes.' For a study of this idea see Panofsky, 'Blind Cupid' in *Studies in Iconology,* IV.

18 Matthew 16:18.

28

1 See Letter 27.

2 This is Ficino's book, *De Christiana Religione.*

29

1 See Letter 27.

2 Soderini was appointed Archbishop of Volterra in 1478.

30

1 Horace, *Art of Poetry*, I, 343.
2 See Letter 46, note 3.

31

1 Cf. Aristotle, *Physics*, VIII, 7, 261b.
2 See Letter 25, note 1.

32

1 John 15:13.
2 The reference is to Piero de' Medici, Lorenzo's eldest son, who was eight years old.
3 Romans 8:32.
4 Ficino is alluding to the death of his father Diotifeci, who died in February or March, 1478. See Gentile, *Un Codice*, op. cit., p. 145, note 200.

33

1 A manuscript copy of this letter is preserved in the Bodleian Library, Oxford: MS Lat. misc. d. 85, which originally belonged to Bartolomeo della Fonte. See Gentile, *Un Codice*, p. 108. See also Notes on the Latin Text, p. 145.
2 Cf. passage in *Asclepius:* 'God does not will anything in vain for he is full of all things and all things that he wills are good. He has all that he wills and wills all that he has.' Hermes, *Asclepius*, 26b (ed. Scott, p. 347).
3 Sassetti's original villa has been substantially altered, but the present owner, Sir Harold Acton, informs us that it did once contain two chapels. See also Notes on Correspondents, p. 169.

34

1 Aristotle, *Nicomachean Ethics*, III, 9.
2 This moral point concerning Hannibal is effectively made by John of Salisbury, *Policraticus*, VIII, 6, 260, who draws on Valerius Maximus, IX, 1; Mark Antony's conduct is described in Macrobius, *Saturnalia*, III, xvii, 15–17, and John of Salisbury, *Policraticus*, VIII, 7, 265. According to one classical tradition Achilles was fatally wounded in the heel by an arrow from Paris as he was seeking the hand in marriage of Paris' sister Polyxena in the temple of Minerva in Troy.
3 Honey and gall are frequent images of pleasure and pain in Ficino; see Letter 15.

4 Homer, *Iliad*, XVII, 570. 'She (Athene) put strength into his (Menelaus') knees and shoulders and made him as bold as a fly which, though driven off, will yet come again and bite if it can, so dearly does it love man's blood – even so bold as this did she make him.' tr. Samuel Butler.

5 See I Kings 11: 1–10.

6 Aristotle, *Nicomachean Ethics*, I, 1094.

7 Cicero, *De Senectute,* XIII, 44: 'The divine Plato calls pleasure the bait of evil because evidently men are caught by it, like fishes on a hook.' He is referring to Plato, *Timaeus,* 69D: 'Pleasure a mighty lure to evil.'

8 Virgil, *Aeneid*, I, 350.

9 Horace, *Epistles*, I, ii, 55: *Nocet empta dolore voluptas* (from Plato, *Timaeus*, 69D).

35

1 Plato, *Ion*, 534; Ficino's Commentary on Plato's *Ion*, *Opera*, p. 1281; letter to Naldo Naldi, *Opera*, p. 830.

36

1 This refers to Book II of Ficino's letters, *Opera*, pp. 675–97. See letter to Gazolti, *Opera*, p. 827.

2 The idea that a man of knowledge possesses all things is frequent in Ficino (See Introduction, p. xiv). He may also have been referring to the fact that Pierleone of Spoleto had a very large library.

37

1 Bembo's first embassy to Florence ended in June, 1476. He was re-elected for a second term of office as Venetian ambassador on the 2nd July, 1478. This letter was evidently written by Ficino to express his jubilation on the re-election of his friend. See A. Della Torre, La Prima Ambasceria di B. Bembo, in *Giornale Storico della Letteratura Italiana*, XXXV, p. 319.

2 Orpheus was the son of the Muse, Calliope, from whom he acquired the gift of music. His father was either Oeagrus, King of Thrace, or the God Apollo, from whom he received a lyre. His skill was such that when he sang and played this instrument rivers ceased to flow, mountains and trees moved, wild beasts became tame and even the Gods were affected. See Horace, *Ars Poetica*, 391–4.

Amphion was the son of Zeus and Antiope. In his youth he studied poetry and music; then Hermes gave him a lyre. At Thebes his playing caused great stones to move and to fit themselves together, so that the city walls were built by his magical powers. See Apollonius of Rhodes, *Argonautica*, 1, 740, 755, and Horace, *Ars Poetica*, 394–7.

3 Bembo's diplomatic missions took him to places as far apart as England, Castile and the northern states of Germany. See Notes on Correspondents, p. 162.

38

1 Probably Antonio's only work on astrology, *Liber de Cometa*, dedicated to Giuliano de' Medici. See Della Torre, p. 783.

39

1 This letter was written shortly after Riario's release from imprisonment on the 12th June, 1478, following the Pazzi conspiracy. (See pp. 86, 169). Apparently Riario wanted Ficino to join him after leaving Florence. Ficino may have hoped that Riario would act as an intermediary between the Pope and Florence during the war between them. See letter to Riario, *Opera*, p. 811, 3.
2 Riario was appointed a Cardinal Priest, one of the three orders of Cardinals; each Cardinal Priest took his title from a church in Rome, in this case San Giorgio.
3 Venus and Jupiter are associated with the benevolent powers of love and justice, Mars and Saturn with the malign influences of violence and misery.
4 Matthew 18: 20: 'For where two or three are gathered together in my name, there am I in the midst of them.'

40

1 See Kristeller, *Philosophy of Marsilio Ficino*, pp. 299–300, for a discussion on this letter.
2 A King of Mycenae who imposed upon Hercules his twelve labours.

41

1 Hesiod, in his *Works and Days* (110–200), describes the legend of the golden race of men who lived in the time of Cronos, free from toil and sorrow, and the succeeding races of silver, bronze and iron, characterised by decreasing degrees of happiness. See also Plato, *Cratylus*, 398A and Virgil, *Eclogues, IV*. Cf. also the Indian tradition of the four ages of man. See especially Mahābhārata, Bhīʃma Parva, Ch. 10.
2 Letters 12, 33 and 40 in the present volume. See Notes on the Latin Text, p. 151. See also *Letters*, **1**, 49. The Pazzi Conspiracy and the suffering which followed may have called forth these letters on the virtue of patience or forbearance. See p. 87.

42

1 According to Ficino love has the magical power to transform the lover into the beloved (Cf. Hermes Trismegistus, *Asclepius*, I, 5–6). The son of Venus, Amor, is represented by Ficino as a magician. See *De Amore*, VI, 9 and 10, and Plato, *Symposium*, 203 DE. References to God as a magician also occur in the Upanishads. See Śvetāśvatara Upanishad, 4, 10. 'One should know that Nature (Prakṛti) is a magic display (Māyā) and that the great God (Maheśvara) is a magician (Māyin).'

2 *Vincire* means 'to bind' in Latin. A play on the correspondent's name, Vinciguerra, may be intended.

3 Ecclesiastes 4:12.

4 Averroes was the Latinized version of the name of Ibn-Rushd (1126–98), an Arabic philosopher who wrote, among other things, a number of commentaries on works of Aristotle, including *De Anima*. The Averroist doctrine of the single mind for all men was in opposition to the Christian belief in an individual mind. Ficino discusses the doctrine in the 15th book of the *Platonic Theology*, refuting some of its conclusions. Quoting this letter Della Torre points out that the Averroist teachings had a powerful advocate in one Gaetano da Tiene, a Venetian friend of Bembo, who lectured in Padua University where Bembo had also studied. See A. Della Torre, 'La Prima Ambasceria di Bernardo Bembo', in *Giornale Storico della Letteratura Italiana*, XXXV, pp. 282–3. See *Letters*, I, 40 and Letter 37.

5 Psalm 133:1.

43

1 'raise myself from the ground' (*tollere humo*): this phrase is part of the poet's opening invocation in Virgil, *Georgics*, III, 9.

2 This simile of the ropes is used by Dionysius with reference to prayer: *The Divine Names*, I, 3. See also Ficino, *Opera*, p. 1049. Cf. Letter 19 and note 3 of that letter.

3 *Aetheria plaga*: Virgil, *Aeneid*, I, 394; IX, 638.

4 *Quid sit lumen*, an essay addressed to Febo Capella; see *Opera*, pp. 717–20.

5 Lucretius, *De Rerum Natura*, IV, 1061; Ficino, *De Amore*, VI, 6.

44

1 This refers to Ficino's *De Christiana Religione*. See Notes on the Latin Text, p. 152.

45

1 John 1:5.

2 Minerva, the goddess of wisdom and the patron of the liberal arts, was represented as arrayed in a robe (*peplum*) woven by her own hand, richly embroidered with mythological subjects. See Plato, *Euthyphro*, 6C. The riches of this robe represent a covering for the truth within. The statue of Minerva in Sais, Egypt, bore this inscription: 'I am all that has been, and is, and shall be, and no mortal has yet removed my robe'. Plutarch, *Isis and Osiris*, 345c. A similar passage is also quoted in Proclus, *Commentary on the Timaeus*, II, 98 (ed. Festugière, pp. 139–40), which describes the allegorical significance of Minerva's robe. Similarly in the Upanishads it is stated that truth is veiled by the golden disc of *Māyā* (illusion) which only the knowers of truth may uncover. Mundaka Upanishad, 2, 2, 9, Īshāvāsya Upanishad, 15.

3 See Plato, *Republic*, VII, 529, where he distinguishes true perceptions through reason and intelligence from mere 'gaping' or 'blinking' with half open eyes (συμμύω), which is often mistaken for knowledge.

4 A play on the words *officina* (workshop) and *Ficino* may be intended.

46

1 A translation of this letter by E. Gombrich is to be found, together with detailed notes, in 'Botticelli's Mythologies', *Journal of Warburg and Courtauld Institutes,* 1945. Recent research suggests that Botticelli's *Primavera* was originally commissioned for Giuliano de' Medici to celebrate his part in the jousts but, on his assassination, it was recommissioned for Lorenzo di Pierfrancesco on the occasion of his marriage to Semiramide Appiani, which was to have taken place in May, 1482 (hence the symbolism associated with Spring). The marriage was postponed to July, 1482.
See Mirella Levi d'Ancona, *Botticelli's Primavera: A Botanical Interpretation including Astrology, Alchemy and the Medici, Florence,* 1983 (Olschki).
See also Umberto Baldini, *Primavera*, p. 94.

2 Virgil, *Aeneid*, VI, 730: *igneus est ollis vigor et caelestis origo.* Ficino has *igneus vigor inest et caelestis origo.*

3 Ficino refers to seven gifts given by God to Man by the agency of the deities who rule the seven planets: contemplation through Saturn, government through Jupiter, magnanimity through Mars, intelligence and prophecy through the Sun, love through Venus, eloquence through Mercury, procreation through the Moon. See *De Amore*, VI, 4 (*Opera*, pp. 1342–3).

4 Cf. Plato, *Epistles*, IV, 321B.

5 A play on words: *Humanitatem, humi natum.*

6 Virgil, *Aeneid*, I, 75. This description of human nature (*humanitas*) by Ficino may have inspired Botticelli to paint the central figure of Venus in his *Primavera*. It is clear from this letter that Ficino attached the greatest importance to the

visual impression. Both the picture and the letter were for the instruction of Lorenzo di Pierfrancesco de' Medici.

47

1 According to Magl. VIII 1441 (M9), this letter was also sent to Naldo Naldi, who with Vespucci was tutor to Lorenzo di Pierfrancesco. See Notes on the Latin Text, p. 155.
2 This refers to Letter 46.
3 Virgil, *Aeneid*, I, 26.

48

1 This letter was written in reply to a letter from Antonio Ivani. See *Sup. Fic.*, II, p. 248 seq.
2 See Eusebius, *Demonstratio Evangelica*, I, 6.
3 In his commentary to the epistles of Saint Paul, Ficino explains the limitations of the Mosaic and Gentile laws compared to the law of Christ, which, being based on spiritual truth, purifies the soul through grace. Ficino, *Commentary on the Epistles of St Paul*, Ch. V (*Opera*, pp. 433–5); Charles Trinkaus, *In our image and likeness*, XVI, 2, pp. 734–53.
4 *Limbo* was traditionally placed on the borders of Hell. The prophets and saints of the Old Testament, not having been baptized under the new law of Christ, died in original sin and were placed in Limbo. They were confined until liberated by Christ on his descent into Hell. This belief was first described in the apocryphal gospel of Nicodemus. Limbo was thus akin to the classical *Hades* or underworld, to be distinguished from *Gehenna*, the place of eternal torment mentioned in the New Testament. Dante placed Socrates, Plato and Virgil and other classical philosophers and poets in Limbo in *The Divine Comedy*, Canto IV. Antonio's letter to Ficino entitled *De Socratis contentissimi anima* (On the soul of the most happy Socrates) questions the belief that the great philosophers of antiquity were automatically excluded from a Christian salvation, on the grounds that their good works would thereby appear to have been futile. In this reply Ficino, following St. Augustine, says that such philosophers had sufficient virtue to merit final salvation through the grace of Christ. See St. Augustine, *Epistles*, CII, 8–12. See also Ficino's letter 'to a faithful friend', *Sup. Fic*, I, pp. 12–15. Antonio still felt the need to consult Friar Simone of Florence on this question, who gave a broadly similar reply to that of Ficino. See P. Landucci Ruffo, 'L'epistolario di Antonio Ivani (1430–82)', *Rinascimento*, 1966, pp. 141–207.
5 Ficino, (*Opera*, p. 808).
6 See *Letters*, **3**, 8.

49

1 The Italian name for Phoebus is Febo, but the translators have preserved the Latin to make the reference to the god clear.
2 Phoebus Apollo, god of light, received the gift of prophecy from Jupiter.

50

1 This may refer to *Letters*, **3**, 25.

51

1 Cf. Horace, *Ars Poetica*, 361.
2 Copies of this letter were sent to Lorenzo de' Medici and Bernardo Bembo (see Notes on the Latin Text, p. 156.)
3 This passage echoes Cicero, *De Officiis*, I, 5. Cf. also Cicero, *De Finibus*, II, xvi, 52. See also Plato, *Phaedrus*, 250D. This passage from Plato is quoted by John of Salisbury, *Policraticus*, VII, 8, 121.
4 Compare this to Cicero, *Tusculan Disputations*, V, xxiv, 68–69, where Cicero says that in the quest for the good the reader must set before his eyes certain tangible images to enable him more readily to understand the good: 'Let us assume a man pre-eminently endowed with the highest qualities and let our imagination play for a moment with the picture.'

APPENDIX LETTERS

A

1 Owing to the fragmentary nature of this dialogue, it is difficult to intepret its meaning. Taken in conjunction with previous correspondence, it implies that Lorenzo had grown apart from Ficino. This letter, which may never have been sent, could have been intended to restore the connection.
2 The reference is to the feast day of St. Cosmas (celebrated on 27th September according to the Latin ecclesiastical calendar). In a letter to Lorenzo de' Medici (see *Letters*, **2**, 15) we are told that such feasts were held over a period of thirty years, throughout a complete orbit of Saturn, in honour of Cosimo de' Medici. From the date that Cosimo had instructed Ficino to begin translating Plato, Ficino had vowed to celebrate the birthdays of Plato and Cosimo with equal honour, treating the feast day of St. Cosmas as their joint birthday.
3 See *Letters*, **2**, 42, and note 3 to that letter.
4 A reference to Matthew 22: 11–13: the parable of the wedding feast at which one of the guests is found to be without a wedding garment and is cast out.
5 Matthew 25: 21.

B

1 The gathering was possibly one of the lay confraternities patronized by the Medici and their friends, such as the *Compagnia dei Magi* or *Compagnia di S. Giovanni Evangelista*, at which orations and sermons were delivered before a chosen audience. See P.O. Kristeller, *Studies in Renaissance Thought and Letters*, Ch.5, pp. 99—122, 'Lay religious traditions and Florentine Platonism.'
2 See Letter 5 for the text of the speech in question. See also Notes on the Latin Text, p. 158.

C

1 Raffaele Riario was made a Cardinal on the 10th December, 1477. Bracciolini, who took part in the Pazzi Conspiracy, became secretary to the Cardinal in January, 1478, ostensibly as his tutor, in fact to further the conspiracy.
2 Iolaus, faithful companion of Hercules who helped him to overcome the Hydra.
3 Probably Niccolo Lelio Cosmico, the poet.

D

1 *Aditus et tempora noras*, Virgil, *Aeneid*, IV, 423.
2 *Our letter*, which presumably accompanied this letter to Rocca, 'full of praise for Riario', may have been intended to support Riario's own letter to Sixtus IV (quoted on p. 86) asking him to forgive Lorenzo and the Florentine people and to lift the interdict upon them.

E

1 The Florentine Council referred to is either the *Otto di Balia*, which was concerned with justice, or the *Otto di Guardia*, which was concerned with public order.

Notes on the Latin Text

It is not intended that these notes should be exhaustive or should supplant a study proper to a critical edition. They have been prepared:

    (a) to give the key variants;

    (b) to allow anyone using the Basle edition (the most accessible) to correct the corruptions of that text, as we have noted each occasion where the Basle text is erroneous and given the readings of the manuscripts and the other printed editions;

    (c) to indicate the path this translation has attempted to follow.

A few points need to be made. As stated in the Translators' Note:

    (i) we give in these notes the comparison between the manuscripts and the three most important printed editions. The most important manuscripts are two in number (M9 and R10) for the book as a whole. But even more important for individual letters are the manuscripts which contain these letters. Details of these, including their sigla, are set out on p. xx. However, Lo4 is not of prime importance. The sigla of the manuscripts which contain the book as a whole and those of the above-mentioned printed editions are given on p. xix and p. xx respectively.

    (ii) we have followed M9 as generally the most reliable source. Occasions where we have departed from this are mentioned.

In the collation for each note it will be seen that the sigla are given in tabular form and in a definite order which reflects our opinion of the relative importance of the manuscripts. The spelling, punctuation and capitals given are those of the main manuscript or edition quoted.

The punctuation in some of the more authoritative Renaissance manuscripts has a great deal more subtlety and many more nuances than that to which we have become accustomed. M9 is an example of such a manuscript. We give just one extract from M9 to illustrate this point. The penultimate paragraph of letter 27 begins:

Domus denique tua sit, Dei templum · prudentiae oculus · libra justitiae · fortitudinis sedes · Regula temperantiae · Honestatis exemplar · and thus it goes on, giving a list of qualities of equal validity. To show this equal validity the scribe used what we have termed a 'spacing stop', a stop equidistant between the words and in the middle of the line, thus indicating the equality. Undoubtedly today this would be reduced to the mundane comma, with what loss of subtlety!

The orthography we have used for the Latin in these notes is as near as we have been able to attain to that used by Ficino (for instance: *Marsilij, uiuit, Vt*). The long 'i' ('j') was introduced by the Renaissance humanists themselves (and was used by Ficino) to indicate a semi-consonantal quality. In other parts of this book the orthography is that now standard in modern Latin (*e.g. Marsilii, vivit, Ut*). This course has been adopted so as not to mislead those who may be unused to the orthography of the Renaissance humanists.

To clarify the form of address in the letters, we point as an example to the address of letter 44. In M9 this reads *Marsilius Ficinus florentinus hieronymo rossio pistoriensi. S.D.* We include *florentinus* and *S.D.* in the translation only when the most important source has them. The same applies to *Vale* if it appears at the end of a letter.

PREFACE

a	M9	R10 Be	L28	V B	read *Prohemium quinti libri*
		G1			reads *Marsilij ficini florentini epistolarum liber quintus* and B has these words but after the preface and before the first letter. Also V has these words but with *Quintus liber epistolarum* before *Marsilij* etc. (ignoring second word which is repeat of *Quintus* misspelled). G1 continues *feliciter incipit: et primo Prohemium*
b	M9	R10 Be G1 L28			read *Marsilius Ficinus Florentinus Bernardo* but V B omit *Florentinus*
c	M9	R10 Be G1 L28	V		read *alibi demonstramus lex* but B has *demonstrauimus* for middle word.

I

a	M9	R10 Be G1	read *Legis diuinae* but L28 V B P have first word *Leges* (erron.) In S the body of this letter actually forms the second part of that published as letter 3. Since S is a copy of what Ficino actually wrote to Ivano, it does not have the

				heading. The one word *Argumentum* underlined, precedes it and separates it from letter 3 as printed. Opposite in the margin appear the words *De Divina Lege*.
b	M9	R10 Be G1 L28 V		read *confirmatur* but B P have *confirmantur* (erron.)
c	M9	R10 Be G1 L28		read *ficinus familiaribus* but V B P add between these two words *Florentinus Reuerendissimis* and the translation follows this latter reading.
d	M9	R10 Be G1 L28 V B P		read *rationum suasionibus: uel* but S has middle word *suasione*
e	M9 S	R10 Be G1 L28		read *palam omnis humanae* but V B P have middle word *omnibus*
f	M9 S	R10 Be G1 L28 V P		read *prorsus auferretur: legem* but B has verb *auferreretur*
g	M9	R10 Be G1 L28		read *Quisquis eiusmodi* but S V B P add *igitur* between these two words.
h	M9	R10 Be G1 L28		read *crediderit, habet et* but S V B P have middle word *habebit*
i	M9 S	R10 Be G1 L28 V		read *ueri quicquam alicubi* but B P have *quiduis* as middle word.
j	M9 S	R10 Be G1 L28 V P		read *boni sperare possimus* but B has *separare* as middle word (erron.).
k	M9 S	R10 Be G1 L28 V P		read *neque sperantes frustratur* but B has *separantes* (erron.)
l	S			gives a date. See note f to letter 3.

2

			All MSS place this letter third, edd. place it second.
a	M9	R10 G1 L28	read *Naldo Naldio poetae. S.D.* but V B P omit *Naldio* and B P omit *S. D.* Be has *Naldio* but omits *S.* at end.
b	M9	R10 Be G1 L28	read *scripsi? Et* but V has full stop in place of question mark. B has comma and P follows B.
c	M9	R10 Be G1	read *scio quod loquor* but L28 has comma after *scio* and V has colon after *scio*. B P have comma.

3

a	M9 S	R10	Be	G1	L28	V	P

read *ut ter argutum te* but B has *argumentum* for third word.

b	M9 S	R10	Be	G1	L28	V	

read *in nostrum illum de religione librum* but B P have *illud* for third word.

c	M9 S	R10	Be	G1	L28	V	P

read *quaedam impertiatur marsilianae* but B reads *impariatur* for middle word (erron.)

d	M9	R10	Be	G1	L28	V B P	

read *amplus affectus. Saepe* but S has *effectus* as middle word. The translation follows M9.

e	M9	R10	Be	G1	L28	V B P	

read *minus spargitur, feruet* but S has middle word *spargit*

f S

gives, after the end of letter 3, the body of letter 1. At the end of this the following appears: *Vale. Ex agro cellano idibus septembris.* – 'Farewell. Celle. 15th September.' What seems like another hand has added *1477* in brackets, although the year looks correct, as this letter appears in a sequence of letters, some of which give the year 1477.
The translation follows S as applying to letter 3.

4

a M9

reads *amico. u.s.* which is to be read *unico salutem.* R10 has *amico unico. S.* which Be G1 follow, V has *amico unico. S.D.* which B P follow.

b M9   R10 Be G1 L28

read at end *legeris. Vale.* but V omits *Vale* and B P follow V.

5

a F

has the heading so the letter had already been thought out by the time F was written.

b	M9 F	R10 Be G1 L28	V	P			read *generis nostri miseria* but B has *nostra*
c	F						reads *Quod illi* thus showing that the words *ut plurimum* between these 2 words in M9 were added later.
d	M9 F	R10					have paragraph mark before the word *Tria*
e	M9 F	R10 Be G1 L28	V	P			read *harum uita habentur* but B gives *uita* indistinctly.
f	M9	Be	L28	V B P			read *summi, ij ut plurimum reuera sunt* but R10 G1 move *ij* to between last two words. F reads *summi, ij reuera sunt* showing that the word *reuera* was an earlier addition to M9 than *ut plurimum*
g	M9						read originally *excellere, ij maxime* but the *ij* which appeared on a new line was crossed out and *ij saepe* added at the end of the previous line in another hand. F has this original version: *excellere, hi maxime*
h	M9						read *in singulis didicere. Et* however F read initially *insingulis dediscere. Et* but the verb was amended to read *dedicere.*
i	F						has a form of paragraph mark before the words *O insipidam* F continues *insipidam sapientiam. Hanc Salomon omnium diuino iudicio sapientissimus affere dolorem inquit atque laborem. Proinde* This makes it clear that the first addition in the margin of M9 (which reads as F), that is from *Nam dum* down to *laborem. Proinde* (i.e.: from the sentence after that in which *ij saepe* appears) was added prior to the writing out of this letter to Bembo and subsequently the words in M9 *Hanc Salomon* down to *laborem. Proinde* were crossed out and *O scientiam* down to *inspicere.* (that is from 'O knowledge' down to 'sees... by the light of the eye

alone.') were added by Ficino himself subsequently to the writing of this letter.

All additions to this letter in sequence after this are incorporated into F except *Voluptas denique falsa* only in part (see note o below).

j M9   R10   G1 L28   V B P   read *inspicere. Proinde qui* but Be omits *Proinde* which probably shows that the scribe was copying from M9 as *Proinde* in that MS is on its own in left hand corner.

k M9   read at first *seruiunt. Qui* but *postremo* was added in front of *qui* possibly by Ficino, although *Postremo* is incorporated into the main body of the letter in F, so this was an early addition to M9.

l   V B P   read *et esuriunt. O* but M9 F R10 Be G1 L28 spell verb *exuriunt*

m M9 F   R10 Be G1 L28   V   P   read *miseriorem. Quonam igitur* but B has middle word *Quoniam* (erron.)

n M9 F   Be G1 L28   V   read *curiosissimam? An ad imperium? An voluptatem?* but B just has a full stop in place of first question mark. R10 P repeat *ad* after second *An*

o   Be G1   P   read *Voluptas denique breuis et falsa, ueris et longibus doloribus inficit. Forsitan* but M9 R10 L28 V omit comma and B puts the comma after *ueris* and has *insicit* for penultimate word (erron.).
F reads *Voluptas denique falsa ueris doloribus inficit. Forsitan* which shows that the additions to M9 were done in stages.

p M9   R10   have paragraph mark before the word *Forsitan*
F has capital in slightly reverse indentation and rubric for the whole word *Forsitan*

q M9   R10 Be G1 L28   V   read *fugiunt, fugiamus. Nusquam* but in B, second punctuation mark is comma with lower case following which P copies.

r	M9		R10 Be G1 L28		V B P			read *,quod mouetur nusquam,* but F adds *quidem* between the first two words.
s	M9		R10 Be	L28		P		read *adest? Ne* but G1 V B omit question mark and have full stop, colon and comma respectively.
t	M9 F		R10 Be G1 L28					read *maneamus. Ethernam* but V has colon in place of full stop and *eternam* which punctuation B P copy as a comma.
u	M9		R10					have paragraph mark before the word *Caeterum* F has new paragraph reverse indentation and rubric for *Caeterum*
v	M9		Be G1 L28					read *amici? Eia* but R10 has full stop but no question mark, V has full stop but also puts question mark before *amici* and B, having put question mark as V, tries to make sense of this by omitting stop after *amici.* P follows B. F reads as M9 but spells second word *Heia*
w	M9 F		R10 Be G1 L28		V			read *Nunquid istud est ipsum* but B omits *istud* and P follows B.
x	M9 F		R10	G1 L28	V			read *bonum? Quod uniuersum implet.* B changes punctuation after *bonum* to comma and moves question mark to after *implet* and P follows B. Be has stop after *bonum* which could be comma and also has question mark after *implet.*
y	M9 F		R10 Be G1 L28		V	P		read *adhaerere nituntur. Bono* but abbreviation mark over *nitunt* in B is indistinct.
z	M9 F		R10 Be G1 L28					read *ipsius ratio ut* but V omits middle word. B P follow V.
aa	M9		R10					have paragraph mark before the word *Quid* F has paragraph in reverse indentation with *Quid* in rubric.
bb	M9 F		R10 Be G1 L28					read *Quid plura? Si* but V has abbreviation *pl'a* for middle word with no question mark or punctuation following. B then misread V as *epistola, si* which P follows.

cc M9 F   R10 Be G1   V   P   read *siquidem deus est* but L28 has
middle word abbreviated to look
like *deum* and B likewise.
Also see initial note to letter 9
concerning MS F.

6

a M9   R10 Be   L28 V   read *Solent dialectici dicere* but B P
reverse first two words and G1 has
Volent (erron.)

b M9   R10 Be G1 L28 V   read *statim altera quaestio.* but B P
have middle word *altior*

c M9   R10 Be   L28 V   read *interim elega uel tragica perago.*
but B P have second word *elegia*
and G1 has fourth word *tragedia*

d M9   R10   have paragraph mark before the
word *Vis*

e M9   R10 Be G1 L28   read *amice saturnum* but V has
question mark between these two
words, which B follows. P has
comma.

f   G1   reads *dicemus amice?* but M9 R10 Be
L28 have the usual vocative mark
"o" over *amice*. V brings this "o"
down into the printed text which B
P follow.

g M9   R10 Be G1 L28 V   P   read *non implentur paruis* but B has
implent with a line over the "*t*"
indicating *implentur*

7

a M9   R10 Be G1 L28 V   P   read *potest sapiens esse* but B has
saqiens (erron.)

b M9   R10   have paragraph mark before the
word *Quoscunque*

c M9   R10 Be G1 L28 V   read *stulte seruire deprehendetis
sapientes* but B has *seruirr
deprehenderis* (erron.)
P corrects the first of these errors
but not the second.

d	M9		R10	Be		L28	V B P	read *copulare conantur. Nam* but G1 has *nituntur*. M9 has *nituntur* crossed out with *conantur* written above. This implies that G1 was copied before the change.
e	M9		R10					have paragraph mark before the word *Haec*
f	M9			Be G1		L28	V P	read *mala mens accepta scientia, malitiam* but R10 has *semina* in place of *scientia* and B has *mentis* in place of *mens*
g	M9		R10	Be G1		L28	V	read *inquit, dici non* but B has *disci* for middle word which P follows.
h	M9							has paragraph mark before the word *Quid*
i	M9		R10	Be G1		L28		read *philosophi? Quid* but V has full stop, B has comma and P has exclamation mark.
j	M9		R10	Be				read *est O sophistae?* and G1 has *o* written above *sophistae* V omits *O* and B P follow this.

8

a						L28	V B P	read *unico. S.D.* but M9 R10 Be omit *S.D.* and G1 has *S.*
b	M9			G1		L28	V	read *Ioannes. ferto precor* but R10 omit *ferto* and Be B read as M9 but Be has question mark instead of full stop and B P have comma.
c	M9		R10	Be G1		L28	V P	read *turba confundor. Ita* but B has *confudor* as middle word.
d	M9		R10	G1		L28	V	read *philosophis. Nam saepe* but Be has no capital letter for new sentence and B P have comma only.

9

a	F		has no heading as this is the original letter sent to Bembo with letter 9 on the first page and letter 5 beginning on the bottom of that

								page. The original letter was of 3 pages. The original fold is evident. The handwriting is the same as that of M9 for these particular letters. Traces of the seal are evident and the pin marks. The address *D. Bernardo bembo iurisconsulto & equiti clarissimo.* is on what would have been the outside of the letter.
b	M9	R10	Be	G1	L28			read *Marsilius ficinus Bernardo Bembo ueneto. S.D.* but V inserts *Florentinus* after *Ficinus* and B P follow V. This insertion immediately prior to publication of the V edition may have been at the instigation of Ficino for the sake of balance and scale. F reads *Marsilius Ficinus Domino bernardo bembo equiti & iuris consulto clarissimo. S.D.* This translation follows V.
c	M9	R10	Be	G1	L28	V	P	read *nonis Septembribus in* but B has typographical error in middle word.
d	M9	R10	Be	G1	L28		P	read *intentio esse et solet* but in the middle V has *esset* which B copies (erron.). F omits the whole of the second sentence of the letter. Thus it reads *gratia. Hic* and thus the addition in M9 to read as published was added after this letter was written out.
e	M9	R10	Be	G1	L28	V	P	read *accepi expectatissimas literas* but B has middle word *exspectantissimas* (erron.)
f	M9	R10	Be	G1	L28	V		read *quo nostra illa decem sunt argumenta quae desiderat phebus dabo operam ut illi argumenta* but B P omit all words after *sunt* down to and including *illi* and F reads *quo decem illa sunt* at the beginning. M9 has the word *illa* deleted after *decem*
g	M9	R10	Be	G1	L28	V	P	read *commendatum. Sine dixero* but B has *Sine* as middle word (erron.).
h	M9	R10		G1	L28	V		read *ab heroe prosperam ualitudinem exoptatam. Cura ut ualeas. At uideo*

bembum meum neque posse neque uelle
absque delitijs suis bene ualere.
Bernarde landinus & bracciolinus tui tibi
bene ualent. Igitur bene. uale. but B
has *prospheram* and BP omit full
stop after *ualere.* Be has colon
instead of full stop. F reads *ab heroe*
felicem ualitudinem exoptatam. Tuus
landinus et bracciolinus tibi bene ualent.
Bene uale. 21 Sept 147 Unfortunately
the last number is lacking: cut off
when the MSS pages were trimmed
for binding in a book, although we
are certain this was a 7.

10

a	M9	R10 Be	L28	V	P	read *astronomo et poetae. S.D.* but G1 has *S.P.D.* instead of *S.D.* and B omits *et*
b	M9	R10 Be G1	L28	V	P	read *discipulis penitus reuelari* but B omits *penitus* (erron.)

11

a		R10 Be	L28	V		read *saepe plectroque lyraque. Alioquin* but G1 has *plectro* for second word. .M9 reads as R10 but the "A" of *Alioquin* is indeterminate upper case. B follows R10 but with comma before *Alioquin* and lower case. P follows B.
b	M9	R10 Be G1	L28	V	P	read *silent, muta sine te* but B has *mutua* for middle word (erron.).
c	M9	R10 Be G1	L28	V	P	read *Phoebus pulsat quidem* but B has *pulsas* for middle word (erron.).
d	M9	R10 Be G1				read *res delira, respondebis* but V B P after *res* have *de lyra. Respondebis* and L28 as R10 but spells middle word *delyra*

e	M9	R10 Be	L28		

read *ne deliremus*. but G1 V B P have *delyremus*

f	M9	R10	L28	

have paragraph mark before the word *Ipse* and start new line. G1 has illuminated letter. V B P indent on new line.

12

a	M9 Ve3 R10		L28	V B P

read *suo. S.D.* but Be G1 have *suo. S.*

b	M9	R10	L28	

have in the margin the words *Item Francisco Bandino* – "the same to Francisco Bandino", indicating that a copy of the letter was also sent to him.

c	M9 Ve3 R10 Be G1 L28	V	P

read *sed patiaris. Quanto* but B has *patiari* (erron.)

d	M9 Ve3 R10 Be G1 L28	

read *malis illatam non* but V B P have *illam* (erron.)

e		B P

read *passurus? Quod* but M9 Ve3 R10 Be G1 L28 V have full stop in place of question mark. B P reading is incorrect.

f	M9 Ve3 R10 Be G1 L28	V	P

read *patieris inuitus, et* but B has *inuitas* (erron.)

g	Ve3

has incorporated into it all the many additions (some of paragraph length or more) to M9 from *O miram patientiam* on, showing that M9 was indeed the working copy.

h	M9	R10 Be G1 L28

read *fatum ipsum immutabilia* but V B P omit *ipsum*
Ve3 as M9 but spelling last word as *immutabilia*

i	M9 Ve3 R10

have paragraph mark before the word *Sicut*

j	M9 Ve3 R10 Be G1 L28	V	P

read *tanquam ueteranus miles* but B has *ueteranus* (erron.)

k	Ve3

reads clearly *prospere contigisse. Prudentis* confirming the abbreviation of *con* in M9 which is somewhat difficult to discern.

l	M9	R10 Be G1	V	read *aere pluuium, et in pluuio expectare* but L28 has *impluuium* near end and B P have *pluuiam, et in pluuia* in middle (erron.)
m	M9 Ve3 R10			have paragraph mark before the word *Errant*
n	Ve3			has in the margin against the line ending *prementem* what we have named the 'Bembo' hand pointing to this passage. This we have seen in other letters actually sent to Bembo and we are convinced that it is his handiwork, showing that he took great heed of what Ficino was saying.
o	M9 Ve3 R10 Be G1 L28	V		read *possumus semper, quae semper et patimur* but B P omit middle two words and comma.
p	M9 Ve3 R10 Be G1 L28	V		read *durissima. Durissima quia* but B omits the stop and second *Durissima* and P follows B but has a comma in place of the stop.
q	M9	Be G1 L28	V		read *nouerunt cedi frangi ligarique* but B has *caedi, frandi* in middle. R10 has cedilla under "*e*" of *cedi* indicating *caedi* otherwise as M9 but with comma after first and second words. P as R10. Ve3 as M9 but with comma after *nouerunt*
r	M9 Ve3 R10			have paragraph mark before the word *Ergo*
s	M9 Ve3 R10 Be	L28 V P		read *iustitia iudice, nullum* but B has *iudise* (erron.)
t	Ve3			has paragraph mark before the word *Vale*
u	M9 Ve3 R10 Be G1 L28	V		read *alios. Ego certe quotiens quae me offendant, in* but B has *Ergo* and *offendunt* (erron.) and P follows M9 for first of these words and B for second.
v	M9 Ve3 R10 Be G1 L28	V		read *ferant. Ferto etiam* but B P have *Fert* (erron.)
w	M9 Ve3 R10 Be G1 L28	V		read *et dicere et* but B P have verb *discere*

13

a M9	R10	G1 L28	V	

read *confugiat. Quo* but Be has *confugiat: quo* and B P have *confugiat, quo*

14

a M9				

reads *Amicitia uera extrinsecis non egit officijs.* but the third word was later amended to read *externis* from which we deduce that R10 was copied from M9 (or a similar MS before this change was made) as it reads *extrinsecis* as does each of the other MSS mentioned. V reads as R10 except it has second word *ueta* and B has tried to make sense of this by following V but putting *uetus* and P follows B.

b M9	R10	L28	V	P	

read *unico. S.D.* but Be B omit *S.D.* and G1 has *S.*

c M9	R10 Be G1 L28	V	

read *respondes. Nescis* but B puts a question mark in place of the full stop. P follows B.

d M9	R10 Be G1 L28	,	

read *nostris epulis condimentum?* but V has second word *populis* (erron.) and B follows V. P follows B.

e M9	

reads *dulce? Johannes.* but either side of the word *Johannes* are four dots placed in approximately the form of a diamond, as if for quotation marks. Something similar appears in L28. The same is repeated at the end of the next sentence. G1 has a small "*o*" over the centre of the word *Johannes* indicating vocative, but this appears to be an erroneous reading. At the end of the next sentence in G1 no vocative is marked.

f M9	R10 Be G1 L28

read *responderes. Vidisti deinde quod* but V reads from second word *Vid*

		einde: quod and B tries to make sense of this with *Vide inde, quod* and P follows B.
g M9		reads *lingua manuique tua.* or rather appears to read *manuique* in the middle when *manuque* is to be expected. R10 Be L28 V B P have *manuque* but G1 has *manuique* which may indicate that G1 was copying from M9.
h M9		reads *admodum diuinaris et* but the middle word was changed to *diuinas* apparently later as R10 also has *diuinaris* amended to *diuinas* However G1 has *diuinas* amended to *diuinaris* Be L28 V B P have *diuinas*
i M9	R10	have paragraph mark at the beginning of *Johannes Marsilio. S.D.* and G1 begins new line with rubric but ends with just *S.*
j M9	R10 Be G1 L28 P	read *beniuolentiae imperfectioris foret* but V has *imperfectiori* as middle word which B follows.
k M9	R10 Be G1 L28 V P	read *silendo. Videris* but B has capital *V* but omits full stop.
l M9	R10 Be G1 L28 V	read *,qualis et est,* but B omits *et* and P follows B.
m M9	R10 Be G1 L28	read *litterarum. Si me* but V has *Sed* for second word which B follows. P follows B.
n M9	R10 Be G1 L28	read *cupis, bene uale.* but V has no comma but a capital letter for *Vale.* B follows V. P follows B.

15

a M9	R10 L28 V B P	read *manetto ciui praeclaro. S.D.* but Be G1 have only *S.* at end and B has *clui* for second word.
b M9	R10 Be G1 L28 B P	read *Sunt amice* but V has *Solent amice*

c M9   R10 Be G1 L28   V   read *confirmatam forte negauerit* but B has *fore* in middle (erron.) and P follows B.

d M9   R10 Be G1 L28   V   P   read *idem ferme nonnullis* but middle word in B looks like *serme* (erron.)

e M9   R10 Be G1 L28   read *litterarum elluonibus lurconibusque* but V has middle word *illiconibus* apparently from a misreading of M9, which error B P then copied.

f M9   R10 Be G1 L28   read *forsitan atram latini bilem*, but V omits *atram* which omission B P follow.

g M9   V B P   read *onerosissimam appellat, addiditque tristitiam* but middle word in M9 is written *appellauit* but has dots under the "*u*" indicating "delete" which is where R10 Be G1 L28 may have obtained their reading *appellauit* (by ignoring deletion mark). L28 has *additque* in place of *addiditque*

h M9   R10 Be G1 L28   B P   read *nucleus. Quid ergo?* but V has *Quod* also M9 R10 have paragraph mark before the word *Quid*

i M9   R10 Be G1 L28   read *temere et importune sectatur*. However V omits *et* and has *importunae* (erron.) and B P have *importuneque* in place of middle two words.

j M9   R10 Be G1 L28   read *uenerem impudenter admiscet*. However V has adverb *imprudenter* which B P follow (erron.).

k M9   R10 Be   L28   V   read *scientiam insciti homunculi* but B P have *inscij* as middle word (erron.).

l M9   R10   have paragraph mark before the word *Proinde*

m M9   Be G1 L28   read *merito bibit.* but V has *bibat* which B P follow. M9 is written *ebibit.* with dot under *e* to indicate omission thereof. R10 has *ebibit* which seems to indicate copying from M9 but misreading.

16

a	M9	R10 Be G1 L28			

read in *dies patiatur aduersa* but V has *patiamur* as the verb (erron.). B follows V. P follows B.

b		Be	L28	

read *iamdiu in me ipso sim expertus* but M9 has what looks like *imme* after *iamdiu* and R10 reads as Be. G1 follows Be but has *ipse* and V B P read in the middle *in me ipso sum* (erron.)

17

a	M9					

read at first *ficinus Francisco Saluiato archepiscopo pisano suppliciter se commendat.* but the words after *ficinus* were all scored out and the reading as R10 substituted:-

		R10	L28	V B P	

ficinus Francisco Cardinali Senensi. S.D. also Be has reading as R10 but with *S.* at end. G1 puts *Cardinali* and *Senensi* in reverse order. The translation follows the original version.

b	M9	R10 Be G1 L28	V	P

read *Quotiens uenerande pater* but B has typographical error in middle word.

c	M9	R10 Be G1 L28	V	P

read *ueras assidue datur* but B has typographical error in middle word.

d	M9	R10 Be G1 L28

read *Illos epistolae, Illos, qui* but V omits first two words. B follows V. P follows B. In our opinion the more correct reading would omit the second *Illos* and the translation follows this reading.

e	M9	R10 Be G1 L28

read *hic faciam nescio* but V has question mark after *faciam* which B follows. P follows B.

f	M9	R10 Be G1 L28

read *ipse duo quaedam* but V omits *duo* which B P follow. The translation follows the MS reading.

g M9   R10 Be G1 L28   read *haec interea nescio* but V has
                                            middle word *interiora* (erron.) and B
                                            has *interim*
                                            P follows B.

18

a M9   R10 Be G1 L28   read *Michaeli patritio ueneto* but V B P
                                            have *Peripatetico* as middle word.

19

a M9   R10 Be G1 L28 V P   read *sine cuius amore* but B has
                                            misspelling *euius*
b M9   R10 Be G1 L28 V   read *amicitia, tanto magis* but B has
                                            amicitia tanta magis and P follows B.
c M9   R10 Be G1 L28 V P   read *bonitas, ibi splendet* but B has
                                            ipsi as middle word (erron.).

20

a M9   L28   read *Ficinus D. Francisco Cardinali*
                                            but all other MSS omit the "*D*". as
                                            do V B P; also V B P have *S.P.D.*
                                            and Be G1 have *S*. Nevertheless at
                                            first after *Ficinus* M9 read
                                            D. Francisco Saluiati archepiscopo pisano.
                                            with no *S.D.* but these words were
                                            all scored out and the published
                                            version substituted.
b M9   R10 Be G1 L28 V P   read *Salue amice dulcissime.* but B has
                                            erroneous spelling *ducissime.*
                                            However M9 first had reading *Salue
                                            Saluiate dulcissime.* but this was
                                            scored out as above.
c M9   R10 Be G1 L28   read *praetermissum: Salue* and V B P
                                            same but V with full stop and BP
                                            with comma and then lower case
                                            salue
d M9   R10   G1   V   read *singularis humanitas potentiam*
                                            but BP omit *humanitas*

e M9	R10	G1		read *praesertim: qui* but V B have question mark (erron.) after *praesertim* but P has no punctuation here.
f M9	R10	G1	V B P	read *Solent amice dulcissime* but M9 first had *Solent ergo Francisce dulcissime* whose middle then scored out as above.
g M9	R10	G1 L28	V P	read *non feliciter uiuere,* but B has typographical error.
h M9	R10	G1 L28	V	read *ipsum arctissime seruiunt, quia liberime seruiunt. Nulla* but B has *actissime* for second word and misread, in setting, the first *seruiunt* for the second, thus leaving out the three central words. P has *arctissime* but follows B thereafter.

21

a M9	R10	G1 L28		read *quem solum gratitudo* but V omits *solum* and B follows V, P follows B.
b M9				read initially *quas hac aurora* the words *in amici nostri causa* being added by Ficino later.
c M9	R10	G1 L28	V P	read *bene fecisse. Quicquid* but B has *fecisset* (erron.)
d M9				read initially *saltem me in* but Ficino obliterated *me* and substituted *nostrum hunc*
e M9				read initially *Sed mei obliuiscantur* but Ficino eradicated the word *mei* and substituted *illius*
f M9				read initially *obliuio. Ego autem obliuisci meorum neque possum neque debeo neque uolo. Compertum* but Ficino eradicated the word *Ego* and the word *meorum* and substituted the words *ille* and *suorum* respectively and also added the word *nequit* after *autem* and obliterated the words that follow *suorum* down to the full stop.
g M9				read initially *fuisse seculis cognitum.* but

the word *seculis* was afterwards obliterated.

h	M9	R10	G1		B P	read *egregij gregi non* but L28 has middle word *greci* (erron.) and V has *graeci* which points to V copying L28.
i	M9					read initially *locum. Natura obruuntur nimio* but *Caligant* was substituted for the words *Natura obruuntur* and for this reading of *Natura* with *obruuntur* we are indebted to Dr. Gentile's thesis *(Un Codice . . . see* p. 161). Since this alteration appears to have been made for reasons of style, the translators have followed the final version of M9.
j	M9					read initially *non quia maximus sim, sed quia minimus, patriae sum ignotus* but *tam* was added after *non* and *sim* was amended to *sit* and *ille noster, quam* replaced *sed* and *censeatur* was added after *minimus* and *sum* was amended to *est*
k	M9	R10	G1 L28	V		has *et ille et nos* added which other MSS & V follow but B adds *nobis* after *ille*
l	M9	R10	G1 L28	V		read *minimus quisquis ab* but B has *quisuis* for middle word (erron.). P follows B.
m	M9	R10				have paragraph mark before the word *Nihil*
n	M9	R10	G1 L28	V		read *sit deus, deus pretium* but B omits second *deus* and P follows B (erron.).
o	M9	R10	G1 L28	V	P	read *nos libere uendiderimus* but middle word in B is unclear.

The translation of the first part of the body of this letter as published would be:

Please accept, Giovanni, copies of two letters which I thought out at dawn this morning in the cause of our friend[b] and gave today to those priests whom you know. I do not know the fate of these letters, and that indeed is not my concern, but I wish at least I knew their Muse. I

am not mercenary. I know that the
reward of being mercenary is to
receive the fruits thereof; but the
end of a liberal art is to have done
the work well.[c]
Whatever happens, at least I will
remember our friend.[d] Perhaps you
will say that it is better to seek to
be forgotten than remembered, and
to be hidden well than viewed
badly. Let others forget him,[e] if
forgetting is what they want, but he
is unable to forget his own.[f] We
know very well that no great man
was ever recognised[g] by his own.
What is remarkable about that?
Outstanding men do not suit the
crowd.[h] Opposites are not loved by
opposites. Envy takes the place of
reverence. Weak eyes are dazzled[i]
by too much splendour. Those who
are filled with small things cannot
receive the great.
But you may perhaps grieve with
me over one thing, my Giovanni,
that our friend is overlooked by his
country, not perhaps because he is
so very great[j] but because he is
considered so little. Let us not
grieve, my friend, provided that both
he and we please Him,[k] who sees
the smallest as He sees the greatest,
and comprehends the greatest as He
does the least.

22

a   M9

reads *principibus conuersarij* but
conuersarij is crossed out and *uiuere*
substituted. This reading i.e.
principibus uiuere G1 L28 follow, but
R10 reads *uiuere conuersarique* and V
has *uiuere: conuersari* and B P have
uiuere et conuersari

	M9	R10	Be	G1	L28	V	B	P	
									The translation follows the final version in M9.
b					L28	V	B	P	read *unico. S.D.* but M9 R10 omit *S.D.* and G1 has just *S.* at end.
c	M9								reads *multis assere* with abbreviation mark over last "*e*" which must be taken to read *asserere* which R10 G1 L28 have but V reads *asserre* which B has copied as *afferre* and P follows B.
d	M9								read at first *cum principibus conuersari.* but this was amended to read *uitam cum principibus agere.* R10 G1 L28 V B P have this latter reading.
e	M9	R10		G1	L28				read *Nempe inueniendae ueritatis* but V has middle word *inueniendo* which B and P follow.
f	M9	R10	Be	G1	L28				read *unquam neque principibus* but V has middle word *ne* which B interprets as *nec* and P follows B.
g	M9	R10	Be	G1	L28				read *sed phidoloxum et* but V B P have middle word *phidolosum* and it seems the word *philodolum* was intended, a latinised version of the Greek φιλοδουλος
h						V			reads *tyranno dionysio uersatum* but M9 R10 Be G1 L28 B P omit *dionysio* (correct reading). M9 has this word crossed out which seems to indicate V was copying M9.
i		R10						P	read *Xenocrates. Apollonius theanus. Plotinus* and M9 appears to have a spacing stop between second and third word but this has been erased. Be G1 V B have this stop.
j	M9	R10	Be		L28	V			read *homines posset philosophia docere.* but G1 has *possent* and B P have *philosophiam* (erron.)
k	M9	R10	Be	G1	L28	V		P	read *leonibus laniandum quod* but middle word unclear in B.
l	M9	R10	Be	G1	L28	V		P	read *omnia nouerant, quae* but middle word unclear in B.
m	M9	R10	Be	G1	L28	V		P	read *ne dixerim imprudenter* but middle word unclear in B.
n	M9	R10	Be	G1	L28	V		P	read *capitis discrimen adducti* but middle word unclear in B.

o	M9	R10 Be G1 L28	V		read *cuiusdam theologici causa quasi* but B has full stop after *cuiusdam* and then capital letter and then omits *causa* also P follows B but with no full stop.
p	M9	R10 Be G1 L28	V		read *quod eos dum tanquam* but B P have middle word *eosdem*
q	M9	R10 Be G1 L28	V	P	read *in crotoniensi rep.* but in B the ending of second word is unclear.
r	M9	R10 Be G1 L28			read *perdidit. Zenonem eleatem methaphysicum* but B omits full stop. V reads as M9 but has line over "*a*" in *eleatem* which B seems to copy as *Eleantem* P follows M9 but has second word *Xenonem*
s	M9	R10 Be G1 L28			read *Hierone. Sub nichocreonte similiter* but B has comma in place of full stop and third word *nichocreante* and P follows M9 but with comma. V follows M9 but with colon.
t	M9	R10 Be G1 L28	V		read *exilium. Mictam* but B omits full stop and P has comma.
u	M9				read at first *tutoque cum principibus conuersarij.* but this was changed to read *tutoque uitam apud principes agere.* and this is the reading R10 G1 L28 V B P have. This change is linked to that in the heading of this letter, and that in note d hereof. Be reads as R10 but adds *Vale.* After the word *agere* in M9 the following was written:- *At siquis rerum nostrarum nescius hic nobis obiciat nostram hanc antiquam cum medicibus consuetudinem, respondabo hos non principes proprie sed maius sanctiusque aliquid quam principes nominandos. Nam at singulares uirtutes suas ac ingentia merita digniores admodum sunt quam quaelibet hominum dignitates, et in libera ciuitate patres patriae.* These words were then lightly marked as deleted, lightly that is except for the words *cum medicibus*

and also the last six words. Both
these last mentioned were more
heavily scored out.

23

a M9	R10 Be G1 L28		read *seruo suo seruit.* however V adds question mark after *seruit.* (erron.). B follows V but omits *suo* (erron.) and P omits *suo* and question mark.
b M9	R10 Be G1 L28	B P	read *diligentissime deligendi antequam* but V has *diligendi* as middle word.
c M9	R10 Be G1	V	read *Nempe ut cum* but L28 B P omit *ut*

24

a   Le M4 — both have the title.

b M9   M4 R10 — read *Marsilius Ficinus florentinus D. Bernardo bembo patritio ueneto iuris consulto et equiti clarissimo. S.D.* but L28 V B P omit *florentinus* and Be G1 follow M9 but omit *D.*
Le has *Marsilius Ficinus D. Bernardo Bembo S.*

c M9 Le   R10 Be G1 L28   V — read *Johannem adhibui Cavalcantem. Verum* but B P have comma only.
M4 reverses the order of the middle two words.

d M9 — read initially *mecum allucinatur, iccirco* but the middle word was under-dotted and *caligare uidetur.* was added above. Both Le and M4 have this original reading. Le has on folio 4 verso this letter written out, probably by Luca Fabiani, with illuminations by Attavanti. The letter is clearly written out as a dedication. On folio 5 recto begins *De raptu Pauli* (from Book II) with superb illuminations by Attavanti, especially of Paul's conversion. The Bembo coat of arms is illuminated below letter 24. There are two instances of 'Bembo' hands in the margin of the pages that follow (see note n, Letter 12).

M4 has a somewhat similar layout to Le: on folio 36 recto letter 12, then on folio 37 recto *De raptu Pauli*.

25

a M9   R10   G1 L28   read *omnium amantissime et amatissime mi* but V repeats *amantissime* a second time in place of *amatissime* and B P omit *et amatissime* (erron.- both V & B P).

b M9   R10 Be G1 L28 V   P   read *enim saepe leuioribusque* but B has last letter of middle word inverted.

c M9   R10 Be G1 L28 V   read *Aut affectus ipsius* but B P have *effectus* for middle word.

d M9   R10 Be G1 L28 V   P   read *Aut certe auaritia* but B has middle word *carte*

e M9   R10   G1 L28 V   read *mercennarius. Qui* and Be has colon and capital *Qui* but B P have comma instead of full stop.

f M9   R10 Be   L28 V   P   read *maxime, tunc tumescit potiusquam adolescat. Ideo* but B has *tum* for second word (erron.) and a comma in place of full stop. P as M9 but with comma as B.

g M9   R10 Be G1 L28   read *celestibus aucta, sublimia* but V has *cuncta* for middle word, and also a colon as punctuation before rather than after middle word. B P follow V but with comma in place of colon. V B P reading is erroneous here.

h	M9	R10	Be	G1	L28	V			read *et fides fidibus* but B P have *fidem* for middle word (erron.).
i	M9	R10	Be	G1	L28	V			read *respondere uidentur, et cithara consonans citharae* but B P have *uidetur* for second word and *consonas* for penultimate word (erron.).
j	M9	R10	Be	G1	L28	V			read *aliquando paries uocitantibus* but B P have *parens* for middle word (erron.).
k	M9	R10		G1	L28	V			read at end *resonat echo.* B has capital for *Echo* and P follows B. Be as M9 but adds *Vale* afterwards.

26

a	M9	R10			L28				read *uolens. Nemo* but V has colon in place of full stop and lower case following. B P have comma and lower case following.
b					L28				reads *Marsilius Ficinus Reuerendo D.R. Cardinali Riario suppliciter se commendat* where *D.* is taken to signify *Domino* and *R. Raphaeli*
						V			reads *Marsilius F. Raphaeli Riario Cardinali Sancti Georgi suppliciter se commendat* and B P follow this reading, putting *Ficinus* for *F.*
	M9								reads *Marsilius Ficinus Reuerendo D.R. Cardinali Riario. S.D.* and has between *D.* and *R.* a mark which may just be a comma written with rather a flourish. R10 G1 follow the first reading of M9 as given above, and so does Be except that it has the third word *Reuerendissimo*
c	M9	R10	Be	G1	L28	V			read *,ut ita dicam,* but B P omit *ita*
d	M9	R10	Be	G1	L28	V		P	read *dicere fas est* but B has *fss*
e	M9	R10	Be	G1	L28	V		P	read *itineris dux erit ueneris* but B has *duxerit* in middle (erron.)
f	M9		Be		L28	V			read *tuum. Forte* but B P have a comma instead of full stop.
g		R10	Be	G1	L28	V	B	P	read *Hei mihi erraui.* M9 however, has exclamation mark after *mihi*
h	M9	R10	Be	G1	L28	V		P	read *maxima non utitur* but B has

i M9	R10 Be G1 L28 V P		middle word *nos* read *tradunt poetae neque* but B unclear.
j M9			after the last words in all other versions *splendore refulgent.* adds the following which was scored out (in some parts very heavily):- *Vale feliciter clementissime domine.* *uerum cur archepiscopi pisani saluiati* *mei nomen mihi dulcissimum* *praetermisi? Quia uidelicet ubi* *nominaui riarium, Saluiatum quoque* *dixisse putaui. Commendarem tibi* *magnanimum bracciolinum, si fidum* *Achatem commendationibus ullis apud* *eneam egere putarem.* *Sed ito iam feliciter epistola mea. Ugos* *alacris petito colles. Ac ne parum ornata* *proficiscaris, tanquam uiaticum ferto* *tecum Cosmi ipsius id est uiri* *ornatissimi nomen. Cosmum poetam* *saluere iubeto.* There is a mark for a complete stop after the word *nomen* near the end. The words *Cosmi* and *Cosmum* are completely inked out.

27

a M9	R10 Be G1 L28 Lo4 V		read *induta. Scit enim* but B has comma and *sic* for second word which P follows.
b M9	R10		read *pulcherimam. Scit* *quemadmodum* but B has *sic* for middle word which P follows. Be G1 L28 Lo4 V as M9 but with first word spelt more correctly *pulcherrimam*
c M9	R10 Be G1 L28 Lo4 V P		read *obfuscat, sic veritatem* but B has middle word *si*
d M9	R10 Be G1 L28 Lo4 V P		read *calumniantur, quod tanquam* but B has middle word *quad*
e	Be G1		read *ueritas, per quam* but R10

Lo4 V P have question mark after first word. M9 has question mark deleted at this point. B has question mark but typographical error in *ueritas*

f M9   R10 Be G1 L28 Lo4 V   P   read *auara sum ullo* but B has *sunt*

g M9   R10 Be G1 L28 Lo4 V   read *inuida. Passim* but B has comma and lower case "*p*". P follows B.

h M9   R10 Be G1 L28 Lo4 V   read *pleni. Aperta* but B has comma followed by lower case "*a*". P follows B.

i M9   R10 Be G1 L28 Lo4 V B   read *hic hostia mihi* but P has *ostia* which reading is followed.

j M9   Be   have *Principio* in reverse indentation marking paragraph,

   R10   G1   V B P   start new line at *Principio*
       L28 Lo4   mark paragraph with place for decorated letter.

k M9   R10 Be G1 L28 Lo4 V   read *fatear, esse non* but B omits *esse* and P copies B.

l M9   R10 Be G1 L28 Lo4 V   read *confidere. Altissima* but B has comma in place of full stop with lower case "*a*". P follows B.

m M9   R10 Be G1 L28 Lo4 V   read *quisquis tutorem eiusmodi* but B has *tutorum* which P follows (erron.).

n M9   Be   have paragraph reverse indentation before the word *Proinde* and R10 G1 L28 V have new paragraph. Lo4 has decorated letter.

o M9   R10 Be G1 L28 Lo4 V   P   read *ecclesiae bono consulere* but B has *booo* (erron.)

p M9   R10 Be G1 L28   read *Dicam ne et* but V has question mark after *ne* which B P follow. Lo4 also follows V.

q M9   Be   have paragraph·reverse indentation before the word *Quantum* and G1 L28 V B have new paragraph. Lo4 has decorated letter.

r M9   R10   G1 L28   V   P   read *seruis intrinsecis id* but B has typographical error in

					middle word and Be Lo4 have *extrinsecis* (erron.)
s	M9	R10 Be G1 L28 Lo4 V	P		read *origine; neque metu* but B has *atque* as middle word.
t	M9	R10 Be G1 L28 Lo4 V	P		read *uideatur. Venatores aucupesque* but B has *Venetores* as middle word (erron.).
u	M9	R10 Be G1 L28			read *prudentia humanitateque mirifica* but V omits the *que* and B P follow V. Lo4 also follows V.
v	M9	R10			have paragraph mark before the word *Natura*
w	M9	R10			have paragraph mark before the word *Nullus*
x	M9	R10 Be G1 L28			read *inuident omnes, his omnes et* but V B P omit *his omnes* and Lo4 follows V.
y		R10 Be L28 Lo4 V			read *contemnere parua. Parua* but B has comma in place of full stop with lower case "*p*". P follows B.
z	M9	R10			have paragraph mark before the word *Neque*
aa	M9	R10			have paragraph mark before the word *Optimum*
bb	M9	R10 Be G1 L28 Lo4 V			read *irasci nunquam. Quid* but middle word in B looks like *nunque* with comma following. P as M9 but with comma.
cc	M9	R10 Be G1 L28 Lo4 V	P		read *signum discipuli unquam* but B has *discipli*
dd	M9				has *Sit* in reverse indentation indicating paragraph. R10 has paragraph mark. G1 L28 V have indentation and Be reverse indentation. Lo4 has space for decorated letter.
ee	M9	R10 Be G1 L28 Lo4 V			read *Grauitas comitati permista.* but B has *comitate* which P copies.
ff	M9				has *Omnino* in reverse indentation indicating paragraph. R10 starts new line. L28 V B P have indentation. Be has reverse indentation. Lo4

gg M9	R10 Be G1 L28 Lo4	V		has decorated letter. read *pretiosissima quaeque munera* but B has *quaecunque* as second word. P follows B.
hh M9	R10 Be G1 L28			read *censemus, qui* but B has a stop in place of comma. Lo4 V P have no punctuation mark here.
ii M9	R10			have paragraph mark before the word *De* and G1 V have larger than usual space.
jj M9	R10 Be G1 L28 Lo4	V	P	read *posse monstraueris.* B however adds *non* between these two words (erron.).
kk M9	R10 Be L28 Lo4	V		read *liminibus tuis procul expellito.* but B has *suis* as second word (erron.). P follows B. G1 as M9 but omits *procul*
ll M9	Be			mark paragraph before the word *Domus* with reverse indentation. R10 starts new line. L28 V B P indent. Lo4 has decorated letter.
mm M9	R10 Be G1 L28 Lo4	V	P	read *sedes · Regula* but B omits spacing stop.
nn M9	R10 Be G1 L28 Lo4	V	P	read *fomentum · Praemium* but B omits spacing stop.
oo M9				has a whole sentence which has been completely obliterated. This was left in the draft page appearing later in the MS. It reads as follows:- *Ama franciscum saluiatum archepiscopum pisanum, & Jacobum bracciolinum, uiros admodum egregios amicosque uerissimos.* After this sentence in both the draft and the fair copy appears the date:- *Sexto kalendas februarias 1477. Florentiae*

28

a M9	R10 Be G1		read *pater? Esto* but V omits

			question mark. B follows V. L28 as V. P has comma and capital letter.
b M9	R10 Be G1 L28		read *Sed tantillum mihi* but V has middle word *tantulum* and B follows V. P follows B.
c	R10 Be G1 L28	V	read *dignitati: quod* but B has comma in place of colon. P follows B. The mark between these two words in M9 may be intended to indicate a question.
d M9	R10 Be G1 L28		read *ipsa veritas. Ipsius* but V B P have no new sentence at *Ipsius*
e M9			reads *eius pedisse* with *quam* written as a separate word in abbreviated form, but Ficino corrected his scribe's version by crossing out separate *quam* and spelling out *quam* in full attached to *pedisse* and R10 Be L28 V B P follow this reading. G1 has correct reading but adds another *quam* afterwards.

29

a M9	R10 Be G1 L28	V	P	read *Veritas Virum reddit* but B has *Veritatis*
b M9	R10 Be G1 L28	V		read *Francisco Soderino Iurisciuilis* but B P have *Sodorino*
c M9	R10 Be G1 L28	V	P	read *nisi Soderinum quoque* but B has *Sederinum*
d M9	R10 Be G1 L28	V		read *accessisse. Nempe* but B P have comma in place of full stop.
e M9	R10 Be G1 L28	V	P	read *saltem declaret iam* but B has *declararet*

30

a		B	reads *Marsilius Ficinus Florentinus Bernhardo Bembo Veneto, S.D.* but V P omit *Florentinus* and M9 R10 omit *florentinus* and *Veneto* while Be G1 follow M9 but omit *D*.
b M9	R10 Be G1 L28		read *quod non leuibus cum grauibus sit commertium*, but V has *animi* in place of *cum* and B has *non leuibus animis*

cum and a question mark after
commertium
P follows B but has *nam*

c M9   R10   G1 L28   V

read *temperari. Summam quoque tum*
but Be omits *quoque* and B has
Summa
P follows B.

31

a M9   R10 Be G1 L28   V   P

read *Malo meis litteris* but B has
Mala meis literis (erron.)

b   Be   L28

read *singulari.* S. and G1 has *S.P.D.*
at end. V B P have *S.D.* whereas
M9 R10 have *singulari.*

c M9   R10   G1 L28

read *amantem, amatum* but Be V
have colon and capital letter for
Amatum
BP have full stop and capital letter
for *Amatum*

d M9   R10 Be G1 L28

read *ipse bene ualeas* but V B P
omit *bene*

32

a   Bo

being the original letter, has no
title. It has all the fold-marks, the
original seal in place and the paper
covering the seal. The words
Laurentio medici uiro magnanimo.
appear on the outside for the
address proper. The outside of the
letter has the following: *1477 marsilij
ficinij Die 22 Martijs* which is the
record by the Medici chancellery of
the date of receipt. This date in new
style is 22nd March, 1478 so the
letter would have been written on
about 21st March, 1478 only just
over a month before the Pazzi
Conspiracy.
This is a remarkable instance of our
being able to ascribe an accurate

date to an undated letter.
All the changes on M9 are
incorporated in Bo showing that
M9 was indeed the working copy in
this instance.

b M9   has some mark written against the
                                         word *charitatem* which may be a
                                         note to use the phrase with
                                         charitatem as the title. The title is
                                         written in by Ficino in his own
                                         hand.

c   Bo R10 Be G1 L28   V B P   read *adeo prospicis, nostra* but
                                         abbreviation for *prospicis* in M9 is
                                         unclear.

d M9 Bo R10 Be G1 L28   V   read *non possimus. Poneremus* but B
                                         has *possumus* with a comma
                                         following. P has *possemus* with a
                                         comma following.

e M9 Bo R10 Be G1 L28   V   P   read *nos nostras pro* but B has
                                         nostrasque instead of the middle
                                         word. B is followed here.

33

a M9   R10 Be G1 L28   V   P   read *uult, qui omnia* but B has
                                         uult, quia omnia (erron.)
                                         O3 which was written out by
                                         Bartolomeo della Fonte, a close
                                         friend of Sassetti, is in our
                                         opinion almost certainly copied
                                         by della Fonte from the letter
                                         actually received by Sassetti
                                         from Ficino. Thus it is of
                                         considerable importance. The
                                         fact that O3 has no heading
                                         lends weight to our opinion.
                                         Ve3 has a heading as it is a
                                         copy of the original letter
                                         written out a little while later.

b   Ve3   originally read *succedunt qui* but
                                         the words. *Soli ad uotum cuncta*
                                         succedunt are in the margin
                                         indicated as added between these
                                         two words (possibly by another
                                         hand).

c M9 Ve3 O3 R10 Be G1 L28   V   P   read *omnia quae uult, habet. Solus omnia quae uult habet, qui* but B omits *quae uult habet. Solus omnia* (erron.)

d M9 Ve3 O3 R10 Be G1 L28   V   P   read *quaecunque uel natura* but B has *uelle* as middle word (erron.).

e M9 Ve3 O3 R10 Be G1 L28   read *nolle debere. Deinde* but V B P have *deberet* as middle word (erron.).

f M9 Ve3 O3   Be G1 L28   read *cuncta fecit bona* but V B P have *facit* for verb.

g M9 Ve3 O3 R10 Be G1 L28   V   read *ut nihil sibi* but B P have *nemo* for middle word. Translation follows M9.

h M9 Ve3 O3 R10 Be G1 L28   read *redigendum. Quaeres forsitan* but V B P have *quaeris* (erron.)

i M9 Ve3   read *praesens, Gaudet enim epistola breuitate, Si* but O3 has *gaudet enim epistola brevitate* in brackets with no other punctuation before or after. This looks like a correction on the actual letter from M9.

j M9 Ve3 O3 R10 Be G1 L28   read *molem tanto tempore* but V B P omit *tanto* however translation follows M9. O3 has *tanto tempore* in commas.

k M9 Ve3   R10 Be G1 L28   V B P   read *bono posse res aliter* but O3 has *bono esse, aliter*

l M9   reads *nihil aestimat esse non bonum* with *aestimat* amended to read *existimat* and O3 has exactly this (that is *estimat* with *xi* added after the 'e') as if copying a correction on the original letter. Therefore it looks as if the amendment to M9 was made at the time of writing out the original letter. Ve3 on the other hand has *existimat* here but *estimare* for the following.

m M9   O3 R10 Be G1 L28   V   read *existimare possimus, ideoque* but B P have *possumus* for middle word.

n	M9 Ve3		R10 Be G1 L28	V		read *quantum hac tuae* but P has *hae* and B has *haec* for middle word. The translation follows P. O3 has *hac* amended very lightly to *hae* (probably contemporary).
o	M9 Ve3 O3	R10 Be G1 L28	V		P	read *continet. Viue religiosior* but B has line over "*e*" of *Viue* (erron.)

34

a	M9	R10 Be G1 L28				read *raphaeli cardinali riario* but V B P omit *cardinali*
b				V B P		read *pisano. S.D.* and G1 has *S.P.D.* All other MSS omit *S.D.*
c	M9	R10 Be G1 L28	V			read *scribit in libro de moribus aristoteles, difficilius* but B reverses *Aristoteles* and *scribit* which order P follows.
d	M9	R10 Be G1 L28	V			read *Quod quidem hac forsitan* but B has *quidam* and omits *hac* and P follows M9 but omits *hac*
e	M9	R10 Be G1 L28				read *reparanda. Propterea uir* but V has *Praeterea* which B P follow. The translation follows the MS reading.
f	M9	R10 Be G1 L28	V	P		read *si optio detur* but B has middle word *potio* (erron.)
g	M9	R10 Be G1 L28				read *mortalium sorte contingat: Vt plerique* but V has *forte contingat. utinam plerique* and B follows this but has *quod* for *utinam* and P follows B.
h		Be L28				read *At quis non ualde miretur? Si* Ficino's writing in the margin of M9 indicates this reading but R10 reads *At uero quis non* at the beginning and with no question mark. The beginning of the sentence in the body of M9 is as R10. V as Be but no question mark. B P as R10. G1 as R10 but omits *non*
i				B P		have question marks after *superauerit* and *subiecerit* but all MSS and V omit these.

j M9   R10   have paragraph mark before the
                                               word *Si* and V has small
                                               indentation.

k M9   R10 Be G1 L28 V   read *ad scelera cunctis procliuiores*. B
                                               has typographical error for *scelera*
                                               and then *cuncta* also P has *cuncta*
                                               The translation follows the MS
                                               reading.

l M9   R10 Be G1 L28 V   P   read *amicam sequimur, eique* but B
                                               has *sequitur* (erron.)

m M9   R10 Be G1 L28 V   P   read *uelut hamo capti* but B has *homo*
                                               as middle word (erron.).

n M9   R10 Be G1 L28 V   read *sicubi nudum nobis* but B has
                                               nondum as middle word which P
                                               follows.
                                               The translation follows the reading
                                               in M9 at this point and in the three
                                               following notes.

o M9   R10   G1 L28   read *ipsa etiam turpitudine* but Be
                                               omits *etiam* and V B P do as well.

p M9   R10 Be G1 L28 V   read *sed uoluptate quae* but B has
                                               uoluptas and P follows B.

q M9   R10 Be G1 L28 V   read *est, opertum hospitio* but B has
                                               middle word *operum* and moves the
                                               comma to follow rather than
                                               precede this word (erron.). P
                                               follows B.

35

a M9   R10 Be G1 L28   B P   read *meas, neuter nostrum* but V has
                                               nouiter as middle word. As the
                                               word *neuter* as written in M9 could
                                               possibly be read as *nouiter* it seems
                                               that V may have been copying M9.

b M9   R10 Be G1 L28 V   P   read *eodem illustrante semper* but B
                                               has *illustante* (erron.)

36

a M9   R10 Be G1   read *Marsilius Ficinus Florentinus
                                               Pierleono spoletino* but L28 V B P
                                               omit *Florentinus*

37

a	M9	Be G1 L28	V	P	read *quondam hinc abeunte populus hic omnis* but R10 has *hic* as second word and B has *populis* as fourth word.
b	M9	R10 Be G1 L28		B P	read *quando diuine senatus* but V has *diuinae* and M9 R10 L28 have "*o*" over *diuine* indicating vocative.

39

a	M9	R10 Be L28			read *ficinus florentinus Raphaeli Riario Sancti Georgij cardinali suppliciter se commendat.* V has this but adds *S.D.* at end (erron.). B follows V except it omits *se*. P follows V. G1 omits *florentinus* and also *Sancti Georgij*
b	M9	R10 Be G1 L28	V	P	read *silentium cadere potuisse?* but B has middle word *cedere*
c	M9	R10 Be G1 L28	V		read *consideraueris. Prodigiosus* but B has question mark after *consideraueris* and P follows B.
d	M9	R10 Be G1 L28	V		read *uides? Prodigiosus nimium agitur* but B omits *nimium* and P follows B.
e	M9	R10 Be G1	V	P	read *uel dissuere temptauerat* but B has middle word *dissueuere* and L28 has *disseruere*
f	M9	R10 Be G1 L28	V	P	read *nostrum Amalphiensem mihi* but B has *Amalphiensis*
g	M9	Be G1 L28	V		read *quem rursus ante omnes haberem* but B omits *omnes* and P follows B. R10 as M9 but with *rursum*
h	M9	R10 Be G1 L28	V	P	read *quando amalphiensem ipsa* but B has *Amalphiensis*
i	M9	R10 Be G1 L28			read *Illius tibi causam* but V omits *tibi* and B follows V. P follows B.
j	M9	R10 Be G1 L28	V		read *suis meritis commendaret. Cum* but B has middle word *meris* (erron.) and a comma before *cum* however P follows M9 but with comma.

40

a	M9		R10		L28	V B	read *quaelibet uertas in bona* but the verb in M9 was first written *ueritas* but the '*i*' was scratched out, so that the word read *uertas* however Be G1 have *ueritas* (erron.). The word in Ve3 is clearly *uertas* not even *ueritas* corrected.
b	M9						read originally *herculi, Aristei parere* but *Aristei* is crossed out and *Euristhei* added in the margin. Ve3 has the original reading.
c			R10 Be G1		L28	V B P	read *quantum proficiat uulgus,* and M9 has an abbreviation at the beginning of the second word which has been taken to read as R10. Ve3 has *proficiat* without abbreviation.
d	M9 Ve3	R10 Be G1		L28	V	P	read *corpusque tantum pertinere* but B has *totum* as middle word. M9 continued in its original reading *ualerent, in* but *ualerent* was under-dotted and *possent* added above. Ve3 has original reading.
e	M9 Ve3	R10					have paragraph mark before the word *Profecto*
f		Ve3					from first *coniungimur.* has *Coniungimur* added in the margin in a different hand, then under-dotted and then *Vbi enim est omne bonum, ibi solum reperitur omnia medicina malorum. Coniungimur* added in the margin.
g	M9 Ve3	R10 Be G1		L28	V	P	read *et nos id* but B had *hos* (erron.)
h	M9	R10					have paragraph mark before the word *Agnoscamus* but Ve3 unusually has no paragraph mark.
i		Ve3					read initially *nihil nobis quae* but middle word was crossed out and *in his* added above. This is the reading M9 has.
j	M9 Ve3	R10 Be G1		L28	V	P	read *ex quo singula* but B has *qua* (erron.)
k	M9 Ve3	R10 Be G1		L28	V		read *Profecto intelligemus quemadmodum* but B P have *intelligimus* (erron.)

l M9	read initially *bene rationabiliterque disposita, ad unam summamque bonitatem et rationem manifeste* but the two words with *ratio* as root are under-dotted and the respective words for *sapientia* are added above. Vc3 has the original reading.
m M9 Vc3 R10 Be G1 L28	read *aetherna. Intelligentia rerum* taking the stop in M9 as a spacing stop. V B P have *intelligentiam* (erron.)

41

a Vc3	has no heading, so is therefore probably the original letter. Vc3 also omits *S.D.* Vc3 contains a large number of letters etc. to Bembo. The Ficino part begins on folio 363 verso with letter 41 written out from the top of the page as if very formally. On the opposite page (folio 364 recto) letter 33 begins. On folio 365 recto letter 12 begins. This ends just over half-way down folio 367 recto when letter 40 begins, ending on folio 368 verso. These 6 pages appear to have been enclosed within a folder since they seem very clearly to be the originals to Bembo but have no fold-marks etc.
b M9	reads *Quotiens hjs temporibus* with the 'i' before the 'j' of *his* apparently scratched out. Vc3 reads *his* but with 'j' scratched out.
c M9	read initially *temporibus accipio calamum* but *accipio* is under-dotted and *summo* added above (to be read as *sumo*). Vc3 has original reading.
d M9 Vc3 Be L28	read *aurum, ut* but V has full stop and capital *V* B follows V and P follows B.
e M9 Vc3 R10 Be G1 L28	read *ueniunt, nobis* but V omits comma and B puts comma after *nobis* and P follows B.

| f M9 Vc3 | | have reverse indent for new paragraph at *Accipe*. V B P have indent at same place. |

42

a M9	G1 L28 V B P	read *imperium Caelestis* and the mark in M9 between these two words seems to indicate an exclamation mark. The other MSS mentioned and V B may be trying to copy this mark. R10 Be just have a stop at this point.
b M9	R10 Be G1 L28 V	read *admodum utrinque cognominabis.* but B has *utrunque* and P follows B.
c M9	R10 Be G1 L28	read *soluitur. Sed* but V has colon in place of full stop. B has comma and P follows B.
d	R10 G1 L28 V B P	read *noster. In* but M9 could be read as a colon but has a capital letter following. Be has colon and capital.

43

a M9	R10 Be G1 L28 P	read *quomodo, qua potissimum* but V has *q* with abbreviation which B copies as *quae*
b M9	R10 Be G1 L28	read *caeli. Prendam igitur* but R10 has *Prehendam* as middle word and V has *Predam* with abbreviation mark over *e* which B read as *Praedam* and P follows B.
c M9	R10 Be G1 V	read *oratorem. lege* but B has comma which P copies.
d M9	R10 Be G1	read *sileat, quod nunc* but V has *qd* with abbreviation mark on *d* which B reads as *quid* and P follows B.
e M9	R10 Be G1 L28	read *surriperes. Johannem* but V has colon, which B interprets as comma. P follows B.
f M9	R10	have –o– over the word *inepte* indicating an adjective in the vocative case and not an adverb.

g M9　　R10 Be G1 L28　　　　read *Age insuper progredere* but V has *nuper* as middle word (?misreading of M9) and B P have *nunc*

h M9　　R10 Be　　L28　　　　read *calame. Exprime* and V has colon, B has comma which P follows.

44

a　　M35　　　　　　has no heading. M35 has on folio 2 recto of printed copy of *De Christiana Religione* once owned by Hieronymo what appears to be the autograph letter of Ficino.

b M9　　R10　　L28　　　　read *Ficinus florentinus hieronymo* but V B P omit *florentinus* and G1 has *S.* at end in place of *S.D.* M35 has at end *pistoiens: S.p.d.*

c M9　　R10 Be　　L28　V B P　　read *Siquid minus tibi forte placuerit, caue* but G1 reverses the position of the second and third words. M35 has *placebit*

d M9　　R10 Be G1 L28　V B P　　read *diuinarum ex humani ingenij humilitate metiri.* but M35 has in the middle *ex ingenioli mei humilitate*

e M9　　R10 Be G1　　V B P　　read *dependent. Viue felix, nostri memor amantissime frater.* but L28 has *Vale* for *Viue* as does M35. M35 has at the end *4° kal nouembr. 1478 florentiae:* 29th October, 1478 Florence

45

a M9　　R10 Be　　　　V B P read *Amalphitano S.D.* but M9 R10 Be omit *S.D.* and G1 has *S.P.D.* at end and L28 has what looks to be *S.se Co.* (suppliciter se commendat?). V P read *ficinus florentinus Reuerendo* but G1 L28 omit *florentinus* and B reads as M9 but has *Reueren*

b	M9	R10 Be G1 L28					read *solent sed oculis ut ita* but V omits *oculis* and B P omit *sed oculis*
c	M9	R10 Be G1 L28	V				read *lynceis uigilantius immorentur;* but B P have *uigilantibus*
d	M9	R10 Be G1 L28	V		P		read *quam uehementer optarem* but B has *uohementer*
e	M9	R10 Be G1 L28					read *saluum fore? Hunc* but V B P do not have question mark.
f	M9	R10 Be G1 L28	V		P		read *oblitum esse mei* but B has *me* for last word.

46

a	M9	R10					read *Marsilius ficinus florentinus Laurentio,* but Be G1 L28 V B P omit *florentinus*
b	M9		L28				have the words *Item Sinibaldo filio Pini foriliuij Domini* in the margin just below the address, indicating that a copy of this letter was also sent to Sinibaldo. R10 Be omit these words and G1 V B P put these words in the address.
c	M9	R10					have paragraph mark before *Principio*
d	M9	R10 Be G1 L28	V		P		read *In Mercurium iterum, id est* but B has *item* for *iterum*
e	M9	R10 Be G1 L28	V		P		read *ut meminerit non posse* but B has *memioerit* for *meminerit*
f	M9						has a paragraph mark beginning after *nympha* and before *Caelesti* and L28 V have full stop between and a capital letter for *Caelesti* R10 G1 and Be have full stop but no capital letter following. BP have comma only.
g	M9	R10 Be G1 L28			P		read *magnificentia. Pedes* but V has a question mark (erron.) in place of full stop and B follows V.
h	M9	R10					have paragraph mark before the word *Denique*
i	M9	R10 Be G1 L28	V		P		read *beatam ages.* but B has *agas* for last word (erron.).

47

a M9	R10		read *Marsilius ficinus Georgio Antonio Vespuccio suo.* but G1 and Be add *S.* and L28 adds *S.D.* while V has *suo. Item Naldo. S.D.* and B P have *suo, Item Naldo, S.D.*
b M9			has in margin, parallel with beginning of body of letter *Item Naldo* indicating that a copy of the letter was sent to Naldo.
c M9	R10 Be G1 L28	V P	read *quoque ut eam ediscat* but B has *eum*

48

a S			being a copy of the letter Ficino actually wrote to Ivano, has no heading.
b M9	R10 L28		read *hynano Sarezanensi. S.D.* but Be G1 have *S.* at end. V has *Serezanensi* which BP follow. S has *suo* before *hynano* and then omits *Sarezanensi*
c M9	R10 Be G1 L28 V		read *Praecepta mosaica in* but B P reverse first two words.
d M9	R10 Be G1 L28 V B P		read *moraleque ius pertinent.* but S omits *ius*
e M9	R10 Be L28		read *moralem? Pythagoras igitur et* but G1 omits question mark. V omits question mark and *igitur* and B P follow V but include question mark.
f M9	R10 Be G1 L28 V B P		read *alij, dei unius cultores* but S reverses the two middle words.
g M9			reads *praesentia Christi superos* but *Christi* was added above the line, later it would seem as S omits this word *Christi*
h M9	R10 Be G1 L28 V B P		read *scribam. Transcribo tibi* but S has middle word *transmitto* and this is followed in the translation as being

more probably what Ficino actually
wrote.

i   Be   after the final word *exemplar.* has
Vale. S has *Vale. Florentia. VII
kalendas februarias.
MCCCCLXXVIIIJ*

49

a   V B P   read *oratori clarissimo S.D.* but M9
R10 omit *S.D.* and Be G1 L28 have
S.

50

a M9   R10 Be G1 L28   V   read *gaudet. Solus* but B has comma
in place of full stop and then lower
case "*s*". P follows B.

51

a M9   has title after the main address.
b M9   R10   V B   read *Marsilius Ficinus florentinus
familiaribus suis,* but L28 omits
florentinus with *s.* after *suis* also Be
after *Ficinus* has *Laurentio Medici uiro
magnanimo*
G1 as Be but continues *et Bernardo
Bembo Veneto jurisconsulto et equiti
clarissimo s.*

M9   R10   have in margin *Item Bernardo Bembo*
and then *Rursus Laurentio medici*
added above, 'the same to Bernardo
Bembo' and 'again to Lorenzo de'
Medici.' This indicates that a copy
of the letter was also sent to each of
these. L28 as M9 but with *item* in
place of *Rursus*
V has words as M9 but placed in
the address and followed by *S.D.*
B P follow V.

c M9	R10	Be	G1 L28	V	P	read *non bonus. Sed* but B has *bonum* (erron.)
d M9	R10	Be	G1 L28	V	P	read *potest quanto facilius* but B has *quando* (erron.)
e M9	R10					have paragraph mark before the word *Finge*
f M9	R10					have paragraph mark before the word *Age*
g M9	R10		G1 L28	V	P	read *animi fortitudinem. corporis* but B has *fortitudine*
h M9	R10		G1 L28	V		read *animi significet temperantiam. Pulchritudo* but B has typographical error in second word and has comma and lower case "*p*". P as M9 but with comma.
i M9	R10		G1 L28	V		read *ipsa perfundit; Atque* but B P have *perfudit*
j M9	R10					have paragraph mark before the word *Collige*
k M9	R10					have paragraph mark before the word *Agite*

Appendix Letters

A

M9   has on folio 5 recto the following fragment of dialogue written out. The beginning is missing and obviously appeared on a previous page or on previous pages now missing. There is a line written diagonally curving right through the page of writing (indicating that it was not to be published). Also every mention of the de' Medici is fairly heavily scored out.

....*accumbitis epulis. Salue ante alios ipse, salus unica patriae medices,*[1] *multosque annos solemnia haec auspiciis semper felicioribus reuoca. Medices: Quisnam adeo procax meas nunc pulsat aures? Quis tam importunus tantum conuiuium interturbat? Amicus: Cosmicus*[2] *quidam sum Laurenti. Cosmica*[3] *sacra quodammodo interpellare equidem forte possum. interturbare certe non possum. Non turbat numerum conuiuarum, qui paulo ante solus iusto deerat numero. Quem modo Cosmus ipse libens inuitauit ex alto. Quem subito misit ad uos, ut beatus suorum numerus impleretur. Excipe igitur me uultu Medices hilari precor, excipe tuum. Medices: Quid huc audes ingredi rustice? Vbi nam uestis est nuptialis? Amicus: Non sum adeo informis. Nuper me tuo in speculo uidi. Introspice igitur Laurenti*

parumper ut soles. Sub rustico palliolo hoc, nisi me fallit opinio, uestem inspicies nuptialem. Spero igitur manus huius pedesque neminem ligaturum, cuius genius in ipsis laribus tuis penes ipsos penates tuos uiuit semper uera tecum pietate ligatus. Scio neminem hunc in exteriores tenebras eiecturum, qui intimo calore flagrat, qui lucem amat interiorem.
Medices: Euge serue bone. Intra in gaudium domini tui.

[1] In his version in the *Supplementum*, Kristeller interprets the placing of an insertion mark differently and this results in the omission of the first *Medices* and putting the word *Laurentius* before the next *Medices*
[2] M9 has the word *Cosmianus* under-dotted (to indicate substitute) to read *Cosmicus* but the version in the *Supplementum* has *Cosmianus*
[3] M9 has the word *Cosmiana* under-dotted to read *Cosmica* but the version in the *Supplementum* has *Cosmiana*

B

M9   has, on folio 26 verso, the following letter, lightly scored out (implying not for publication). It follows letter 29 in M9.

Marsilius Ficinus Patribus dominisque suis plurimum uenerandis Raphaeli Cardinali Riario et francisco saluiato archepiscopo pisano suppliciter se commendat.

Orta nobis est nuper in ipso familiarium cetu[1] moralis declamatio quaedam etsi auribus delicatis inepta, tamen his forsitan apta diebus. Solent philosophi dicere, eam contrariorum esse naturam, ut in eodem simul manere non possint. Ego autem contra paulo ante perpendi. Vidi equidem nonnullos audientium dum declamarem, ineptias quidem meas aperte ridentes, ac simul propriam de qua uerba tunc agebantur, miseriam lachrimantes. Me tamen ineptum his apparuisse non penitet, dum glorior ea me miracula quae natura ipsa non facit, in coniungendis contrarijs effecisse. Verum nequis ulterius declamatorem me iudicet deridendum, declamationem eiusmodi dominis meis, hodie patribusque pijs et grauissimis recitabo. Scio insignes grauitate et pietate uiros, pia nunquam uerba risuros. Confido praeterea, quem maxime auctoritatis uiri non riserint, neminem ulterius derisurum.
Tragedie miseram etc.[2]

[1] This word should be read as *coetu*
[2] These words indicate that the body of letter 5 should follow, i.e. that a copy of letter 5 was sent with this "appendix letter" specifically to Riario and Salviati.

C

M9   has the following letter, beginning at the top of folio 27 verso. There are lines written horizontally, vertically and diagonally through the body of the letter (indicating that it was not to be published).

In M9, letter 30 follows this letter.

Non est dicenda ueritas nisi auscultanti.
Marsilius Ficinus Jacobo bracciolino. S.D.

Exhortatus suasionibus tuis braccioline magnanime ueritatem ipsam oraui nuper et exoraui, ut ad instituendum riarium cardinalem, si modo opus fuerit, Pisas accederet. Quod quidem cum uultu primum[1] hilari annuisset, uisa tamen nobis est paulo post nescio quomodo iter hoc paulo diffidentius aggredi. Nam etsi plane intelligebat cardinalis domesticos omnes esse ueritatis amicos, uerebatur tamen ne quis[2] alienus interueniret[3] uerborum eius malignus interpres.[4] Verum deinde cum meminisset Bracciolinum istic iam esse ueritatis acerrimum[5] defensorem, maxima[6] subito cum fiducia iter arripuit. Sed heus tu mi hercules, si res postulauerit, ad huiusmodi patrocinium mox Iolaum aduocato. Cosmicum scilicet strenuum palladis militem. Sed quidnam frustra diffidimus? Quasi sub amplo patroni mei saluiati tecto mea minus tuta sint omnia.[7] Inter amicos feliciter cuncta succedunt.[8] Valete felices.

[1] The word *primum* was added afterwards by Ficino, at which time presumably the word *primo* which appeared after the word *annuisset*, was deleted.

[2] The word *quis* was added by Ficino, deleting *forte* after *ne* and indicating that *quispiam* should be omitted after the word *alienus*

[3] The word *interueniat* was amended to read *interueniret*

[4] The words *uerborum eius malignus interpres.* were added, mainly in the margin, deleting the words *qui benignissima ueritatis falso maligneque nimie interpretetur.*

[5] This word should be read as *acerrimum*

[6] The *Supplementum* version omits this word.

[7] The word *omnia* was added afterwards.

[8] The words *cuncta succedunt.* are written in Ficino's hand over the deleted words *omnia cedunt.*

D

In M9   the end of letter 34 comes at the bottom of folio 30 recto. On folio 30 verso appears the following letter (which has been lightly scored out). The letter breaks off abruptly at the bottom of the page.

Marsilius Ficinus Petroguglelmo rocho archepiscopo Salernensi plurimum uenerando.

Quam inuidi est, rem laude maxima dignam nolle laudare, tam temerarij est, egregiam singularemque uirtutem uulgari quodam stilo comprehendere uelle. Ego igitur uenerande pater ne inuidus essem, Raphaelem riarium cardinalem iampridem laudare constitui. Rursus ne forte temerarius iudicarer, nolui personam mihi laudatoris assumere. Sed dignitas ipsa cardinea, quae uirum ostendit, quae Raphaelem iam omnibus comprobat eadem illum omnium quoque pastori laudet et probet. Ille siquidem adeo digne cardineam dignitatem gerit, ut sola haec digna esse uideatur, quae laudandi illius sibi prouinciam uendicet. Quam ob rem sub dignitatis huius persona scribo ad pontificem breuibus longas riarij laudes. Elegli[1] uero te prae ceteris tanquam fidum pastoris acatem,[2] ut cum faciles aditus et tempora noris, nostram illi reddas epistolam. Significes praeterea quod hic a me scriptum legit, idem ab omnibus quoque florentinis atque pisanis putet esse conscriptum. Siquidem cuncti Raphaelem nostrum quasi quoddam et morum specimen et spectaculum gratiarum ardenter amant, mirifice laudant, officiosissime colunt et uenerantur. Solent ut plurimum, mercennarij esse laudatores principum atque ministri. Huic autem tantum gratiae benignus ipse deus infudit, ut ei gratis omnes seruire parati sint, eum gratis amare. Equidem nisi scirem uobis non ...

[1] This word should be read as *Elegi*
[2] This word should be read as *achatem*

E

M9   ends Book 5 proper where letter 51 finishes at the bottom of folio 38 verso.

After letter 51, M9 has the following letter written in a hand different from any of those in the rest of the MS. The letter begins at the top of folio 39 recto.

De libertate et seruitute

Marsilius ficinus Marchioni donato ottouiratus Mercurio. S.

Quaeris amice, cur nulli seruiam. Quia non cupio dominari. Rursum quare dominari non optem. Ne perpetuo seruiam. Plerique dominationem falsam emunt seruitute perpetua. tunc grauissime seruituri, quando dominari maxime uideantur. Nos autem libertatem ueram sola temperantia sumus adepti. Magnanimi est, quae pusillanimes multi faciunt paruifacere. hic solus uiuit liber. Qui seruit, se non possidet. Qui non possidet se ipsum, nihil possidet.

Notes on Ficino's Correspondents
and other Contemporaries mentioned in this Volume

ABBREVIATIONS

The same abbreviations for references are used here as for the Notes on the Letters: see p. 93.

Girolamo Amazzi: physician, musician and member of the Academy. Ficino called him *comes noster in medicinae citharaeque studio valde iucundus* — 'our delightful companion in the study of medicine and the lyre' — and declares that they are united by a deep love, using a pun on *amati*, the Latin form of his name. He apparently helped Ficino to resolve the difficult question of whether a cause can produce contrary effects in one and the same subject (see Letter 31).

Della Torre, p. 779; Cosenza, p. 158.

Giovanni Pietro Apollinare of Cremona: professor of philosophy and mathematics at Pisa University, 1474, his predecessor being Niccolo Tignosi of Foligno; it was Lorenzo de' Medici who in 1473 instructed Oliviero Arduini, the Aristotelian philosopher, (see *Letters*, Vol. 1) to search Italy for teachers for the new university of Pisa, and Apollinare was among those chosen.

Fabroni, *Historia Academiae Pisanae*, Vol. I, p. 288 *seq.*; Della Torre, p. 744; Cosenza, p. 232.

Marco Aurelio of Venice: scholar who held public office. He was Secretary to the Venetian Senate (*Secretario Ducale*), and succeeded Giovanni Pietro Stella as Grand Chancellor of Venice. He went on an embassy to the Turks. Ficino sent him a letter in praise of philosophy and one in praise of medicine (*Opera*, pp. 757, 759; see also *Letters*, **3**, 13 and 14). Many letters from Filelfo are addressed to him. He also corresponded with Giuliano de' Medici, Bernardo Bembo, Guarino and Niccolo Sagundino.

Sup. Fic., I, p. 119; Cosenza, p. 336; *Iter Ital.*, II.

Bernardo Bembo (1433–1519): eminent Venetian statesman, diplomat and man of letters, father of the celebrated poet Cardinal Pietro Bembo. He was born on the same day and year as Ficino (see *Opera*, p. 821). He studied philosophy and jurisprudence at Padua University. He travelled on various legations for the Republic — to Henry IV of Castile in 1468, to Charles the Bold in 1471, and later to Duke Sigismund of Austria, returning to Venice in 1474. His first embassy to Florence commenced in January 1475, during which period he cultivated the friendship of the Florentine humanists, especially the circle of Lorenzo de' Medici, and was introduced to Ficino's Academy. Bernardo was re-elected for a second term of office as Ambassador to Florence in July, 1478. Letter 37 refers to the pleasure of Ficino and the Florentines at this event. This period was a critical one; the Pazzi Conspiracy had sparked off a war between Florence and the Pope, and Venice found herself torn between her allegiance to her ally Florence and her traditional loyalty to the Holy See. These were therefore difficult years for Bembo, who favoured Florence, and his relations with the Venetian Senate were not altogether harmonious. In 1481–3 Bembo was *Podesta* and Captain of Ravenna, during which time he had Dante's sepulchre there restored. In 1483 he was chosen to go on a diplomatic mission to Henry VII of England.

In 1497 whilst acting as Visdomino (protector) of the Venetian Republic at Ferrara, he succeeded in appeasing the hostility of Duke Ercole d' Este and the citizens of Ferrara and so averted a possible revolt against Venice. He thus seemed to fulfil Ficino's words about his ability to 'subdue distant nations' through his love of mankind. Ficino dedicated his fifth book of letters, the Oration in Praise of Philosophy (*Letters*, **1**, 123), and a letter on the Convivium (*Letters*, **2**, 42) to Bembo. Alessandro Braccesi celebrates in his elegies Bernardo's love for Ginevra de' Benci who was painted by Leonardo da Vinci. Bembo's devotion to Dante inspired his unsuccessful attempt to have Dante's remains removed from Ravenna to Florence.

He also possessed an impressive library with many Greek and Latin codices. His letters (unedited) are preserved in the Marciana library, Venice.

F. Pintor, 'Le due ambascerie di B. Bembo a Firenze, e le sue relazioni coi Medici' in *Studi Letterari e Linguistici a Pio Rajna*, Florence, 1911, pp. 785–813; *Sup. Fic.*, p. II, p. 386; *Diz. Biog. Ital.*, Vol. 8, pp. 103–109; Della Torre, 'La prima ambasceria di Bernardo Bembo a Firenze', in *Gior. Stor. della Lett. Ital.*, Vol XXXV, p. 269 seq.; V. Cian, 'Per Bernardo Bembo; le sue relazioni coi Medici', in *Gior. Stor. della Lett. Ital.*, Vol. XXVIII, p. 348 *seq.*

Antonio di Paolo Benivieni (1443–1502): greatest Florentine physician of the second half of the 15th century and important for his studies in pathological anatomy. He was a member of Ficino's Academy and a friend of Lorenzo and Giuliano de' Medici. He possessed an excellent library of philosophical and medical works, and was interested in astronomy and astrology. Both he and Ficino were consulted by Filippo Strozzi as to the right time and place for laying the foundation stone of the Strozzi Palace in 1481. Antonio wrote one work on astrology, *Liber de Cometa*, dedicated to Giuliano de' Medici.

Della Torre, pp. 780–3; Cosenza, pp. 512–3; *Diz. Biog. Ital.*, Vol. 8, pp. 543–5.

Jacopo Bracciolini (1441–1478): son of Poggio, the famous humanist. He was a scholar and member of Ficino's Academy and secretary to Cardinal Raffaele Riario. The Bracciolini family had been deprived of their estates because Jacopo had been implicated in the anti-Medici conspiracy of 1466 led by Dietisalvi Neroni and sentenced to internal exile. In 1478 he took part in the Pazzi Conspiracy against the Medici and was executed (see p. 84).

Jacopo's writings include an Italian translation of his father's *Historia Florentina* as well as translations of classical texts, including the 'Lives of the Two Antonines' from *Scriptores Historiae Augustae*. He also wrote (in Italian) *On the origins of the War between the English and French*, which is based on a Latin novel by Bartolomeo Fazio. An earlier letter of Ficino's in praise of history is addressed to Jacopo (see *Letters*, **1**, 107).

    Iter Ital., 1, pp. 124, 126; Cosenza, pp. 693–4; *Diz. Biog. Ital.*, Vol. 13, pp. 638–9 (full bibliography). See also A. Poliziano, *Della Congiura dei Pazzi*, ed. A. Perosa, Padova, 1958; R. Fubini, 'Ficino e i Medici all' Avvento di Lorenzo il Magnifico' in *Rinascimento*, XXIV, pp. 3–52; *Poggio Bracciolini nel VI centenario della Nascita*, Mostra di Codici e documenti, Biblioteca Medicea Laurenziana (Catalogue), ed. R. Fubini and S. Caroti, Florence, 1981.

Lorenzo Buonincontri of San Miniato (1411–1492): philosopher, astronomer and poet. He was a member of Ficino's Academy and a close friend of Lorenzo de' Medici. Ficino sought Buonincontri's advice on questions of astronomy. Buonincontri wrote many works on philosophy and astronomy, including an important commentary on Manilius' *Astronomicon* and a poem 'Atlante' in *ottava rima*. He was also a soldier of fortune, and served in the army of Costanzo Sforza.

    Della Torre, pp. 681–7; Thorndike, *History of Magic and Experimental Science*, IV, p. 405 *seq.*; Cosenza, p. 659 *seq.*

Febo Capella: Venetian humanist. For many years he was scribe or *cancellarius* to the Venetian Republic and was made Grand Chancellor in 1480. In 1463 he went on a mission to Florence. Ficino dedicated his *Quid Sit Lumen* (*Opera*, p. 717) to Capella. Febo also corresponded with Sagundino, Filelfo and Francesco Barbaro. Naldo Naldi wrote verses to him.

    Sup. Fic., I, p. 119.

Giovanni Cavalcanti (1444–1509): a son of a Florentine nobleman, he studied rhetoric under Landino and became a statesman and diplomat, going on an important mission to King Charles VIII of France in 1494. Ficino knew and loved Giovanni from the time when Giovanni was only three years old. Ficino dedicated his translations of Alcinous and Speusippus to him in 1463 (see Vol. I, letter 51). In Cavalcanti's company Ficino wrote many of his works, such as the *Platonic Theology*. Cavalcanti remained devoted to Ficino all his life. When Ficino was afflicted with a 'bitterness of spirit' (*Letters*, **3**, see p. 139), Cavalcanti advised him to write a book on love as a remedy for his illness and to 'convert the lovers of transitory beauty to the enjoyment of eternal beauty.' This work became the first version of *De Amore*, the commentary on Plato's *Symposium* which is dedicated to Cavalcanti. He should not be confused with the famous Florentine historian Giovanni Cavalcanti (1381–1451) who wrote the *Istorie Fiorentine*.

Della Torre, p. 647 *seq.* & index; *Sup. Fic.*, I, p. 118; Marcel, pp. 340–6 & index; Cosenza, pp. 951–3.

Giorgio Ciprio: physician to the Medici, especially to Cardinal Giovanni de' Medici, and a member of Ficino's Academy. He was also Ficino's doctor during a serious illness in 1480. Ficino calls him *antiquum familiae nostrae medicum* ('our old family doctor') and sent him a copy of *De Sole*. Ficino also dedicated his *Fables* to Giorgio. A celebrated Platonic banquet (*convivium*) was held in his house (*Opera*, p. 865).

Della Torre, pp. 779–80; Cosenza, p. 1582.

Antonio di Donato Cocchi: professor of canon law at Pisa University from 1473–1490. He became Vicar of Pisa Chapterhouse after the death of its titular holder, the archbishop Francesco Salviati.

Fabroni, *Historia Academiae Pisanae*, Vol. I, p. 133; Della Torre, p. 719; Cosenza, p. 1029.

Marchionne Donati: Florentine notary and member of the magistrature from 1446–1474; father of Alamanno, whom Ficino praises.

Sup. Fic., I, p. 126.

Luca Fabiani: married a daughter of Agnolo di Giusto Ficino; notary and scribe in the Florentine chancery and friend of Bartolomeo Scala. For many years he was Ficino's scribe; in two months he completed a transcription of Ficino's translation of, and commentary on, Plotinus' *Enneads*, for Lorenzo de' Medici. He also copied books for the library of King Matthias Corvinus of Hungary. He is mentioned in Ficino's will. Poems and letters were addressed to him by Poliziano and Braccesi.

Della Torre, p. 102; *Sup. Fic.*, II, p. 333; Cosenza, pp. 2017–8; Gentile, *Un Codice*, p. 87.

Sebastiano Foresi (born 1424): Florentine poet and musician, much admired by Ficino for his playing on the lyre. He addressed two poems in Italian to Lorenzo de' Medici, one a paraphrase of Virgil's *Georgics*; the other, *Il Trionfo delle Virtù*, in praise of Cosimo de' Medici. As a notary he served in the magistrature between 1456 and 1497.

Della Torre, pp. 792–3; *Sup. Fic.*, I, p. 117.

Antonio Ivani of Sarzana (1430–1482) : scholar who held public offices. He was Chancellor of Volterra, 1466–71, and Pistoia, and was present at the sack of Volterra, after which he devoted himself more to philosophy. A friend of Guarino da Verona, he was very interested in the study of classical antiquities and archaeology, and once recommended Piero Pollaiuolo, the artist, to Guarino (*Sup. Fic.*, II, p. 250). He wrote a work on the education of a prince, *De Claro Adolescente Instituendo*, and a treatise on the family, *Del Governo della Famiglia*. His *De Antichristi Nativitate* — the birth of the Antichrist — discusses the greatly feared conjunction of Saturn with Jupiter which took place in 1484. His letters, including his correspondence with Ficino, are preserved in Sarzana (*Cod. Sarzan. XXVI*).

Sup. Fic., II, p. 324; Iter Ital., pp. 144–5; P. Landucci Ruffo, 'L' Epistolario di Antonio Ivani' in *Rinascimento*, II, ser. VI, 1966, pp. 141 *seq*.

Pier Leone (Pietro Leoni) of Spoleto (d. 1492): physician and astrologer, learned in Greek and Latin. He lectured on Manilius' *Astronomicon* at Florence University (1476–8). He was twice professor of medicine at Pisa University and also lectured at Rome and Padua. He was a close friend of Lorenzo de' Medici and was the physician in attendance on Lorenzo during his last illness. After Lorenzo's death in 1492, he was accused of misdiagnosing his illness and apparently committed suicide by throwing himself down a well, although murder was also suspected.

He was a close disciple of Ficino and member of the Platonic Academy. Ficino sent him a copy of *De Vita Libri Tres* and his commentary on Plotinus. Pier Leone asked Ficino to translate the *Aphorisms* of Hippocrates; Ficino declined and they were later translated by Poliziano. He possessed a fine library of Greek and Latin texts.

L. Dorez, 'Recherches sur la bibliothèque de Pier Leoni, Médecin de Laurent de' Medicis' in *Revue des Bibliothèques*, VII (1897), pp. 80–106; *ibid.*, IV (1894), pp. 73–83. On his death—see L. Frati, 'La morte di Lorenzo de' Medici e il suicidio di Pier Leoni' in *Rinascimento*, 6, p. 333, and *Archivio Storico Italiano*, Ser. 5, Vol. 4 (1889), p. 255 *seq.*; Della Torre, pp. 785–7; Sup. Fic., I, p. 123; Cosenza, pp. 2782–3.

Angelo Manetti: son of the famous historian and scholar of Hebrew, Gianozzo. Even as a boy he could speak and write Latin, Greek and Hebrew. He possessed many manuscripts, some of which are now kept in the *Fondo Palatino* of the Vatican Library (*Vat. Pal. Lat.* 958). He lived in Naples from 1460–68. He was a friend of Lorenzo de' Medici and of Vespasiano da Bisticci.

Vespasiano, pp. 305–10; Cosenza, p. 2109.

Cosimo de' Medici (1389–1464): statesman, banker, scholar, and patron of the arts. Cosimo as a man towers above the many functions which he so ably performed. At the death of his father he was possessed of a vast fortune and wide experience both in commerce and diplomacy. Of gentle and kind manners, and immensely generous, he was also blessed with the widest vision and a spirit of philanthropy that deployed his resources with remarkable effectiveness. He was particularly generous towards artists and scholars.

From 1429 Cosimo was head of a great banking house with interests all over Europe and the Orient; from 1433 an active and devoted collector of ancient manuscripts; and from 1434, the first citizen of Florence. Inspired by Gemistos Plethon with renewed enthusiasm for the study of Plato, Cosimo determined to establish a new Platonic Academy in Florence. To lead the Academy he chose Marsilio Ficino, entrusting him in 1462 with the translation and interpretation of the Platonic dialogues. Two years later, as he lay dying, Cosimo heard Ficino read to him the words of Xenocrates, a disciple of Plato, on the consolation of death. Thus, at the age of seventy-five, died a man exemplary in private and public affairs, honoured as *Pater Patriae*.

A. Fabroni, *Magni Cosmi Medicei Vita*, Pisa, 1789; Della Torre, p. 559 *seq.* & index; C. S. Gutkind, *Cosimo de' Medici, Pater Patriae*, Oxford, 1940; Alison Brown, 'The Humanist Portrait of Cosimo de' Medici, Pater Patriae' in *Journal of the Warburg and Courtauld Institute*, 24, 1961, pp. 186–221; Marcel, pp. 255–62 & index.

Giuliano de' Medici (1453–1478) : son of Piero de' Medici and younger brother of Lorenzo by four years; murdered in the Pazzi Conspiracy. His tutor was Gentile de' Becchi. Distinguished in appearance, a keen horseman, he enjoyed hunting and jousting; after the jousts in his honour of 1475 Poliziano sang his praises in the celebrated poem *Stanze per la Giostra*. He also enjoyed painting and music, according to Poliziano, and wrote poetry in the vernacular, which he recited on occasion with much feeling (*Letters*, I, 72). Giuliano and Lorenzo were referred to as the twins Castor and Pollux on account of the harmony which prevailed between them (*Letters*, 2, 54). Although Giuliano took no part in affairs of state, he did go on minor diplomatic missions, one being to the Gonzagas of Mantua. Lorenzo tried to obtain the Cardinal's hat for Giuliano, without success. Giuliano was a member of Ficino's Academy, and Ficino dedicated the first book of his letters to him. Giuliano was patron (*governatore*) of the *Compagnia de' Magi*, a lay confraternity to which members of the Medici family belonged. One letter of Ficino's to Giuliano (*Letters*, I, 72) mentions an oration delivered by Giuliano at such a gathering which had a profound effect on those present. Giuliano's correspondence is preserved in the State archives of Florence.

Della Torre, p. 237; Poliziano, *Della Congiura dei Pazzi*, ed. A Perosa, Padova, 1958; A Rochon, *La Jeunesse de Laurent de' Medici*, Paris, 1963, pp. 26–29 *et passim*.

Lorenzo de' Medici (1449–1492): grandson of Cosimo and son of Piero. Lorenzo was one of the most versatile and talented men of his time: perhaps the finest Italian poet of the century, he was equally accomplished in philosophic and religious poetry, love poetry and comic poetry. An eminent statesman, his principles, particularly his respect for justice, arose from his love of religion and philosophy. Ficino, his boyhood tutor, he had regarded as a close friend. Their friendship appears to have been strongest at the time the letters in Book I were written.

He was only 21 when he found himself the effective ruler of Florence. He was faced with enemies both in Florence and outside. The most critical period of his rule was that of the Pazzi conspiracy (1478) in which his brother Giuliano was assassinated in Florence Cathedral and he only narrowly escaped. After the conspiracy he was opposed in war by a powerful alliance of Italian states under the leadership of the Pope, a war which his courage and statesmanship brought to a satisfactory conclusion. After this, through his statesmanship and the respect in which he was held, Italy enjoyed a period of comparative peace until his death.

From his love of knowledge and the arts Lorenzo revitalized the University of Pisa, discerned the latent talent in Michelangelo, and supported that group of artists, sculptors, poets, scholars and philosophers who were close to the heart of the Renaissance.

A. Fabroni, *Laurentii Medicis magnifici vita,* Pisa, 1784; A. Von Reumont, *Lorenzo de' Medici,* Leipzig, 1883, and London, 1876; see the edition of the letters of Lorenzo de' Medici edited by N. Rubinstein, Florence, 1977, in progress; Della Torre, pp. 737–42 & index; Marcel, p. 372 *seq.* & index; Cosenza, pp. 2272–5. See also bibliography at the end of this volume.

Lorenzo di Pierfrancesco de' Medici (1458–1503): the second cousin of Lorenzo de' Medici, referred to as Lorenzo the Younger. His fame has been assured for posterity by a letter to him from Ficino (Letter 46) linking him with Botticelli's *Primavera,* as the letter describes the figure of Venus which is thought to have inspired Botticelli's Venus in the *Primavera* (see Letter 46, Note 6). Ficino sent Lorenzo a copy of *De Vita Libri Tres* in 1489 as soon as it was published; and in his will Ficino bequeathed him a manuscript copy of the Dialogues of Plato in Greek originally presented to him by Cosimo. Giorgio Antonio Vespucci was one of Lorenzo's tutors, and his friends included Poliziano and Bartolomeo Scala. His letters are preseved in the Florentine Archives. Lorenzo was sent on a diplomatic mission to France in 1493. He deplored the tyranny of Lorenzo's successor, Piero, and subsequently gave his support to King Charles VIII of France, who finally deposed Piero.

G. Pieraccini, *La Stirpe de' Medici di Cafaggiolo,* Florence, 1924, Vol I, pp. 353 *seq*; Della Torre, p. 542. *Sup. Fic.,* II, pp. 331–2.

Piero de' Medici (1472–1503): eldest son of Lorenzo de' Medici, he succeeded his father as ruler of Florence in 1492 but was deposed by the French in 1494. He died in exile at the age of 31.

In youth Piero showed great promise, having had as his tutors some of the outstanding scholars of his time: Poliziano (from 1475); Gentile de' Becchi; and even Ficino seems to have taken considerable interest in the young man. (See

Letters, **I**, 3, 10).

However, Guicciardini, the famous Florentine historian, quotes Lorenzo as saying that the pride and arrogance of Piero would bring ruin upon his house.

Guicciardini, *Del Reggimento di Firenze* in *Opera*, II, pp. 45–6.

Naldo Naldi (*c.* 1435–1513): Professor of Poetry and Rhetoric at Florence University from 1484, and a member of Ficino's Academy. He was one of the most prolific poets of the Medici circle, and an intimate friend of Ficino who sent him the *De Christiana Religione* (see *Letters*, **2**, 57). Naldi praised Ficino in his poetry and once for a platonic symposium he rendered Ficino's *Life of Plato* into verse. He wrote religious and pastoral poetry, and love poems addressed to friends; three books of his Latin elegies were dedicated to Lorenzo de' Medici. He supervised the work of copyists preparing illuminated books for the library of King Matthias of Hungary at Buda.

    Elegiae, ed. L. Juhasz, Leipzig, 1934; *Epigrammata*, ed. A. Perosa, Budapest, 1943; *Bucolica, Carmina Varia, Volaterrais*, ed. W. L. Grant, Florence, 1974; Della Torre, pp. 503–5, 668; *Sup. Fic.*, II, p. 328; Marcel, pp. 170–2; Cosenza, pp. 2408–11.

Lotterio Neroni: Florentine humanist of noble family, exiled in 1466 after being involved in a conspiracy against Piero de' Medici. He returned to Florence but held no public office. Friend of Ficino, Platina and the poet Ugolino Verino, he compiled excerpts from Cicero's letters. Ficino wrote an important letter on the soul to him, *Anima in corpore dormit, somniat, delirat, aegrotat (Opera Omnia*, p. 926). *Sup. Fic.*, I, p. 120; Cosenza, p. 2430.

Giovanni Niccolini (1449–1504): Florentine, son of Ottone, distinguished churchman and man of letters, he became Canon of Florence Cathedral at the age of 18 and Archbishop of Amalfi at the age of 25 (1475–1484). He was created 'titular' Patriarch of Athens in 1482 and Bishop of Verdun in 1498. Niccolini was made *Referendarius* to Pope Sixtus IV (one instructed to receive briefs and requests on the Pope's behalf). As a young man Niccolini visited Ficino at Careggi in the company of his teacher, Cherubino Quarquagli, when Ficino studied his horoscope and predicted a brilliant career for him in the church (*Letters*, **I**, 12). Ficino sent Giovanni a copy of his *Theologia Platonica* with a letter emphasizing the importance of St. Augustine (*Opera*, p. 855). Niccolini also corresponded with Salviati (*Vat. Lat.* 5140) and Campano. Letters of his are preserved in the Florentine archives.

    Della Torre, pp. 72, 574; Passerini, *Genealogia e Storia della Famiglia Niccolini*, Florence, 1871, p. 40 *seq*; Cosenza, p. 2435.

Cherubino Quarquagli of San Gimignano: grammarian, musician and poet. He was one of the first members of Ficino's Academy, and for many years lived in Rome in the service of Cosimo Orsini, protonotary or Apostolic secretary. He continued to correspond with Ficino. His Latin poetry is preserved in Urbino (*Cod. Urbin.* Lat. 1193) and Florence (*Laur.* 90 sup. 2, *Ricc.* 915, etc.). He numbered among his friends Antonio Campano and Ugolino Verino. Paolo Cortesi names Cherubino in his dialogues *De Hominibus Doctis* and *De Cardinalatu.*

Della Torre, pp. 795–6; *Sup. Fic.*, I, p. 118; Cosenza, pp. 2978–9.

Raffaele Riario (Sansoni-Riario) (1461–1521): Cardinal of San Giorgio and young nephew of Girolamo Riario; he was made a Cardinal by Sixtus IV in 1477 at the age of 16 whilst still a student at Pisa University. In the following year he was summoned to Florence. Jacopo Bracciolini, one of the Pazzi conspirators, became his secretary, and Raffaele was used as a tool in the plot against the Medici. He was consequently imprisoned by the Signoria after the abortive attempt to assassinate Lorenzo in the Cathedral, and kept in confinement for six weeks for his own safety from an angry mob, and as a surety for Florentine citizens in Rome. (See p. 85). When finally permitted to return to Rome, on 12th June, 1478, he was said to be more dead than alive from the terror he had endured and still feeling as if the rope were about his neck, as he had repeatedly been threatened with hanging by the mob.

Riario became the *camerarius* (Chamberlain) of Sixtus IV, and Leo X made him Chancellor of Rome University. In 1498 he was appointed Bishop of Viterbo. In the conspiracy of Cardinal Petrucci against Pope Leo in 1521, Riario was accused of complicity, arrested and stripped of his office, but on paying a large sum of money he was pardoned and reinstated as a member of the College of Cardinals. He died shortly afterwards (July, 1521) in Naples, where he had taken up residence.

The patron and friend of humanists and one of the most long-standing members of the College of Cardinals (a member for over 40 years), he was a man of considerable wealth. The Chancery at Rome was built on his orders to the designs of Bramante, as well as a splendid hunting lodge at Bagnaia near Viterbo. The plays of Terence and Plautus were performed at his villa in Rome and he was responsible for a revival of classical drama. Ficino corresponded with Riario for many years. His friends included Pomponio Leto and Lorenzo Buonincontri, who dedicated his commentary on Manilius' *Astronomicon* to Riario.

Della Torre, pp. 93, 805: *Sup. Fic.*, I, p. 125; Reumont, *Lorenzo de' Medici*, tr. R. Harrison, pp. 324, 340–2.

Pietro Guglielmo Rocca (died 1482): Spaniard, apostolic protonotary. He was made Archbishop of Salerno in 1471. He represented the King of Naples at the Roman Curia.

Sup. Fic., I, p. 126; Gentile, *Un Codice*, p. 143.

Girolamo Rossi of Pistoia: a Dominican of the Congregation of Lecceto and member of Ficino's Academy. Ficino dedicated his *De Christiana Religione* to Girolamo, and also the twelfth book of the *Epistolae*, as well as the Venice edition of the *Epistolae*, which was probably printed at Rossi's expense.

Della Torre, pp. 769–70; *Sup. Fic.*, I, lxvii, cvi, cvii; Cosenza, p. 3096.

Francesco Salviati (died 1478): first cousin to Jacopo de' Pazzi, he was orphaned and reduced to poverty at an early age. He became a priest and sought a career in the Roman Curia with the financial assistance of the Pazzi family who wanted to further their political influence in Rome and over the Tuscan clergy. He was appointed Archbishop of Pisa by Pope Sixtus IV in October 1474 on the death of the previous incumbent Filippo de' Medici. Because this appointment was made against the wishes of Lorenzo de' Medici, the Signoria of Florence prevented Salviati from taking office until 1476. Previously Salviati had sought to obtain the archbishopric of Florence on the death of Cardinal Pietro Riario, but Lorenzo's brother-in-law, Rinaldo Orsini, had been appointed instead. As a result of grievances which Salviati bore against Lorenzo, he played a leading part in the Pazzi Conspiracy to overthrow the Medici, and was ignominiously executed in 1478 (see p. 84). Poliziano dedicated his Latin epigrams to Salviati; and Jacopo Ammanati (Cardinal of Pavia) and Antonio Campano (Apostolic Protonotary) addressed Latin epistles to him. His letters are preserved in the Florentine archives.

    Sup. Fic., I, p. 121; Cosenza, p. 3158; R. Fubini, 'Ficino e i Medici all' avvento di Lorenzo il Magnifico' in *Rinascimento*, XXIV, pp. 3–52.

Sebastiano Salvini of Castel San Niccoli: Ficino's cousin, priest and member of the Florentine college of theologians. He acted as Ficino's secretary. When Ficino was invited in 1482 to go to Hungary by King Matthias to teach Plato's philosophy, he declined the invitation and tried unsuccessfully to induce Salvini to go instead. Salvini's letters are preserved in a Vatican library manuscript (Vat. Lat. 5140).

    P. O. Kristeller, 'Sebastiano Salvini, a Florentine humanist and theologian, and a member of Marsilio Ficino's Platonic Academy' in *Didascalie*, ed. Sesto Prete, New York, 1961, pp. 205–43; Della Torre, pp. 94–104; Cosenza, p. 3164–5.

Francesco di Tommaso Sassetti (1421–1490): a wealthy Florentine merchant and patron of the arts. As an agent of the Medici he spent many years in France, where he made a collection of manuscripts which made his library one of the finest of his day. He corresponded with Ficino, who wrote his *Ricepte contro alla peste* ('Remedy against the plague') with the aid of Francesco's library. He was also a friend of Bartolomeo della Fonte with whom he shared an interest in classical inscriptions.

Francesco became general manager of the Medici bank soon after Cosimo's death. His interest in culture and patronage of artists and writers led him to neglect his business duties, and he has been held partly responsible for the general decline of the bank.

The Sassetti chapel in the church of Santa Trinita, in Florence, is decorated with frescoes painted by Domenico Ghirlandaio in 1485. Members of the Sassetti family appear in the painting together with Lorenzo and Giuliano de' Medici and Poliziano.

    Della Torre, p. 781; *Sup. Fic.*, II, pp. 175–182; Sabbadini, *Scoperte*, I, p. 139; Cosenza, p. 3204; A. De La Mare, 'The Library of Francesco Sassetti (1421–1490)' in *Cultural Aspects of the Italian Renaissance, Essays in Honour of P. O. Kristeller*, ed. C. H. Clough, Manchester, New York, 1976; De Roover,

'Francesco Sassetti and the Downfall of the Medici Banking House' in *Bulletin of the Business Historical Society*, XVII, 1943, pp. 65–80; Aby Warburg, 'Francesco Sassettis Letztwillige Verfügung' in *Gesammelte Schriften*, Leipzig, Berlin, 1932, I, 145 *seq.*

Francesco di Tommaso Soderini (1453–1524): distinguised Florentine diplomat and scholar; he was professor of jurisprudence at Pisa University, 1485–1504. At the age of 25 he was made Bishop of Volterra in 1478, and Cardinal in 1503. He travelled on numerous legations for Florence: as ambassador to Sixtus IV (1480), to Innocent VIII (1484), and to King Charles VIII in 1495. He was twice imprisoned on being implicated in plots: by Leo X in 1517 and Adrian VI in 1523.

Francesco was a devoted disciple of Ficino, as their long correspondence testifies, and a close friend of Francesco da Diacetto. Soderini successfully defended Ficino against a charge of heresy following the publication of Ficino's *De Vita Libri Tres*. In return for this favour Ficino tried to get Francesco exempted from the tax which all clerics were obliged to pay in support of Pisa University.

Della Torre, pp. 624, 720; *Sup. Fic.*, I, pp. 127–8; Fabroni, *Historia Academiae Pisanae*, Vol. I, p. 384 *seq.*; Litta, *Le Famiglie Celebri Italiane*, Tav. VII, Soderini; Cosenza, p. 3291.

Carlo Valguli of Brescia: Scholar and tutor to the sons of Tommaso Minerbetti; Secretary of Cardinal Cesare Borgia and friend of Poliziano and of Cardinal Piccolomini of Siena.

Sup. Fic., I, pp. 114–15.

Giorgio Antonio Vespucci (1435–1514): priest and Canon of Florence Cathedral, he was an early member of Ficino's Academy, and became an eminent tutor of the classics. He built up a rich library of Greek and Latin manuscripts. Ficino gave Vespucci his Latin translation of Plato to revise. He was an uncle of the navigator and explorer, Amerigo Vespucci (after whom America is named).

Bandini, *Vita e lettere di Amerigo Vespucci*, Florence, 1745; Della Torre, pp. 772–4; *Sup. Fic.*, I, pp. 111–12; Cosenza, pp. 3654–5.

Antonio Vinciguerra (1440–1502): scribe and humanist, secretary to the Venetian Senate from 1470 to 1500. He was official secretary to Bernardo Bembo during his second embassy to Florence. Antonio was present at a Platonic banquet held in the house of Bembo in 1475 at which the immortality of the soul was discussed (*Opera*, p. 157.) Ficino dedicated his *De Christiana Religione* to Antonio. He wrote satires and *Canzoniere*. Among his friends were the poets Filelfo, Merula and Landino.

A. Della Torre, *Di Antonio Vinciguerra e delle Sue Satire*, Rocca S. Casciano (1902); Della Torre, p. 820; Cosenza, p. 3691.

Bibliography

In addition to the publications listed below, the reader is also referred to the bibliography in *The Letters of Marsilio Ficino*, Vols. 1–3, to that in *The Philosophy of Marsilio Ficino* by P. O. Kristeller, German ed. 1972, p. 387, *seq.*, and to that in *Marsilio Ficino e Il Ritorno di Platone* (Studi e Documenti, I), p. 50 and Appendix III, p. 81, for a list of manuscripts.

TEXT OF WORKS BY FICINO

Ficinus, Marsilius: *Opera Omnia*, 2 vols., Basle, 1561; 2nd ed., 1576; Paris, 1641. 1576 ed. reprint in 1959, Bottega d' Erasmo, Turin.
—— *Epistolae Libri XII*, Venice, 1495; Nuremberg, 1497; Prague, 1500.
Ficino, Marsilio: *Consilio Contra la Pestilenza*, ed. E. Musacchio, Bologna, 1983. The Italian text as printed in the *Editio Princeps* of 1481.
Ficino, Marsilio: *Sopra lo amore over' Convito di Platone*, ed. G. Ottaviano, Milan, 1973. Ficino's Italian text of the *Commentarium in Convivium Platonis de Amore*, first published (in Italian) in 1544.
Kristeller, P. O. (ed.): *Supplementum Ficinianum—Marsilii Ficini Florentini opuscula inedita et dispersa*, Florence, 1937. Reprint in 1973.
—— *Studies in Renaissance Thought and Letters*, Rome, 1956, 1969; containing unpublished writings of Ficino, with additional notes on the manuscripts and printed editions of his works not included in the *Supplementum*.

TRANSLATIONS

Allen, M.: *Marsilio Ficino: The Philebus Commentary*, University of California, Los Angeles, 1975. Text and translation of Ficino's *Commentarium in Philebum Platonis de Summo Bono*.
—— *Marsilio Ficino and the Phaedran Charioteer*, University of California, Los Angeles, 1981. Text and translation of Ficino's *Commentarium in Phedrum Platonis*.
Boer, C.: *Marsilio Ficino: The Book of Life*, Irving, Texas, 1980. An English translation of Ficino's *De Vita Libri Tres*.

Figliucci, F.: *Le Divine Lettere del Gran Marsilio Ficino*, Venice, 1546, 1563. An Italian translation of the twelve books of letters.

Jayne, S. R.: 'Marsilio Ficino's Commentary on Plato's Symposium', *University of Missouri Studies* XIX, no. 1, Columbia, 1944. Text and translation of Ficino's *De Amore*.

—— *Marsilio Ficino: Commentary on Plato's Symposium on Love*, Dallas, Texas, 1985: A new translation of Ficino's *De Amore*.

Marcel, R.: *Commentaire sur le Banquet de Platon*, Paris, 1955. Text and French translation of Ficino's *De Amore*.

—— *Théologie Platonicienne de l'Immortalité des Ames*, 3 vols., Paris, 1964–70. Text and French translation of Ficino's *Theologia Platonica Sive de Immortalitate Animorum*, the third volume containing the text of *Opuscula Theologica* from the second book of letters.

SELECTED STUDIES ON FICINO, HIS SOURCES AND RELATED MATERIAL

Acton, H.: *The Pazzi Conspiracy: The plot against the Medici*, London, 1979.

Allen, M.: *The Platonism of Marsilio Ficino*, a Study of his Phaedrus Commentary, University of California, Los Angeles, 1984.

Chastel, A.: *Marsile Ficin et l'Art*, Geneva, 1954. Reprint, 1976.

—— 'Marsile Ficin. Lettres sur la Connaissance de Soi et sur l'Astrologie' in *La Table Ronde*, 2(1945), a French translation of selected letters, including letters 10, 22, 23 and 24 of Volume 2.

—— 'L'Apocalypse en 1500: La Fresque de l'Antéchrist à la Chapelle Saint-Brice d'Orvieto, in *Bibliothèque d' Humanisme et Renaissance*, XIV (1952), pp. 124–40, a French translation of Ficino's *Apologia Contra Savonarolam*.

Della Torre, A.: *Storia dell' Accademia Platonica di Firenze*, Florence, 1902. Reprint 1969. Bottega d'Erasmo, Turin.

Ficino, Marsilio: *Lessico Greco-Latino*, ed. R. Pintaudi, Rome, 1977 (Ateneo e Bizzarri).

Ficino and Renaissance Neoplatonism, ed. O. Pugliese, K. Eisenblicher, Ontario, 1987.

Marsilio Ficino e il Ritorno di Platone, Studi e documenti, Florence, 1986, 2 vols., ed. Gian Carlo Garfagnini (Istituto Nazionale di studi sul Rinascimento): papers read at an international conference on Ficino held in 1984 in Florence and Naples.

Fubini, R.: 'Ficino e i Medici all' Avvento di Lorenzo il Magnifico', *Rinascimento*, Vol. XXIV (1984).

Garin, E.: *La Cultura Filosofica del Rinascimento Italiano*, Florence, 1979.

—— *Prosatori Latini del Quattrocento*, Milan, 1952. Contains an Italian translation of Ficino's *De Sole*.

Gentile, S.: 'In Margine all' Epistola "De Divino Furore" di Marsilio Ficino', in *Rinascimento*, Vol. XXIII, 1983, pp. 33–77. A discussion of the sources of the letter on divine frenzy to Pellegrino degli Agli (*Letters*, I, 7).

—— 'Un Codice Magliabecchiano delle Epistole di Marsilio Ficino', in *Interpres*,

III, 1980, pp. 80–157. A study of the archetype manuscript M9 containing books V–VI of the *Epistolae*.

The Hymns of Orpheus, tr. T. Taylor, in *Thomas Taylor, Selected Writings*, ed. Kathleen Raine, G. M. Harper, London, 1969.

Iamblichus: *Giamblico Vita Pitagorica*, tr. L. Montenori, (Laterza), Rome-Bari, Italian translation of his Greek *Life of Pythagoras*.

Iamblichus: *Life of Pythagoras*, tr. T. Taylor, London, 1818. Reprint, 1986.

Il Lume del Sole. Marsilio Ficino Medico dell' anima, Opus Libri, Florence, 1984. A volume of essays on Ficino's medicine and astrology to commemorate the 550th anniversary of his birth. Contributors: P. Castelli, P. Ceccarelli, A. Mazzanti, C. Paolini.

John of Salisbury's Frivolities of Courtiers and Footprints of Philosophers, tr. J. B. Pike, Minneapolis, 1938, repr. New York, 1972. A partial translation of the *Policraticus, sive de nugis curialium et de vestigiis philosophorum*.

John of Salisbury: *The Statesman*, tr. J. Dickinson (Books IV, V and VI of the *Policraticus* and selections from VII and VIII comprising the 'political' sections).

Klibansky, R.: *The Continuity of the Platonic Tradition during the Middle Ages*, London, 1939. Re-issued Munich, 1981.

Kristeller, P. O.: 'Domenico Sforazzini (1686–1760) e La Sua Biografia di Marsilio Ficino' in *Interpres*, VI, 1985–86.

—— *The Philosophy of Marsilio Ficino*, Columbia University, 1943. Reprint 1964, Italian ed., Florence, 1953; German ed., Frankfurt, 1972.

—— *Renaissance Thought and its Sources*, Columbia Univ. Press. New York, 1979.

—— 'Sebastiano Salvini, a Florentine Humanist and Theologian, and a Member of Marsilio Ficino's Platonic Academy' in *Didascalie*, ed. Sesto Prete, New York, 1961, pp. 205–43.

—— 'Some Original Letters and Autograph Manuscripts of Marsilio Ficino' in *Studi di bibliografia e di Storia in Onore di Tammaro de Marinis*, Vol. III, Verona, 1964, pp. 5–33.

—— *Marsilio Ficino letterato e le glosse attribuite a lui nel codice Caetani di Dante*, Rome, 1981. (English translation: 'Marsilio Ficino as a man of letters and the glosses attributed to him in the Caetani Codex', *Renaissance Quarterly*, XXXVI, 1983; pp. 1–47).

Lorenzo de' Medici: *Lettere*, ed. N. Rubinstein (Florence, 1977–). In progress; 3 volumes printed to date.

Macrobius: *Commentary on the Dream of Scipio*, tr. W.H. Stahl, Columbia University Press, 1952.

Marcel, R.: *Marsile Ficin*, Paris, 1958.

Moore, T.: *The Planets Within: Marsilio Ficino's Astrological Psychology*, Lewisburg, (Bucknell University Press), 1982.

Novotny, F.: *The Posthumous Life of Plato*, Prague, 1977, Ch. 20, 'Marsilio Ficino. The Florentine Academy'.

Pastor, L.: *History of the Popes*, Vol. IV, 5th edition, London, 1950. See section on Sixtus IV, Lorenzo and the Pazzi Conspiracy.

Plato: *The Dialogues of Plato*, tr. Benjamin Jowett (3rd ed.).

—— *The Epistles*, tr. G. R. Morrow, Library of Liberal Arts, 1962.

Porphyry: 'Life of Pythagoras', tr. M. Hadas and M. Smith, in *Heroes and Gods*, London, 1965.

Reumont, A. von: *Lorenzo de' Medici*, Leipzig, 1883 and London, 1876.

Rochon, A.: *La Jeunesse de Laurent de Medicis* (1449–1478), Paris, 1963.

Roscoe, W.: *Life of Lorenzo de' Medici*, London, 1884.

St. Augustine of Hippo: *City of God*, tr. H. Bettenson, 1972.

Saitta, G.: *La Filosofia di Marsilio Ficino*, Messina, 1923, 3rd ed., Bologna, 1954.

Saturn and Melancholy, Studies in the history of natural philosophy, religion and art. R. Klibansky, E. Panofsky, and F. Saxl, London, 1964. Italian reprint, Turin, 1983.

Schiavone, M.: *Problemi Filosofici in Marsilio Ficino*, Milan, 1957.

Shumaker, Wayne: *The Occult Sciences in the Renaissance*, California, 1972.

Thorndike, L.: *A History of Magic and Experimental Science*, 6 vols., New York, 1923–41.

Trinkaus, C.: *In Our Image and Likeness. Humanity and Divinity in Italian Humanist Thought*, 2 vols., London, 1970.

Zanier, G.: *La Medicina Astrologica e la sua Teoria*, Rome, 1977 (Ateneo e Bizzarri).

Index

Absolute: a. goodness and wisdom, 56; a. heat and light, 55

Abundance: Virtue will completely fill us with an a. of all that is good, 67; makes men unrestrained and neglectful, 47

Achates, 37, 71

Achieve, the power to a. whatever man wishes, 26

Achilles, 48

Act, more difficult to a. well than to suffer well, 17

Acting, refrain from, 9

Adversity: 48; suffered a. perversely, 24; tested and made bright by, 18

Advice, philosophers often forget to ask for, 13

Aeneas: 37; my A., 44

Affairs, public, 53

Ages: iron a. bring us nothing but evil, 56; the worst a., which come as iron because of suffering, 56; made as golden, 56

Alchemy, transforming a. of patience, 56

Alexander of Macedon, 31, 32

Amalfi, Archbishop of: Ficino's regard for, 53; letter to, 60

Amazzi, Girolamo: 45, 161; letter to, 35

Ambrosia, 36

Amphion, 52

Anaxarchus, 32

Anger: best never to be roused to, 41; surge of, 35

Antisthenes, 31

Apollinare, Giovanni Pietro: 162; letter to, 45

Apollo, 23

Apollonius of Tyana, 31

Apostles, Cardinals as vicars of the, 39

Appetite: every a. chooses and pursues the good, 49

Archbishop: of Amalfi, 53; of Florence, 60; of Pisa, 24, 28, 48, 69; of Salerno, 71

Argus, 40

Aristippus of Cyrene, 31

Aristotelian, Apollinare the distinguished, 45

Aristotle: 11, 23, 31, 32; on melancholy, 23; A.'s book on Ethics, 48

Art, the end of a liberal a. is to have done the work well, 29

Asleep, eyes that are half, 60

Astrologers: 61; wicked men are never able to become true a., 15

Astronomy, 15

Attributes, of men, 19

Aurelio, Marco: 14, 162; letter to, 51

Authority, dictatorial, 3

Autumn, 9

Averroes: heresy of, 57; implies that mind in the many is one, 57

Beauty: follows the light of the good, 27; calls forth love more easily and powerfully than words, 66;

determined by the proportions of the body and a becoming complexion, 67; shows the harmony and splendour of justice, 67

Bees, men totally devoted to study likened to, 22

Being still and being one, 8

Bembo, Bernardo: 30, 51, 57, 162; letters to, 2, 14, 34, 44, 50, 56; a man of David, 57; an Averroist rather than a Platonist, 57; and Ficino slow to write to each other, 50; joined to us, 2; dedication of fifth book of letters to, 2; Ficino asks B. to return to Florence, 52; his captivating humanity, 52; his departure grieved people, 51; most patient of men, 56

Benivieni, Antonio: 163; letter to, 52

Best, accept whatever happens as the, 56

Bile, or melancholy, 23

Blame, 52

Body: the shadow of the soul, 67; enslaved to the, 33; form of the b. represents the form of the soul, 67; serving the, 11

Bondage, perpetual, 72

Bracciolini, Jacopo: 14, 37, 163; letter to, 70; keen defender of truth, 70

Buonincontri, Lorenzo: 163; letter to, 15

Busy, better to be b. when idleness oppresses, 13

Caesar, 52

Callisthenes, 31

Capella, Febo (Phoebus): 14, 163; letter to, 65

Capponi, Bernardo, letter to, 65

Cause, the same c. bringing about opposite effects in the same subject, 45

Causes, truest c. of things, 11

Cavalcanti, Giovanni: 14, 25, 34, 164; letters to, 6, 9, 13, 20, 24, 29, 30; as Ficino's eye, 17; bound by Neroni to himself, 58

Celestial minds, 55

Celle: 45; Monte, 14

Choler, 35

Christ, 15, 64

Christian: flock, 39; church, 39

Cicero, 31

Ciprio, Giorgio: 164; letter to, 33

Civility, dexterity indicates to us c. and courteousness, 67

Cocci, Antonio: 164; letter to, 54

Concord, 45

Conduct: no great man ought to believe his c. can be hidden, 40; moral, 33

Contemplation, 11

Contempt, avoided by knowledge, worth and integrity, 40

Contradiction, nature of a, 9

Convenience of living, 3

Convictions, do not trust your own c. in anything, 41

Cord, triple c. is difficult to break, 57

Corruption of the mind, 49

Cosmico: the poet, 37; the vigorous soldier of Pallas, 70

Council of Eight, 72

Counsellor, 41

Courteousness, dexterity indicates to us civility and, 67

Crates, 31

Croton, 32

Cupid, 37

Cyrus, King of Persia, 32

Darkness: of the lower world, 11; in which all things are hidden, 38; outer, 69

David, 57

Deformity of Vice, 67

Delight: in good things by using them well, 55; is in the will, 9

Democritus, 31

Desires, only he has all he d. who d. all he has, 47

Devotion to God, 48

Dialecticians, words the practice of, 45

Diogenes, 31

Dionysius: the tyrant of Syracuse, 31; the elder and the younger, 32

Divine: cannot be spoken or learned as other things are, 12; does not

depend upon the human but the human upon the, 59
Dominion, no d. safer and easier than that which is loving, 28
Domitian, 32
Donati, Marchionne: 164; letter to, 72
Duty of a priest, 6

Ears, delicate, 69
Easier, nothing is e. than to please Him, 29
Effects, opposite e. from same cause, 45
Enslavement, 33
Envy: allayed by generosity, liberality and greatness of action, 40; mark of, 71
Eternal unity, 8
Ethereal: god, 63; realms, 58
Ethics, Aristotle's book on, 48
Eurystheus, 54
Evil: 17, 26, 54; has no true place anywhere, 47; in the mind, 47; not in nature, 47; nature of, 49; nothing escapes the touch of, 19; nothing e. without due punishment, 19; to make use of, 18
Eye, light of the, 7

Fabiano, Luca, 164
Faith: divine f. more certain than human wisdom, 3; made sure by knowledge, 3; Ficino's book on holy, 59; more faithful than, 59; rather trust with divine f. than know with human knowledge, 3; true, 34
Fame, striking from behind, 43
Fate: 62; changed by patience, 18; more miserable than misery itself, 8; brings about the truest tragedy of mortals, 7
Fates, menaces of the, 63
Father: heavenly F. embraces everything, 39; who disregards the merciful F.'s light discovers in this same F. a fiery judge, 39
Feast: of the gods, 36; sacred, 68
Ficino, Marsilio: commended by Truth, 42; bound to no man, 72; overlooked by his country, 29;

ridiculed as absurd, 69; summary of his *Platonic Theology*, 5; summary of his *On Religion*, 4, 5; summary of his *On the Highest Good*, 5; symposium *On love*, 5; transformed into Bernardo Bembo, 57; summoned to follow Riario to Pisa, 53
Fire, inward, 69
First, whatever is f. owed to him who is, 6
Flatterers and ministers of pleasure to be banished as enemies, 42
Foresi, Sebastiano: 165; letter to, 16
Forgiveness, 57
Forms, incorporeal, 12
Fortune, overcoming, 19
Free-born, 62
Freedom: 30; attained through restraint, 72; only such a man lives in, 72
Free will, 57
Frenzy, nothing may be said or done in a, 41
Friends: in that One, 27; letter to Ficino's, 7; letter to Ficino's reverend, 3; among f. all things have a happy issue, 70
Friendship: true, 26; unity of minds in, 20

Galen, 12
Gall of opinion, 23
Gentiles, 49, 64
Gentleness, 63
God: 26, 42, 64, 71; in the likeness of, 11; Himself, 39; Himself is love, 9; Himself pleases us in things that please, 55; is the good itself, 8; is the law for love and praise, 33; the helmsman, 47; office of G. alone, 54
Gods, household, 69
Golden age, 56
Good: 25; abundance of all that is, 67; everything everywhere disposed for the, 47; does no evil, 4; itself fills the universe, 47; itself which all things seek, 8; men praise good things, 66; the remedy for all evils, 55; how to enjoy the, 18; infinite

g. bought by mere will, 30; let us place our hope in the g. itself, 4; it is the very nature of the g. to be sought after, 8; movement towards the g. can depend on no other source than the g. itself, 4; nothing g. can be without just reward, 19; nothing g. that should not be desired, 47; nothing other than, 48; the first g., namely God, 26; the g. has given them light that they may hope, 4; the g. has set them afire that they may love, 4; the g. never abandons those who love it, 4; the g. never disappoints those who hope for it, 4; the g. suffers no injustice, 4; that g. part, 26; to love the g. itself, 25; whatever has any part of the g. must clearly come home to that one absolute goodness and wisdom, 55; wisdom the light of the highest, 12

Grace: of the splendour of Virtue, 67; without God's g. nothing is worthy of praise, 59

Graces: 42; 61; embodiment of the, 71

Gravity and levity, 16

Greatness in action, 63

Hannibal, 48

Happiness: dwell in, 59; freely available, 63; is true joy, 66; perfect, 56; serene h. represented by gracious laughter, 67

Happy: the h. man, 47

Harmony: 40, 63; and proportion of Virtue, 67

Hatred softened by innocence and humanity, 40

Head alone furnished with the powers of all the senses, 40

Health of body signifies a temperate mind, 67

Heart, response of the human, 35

Heat, particles of, 55

Heaven: heights of, 58; origin of, 62; power higher than, 3; the third, 34

Heavens: in their entirety are within us, 62; the temple of God, 15; middle of the, 36; their price, 61

Hebrews, 49

Heraclitus, 31

Hercules: 49, 54; my, 71

Hero: of ours, 14; my, 13

Hiero, 32

Him: act in H. who cannot fall, 39; all things shine in H., 29; hold fast to H. who is not moved, 39; whoever is approved by H. will not be the least, 29

Homer, 49

Honey, 22, 23, 49

Honour, 63

Hope, let us place our h. in the good itself, 4

House, let your h. be a temple of God, 42

Human: affairs prosper only by the favour of men, 40; laws, 3; nature described, 62; species only united by love, 39; you are h. and always have within you some false things, 42

Humours, health consists in the tempering of, 67

Idleness, 13

Impatience: the culmination of all evils, 55; alone causes adversities to pass to the soul, 55

Indolence, 10

Infinite: 9; nature of men, 10

Inspiration: by love, 50; to write, 50

Integrity, 63

Invention shines by the light of love, 50

Iolaus, 70

Iron age made so by suffering, 56; ages bring us nothing but evil, 56

Isaiah, 7

Ivani, Antonio: 165; letters to, 5, 64

Jews, laws binding the, 64

Jove, 61

Joy: for the sake of j. everyone pursues everything, 66; of thy Lord, 69; to the full, 9; perfect j. showered upon us by Virtue, 67; perfect j. represented by gracious laughter, 67; true, 12

Joyful, be j. in truth alone, 66

Judgements stand the test of time, 41

Jupiter: 44, 53; cannot tame Cupid, 37; signifies law, 62; that is, laws divine and human, 62

Justice: administration of, 64; operation of, 19; portrayed by beauty, 67

Kindle a light in the mind, 12
Kinship, 63
Knowing, 10
Knowledge: a man without, 62; companion of k. is sorrow, 23; human k. sometimes wavers through lack of trust, 3; as the mother of his faith, 3; tree of k. indeed has bitter roots but the sweetest fruit, 23

Landino, 14
Law: divine, 2, 38; divine l. has its origin in a power higher than heaven, 3; human and divine, 3; human l.s kept in being by three means, 3; Jupiter as, 62; of the heavens, 2; natural, 64
Leone, Pier, 36, 165; letter to, 51
Letter: a l. delights in brevity, 47; this l. should speak to the people, 25
Letters: reason for, 21; three ls. which discuss patience, 56
Levity and gravity, 16
Liberality, 51, 63, 67
Licence, 49
Life: blessed, 63; eternal, 56; dedicated to action, 7; dedicated to pleasure, 7; dedicated to study, 7; of men seems to be their truest tragedy, 7; is a form of suffering, 18; under divine auspices, 63; light of, 62; three kinds of, 7
Light: Ficino's little work on, 58; of the good, 8; of the mind, 18; of Truth, 38; and heavy qualities, 44; within, 69; particles of, 55
Limbo, 64
Limitless, 10, 47
Little, dangerous to despise l. things in great matters, 40
Liveliness in the body represents wisdom and far-sightedness of mind, 67

Living, instructions for, 65
Logicians, 9
Lord and his servant are at one, 25
Love: as blind, 41; brings forth invention, 50; divine, 35, 57; extreme, 35; Ficino's l. for Naldi, 4; greater, 46; heavenly, 34; human l. full of anxious fear, 35; injured, 35; born of the Graces, 61; is good, nearest of all to the highest good, 8; is the flame of the good, 8; itself is God, 9; offspring of heavenly Venus, 36; of God, 6; of mankind alone the food by which men are won, 40; men in God, 33; moderate, 35; mutual, 35; nature of, 35; not to l. briefly, 5; where l. overflows, forgiveness abounds, 57; where speech is restricted, l. is abundant, 5
Loving: in l. all things, we shall realise beyond doubt that it is God Himself who is being loved, 55; in l. individual good things we really l. the supreme divine good itself, 55;
Luca, Marsilio's scribe, 17
Lucan, 32
Lust, 49
Lute, 16
Luxury, 39
Lynceus, 60
Lyre: 16, 35; making and playing the, 16; well-tempered, 16

Magnanimity: 63; represented by stature, 67
Malicious, interpretation of the truth, 70
Man: a m. pictured, 66; of David, 57; m.'s life in this region of the universe, 55; no great m. recognised in his own age, 29; no great m. ought to believe that his conduct can be hidden, 40; the happy, 47; the prudent, 18
Manetti, Angelo: 15, 165; letter to, 22
Mankind, Ficino's short address to, 65
Mark Antony, 48
Mars: 53, 61; cannot tame Venus, 37; signifies swiftness, 62

Master: no one is truly m. except he
be m. of the willing, 37; not
enslaved by anything but m.s of
everything, 9; one M. of all who
serves no one, 9; who does not m.
himself is m. of nothing, 72
Measure in study, 22
Medici, Ficino's friendship with the,
32
Medici, Cosimo de': 166; sacred feast
in honour of, 68
Medici, Giuliano de': 77–82, 166
Medici, Lorenzo de': 167; as Ficino's
sole father, 46; his son, 46; letter
to, 46; as speaker in a dialogue,
68–69; probable letter to, 68
Medici, Lorenzo di Pierfrancesco de',
the Younger: 63, 167; letter to, 61
Melancholy: 35; or bile, 23
Memory, hives of, 22
Men: apostolic, 39; few are fit to be
praised, 33; happiest of m. are
usually most miserable, 7; created
for great things, 10; deceived by no
one more than themselves, 41; may
be exalted but not idolized, 33; not
fully satisfied by anything limited,
10; outstanding m. do not suit the
crowd, 29; should be tested over a
long period, 33
Mercury: 45, 61; makes the lyre, 16;
as counsel and reason, knowledge
and discernment, 62; signifies
reason, 62; the M. of the Council
of Eight, 72
Messiah, 64
Michaeli, Leone, letter to, 25
Mind: captivated by the light of the,
7; choice of a man of sound, 48;
clear m. disperses darkness, 18;
clouded, 11, 38; corruption of the,
49; delight in a m. ordered by fine
language and conduct, 40; desire of
the erring, 35; evil m. on receiving
knowledge produces evil, 12; a
blend of dignity and courtesy, 41;
and the light of truth and wisdom,
12; at once humble and exalted, 41;
can attain all things, 26; has
become physical, 11; opposing
states of, 45; reflect upon divine

aspect of, 67; temper the desires of,
40; wisdom and far-sightedness of,
67
Minerva, 20, 60
Miracles, 69
Mirror, your, 69
Misery: 7; inner, 69; where to flee, 8
Moon: 36, 61; directed to Mercury,
62; fix its gaze on Venus, 62;
within you, 62; observe Jupiter, 62;
the continuous movement of mind
and body, 62
Montughi, hills of, 37
Moral: conduct, 33; law, 64
Morals, Ficino's speech on, 69
Moses, his precepts, 64
Mugello, mountains of, 20
Muse, 29, 50
Muses: 22, 23, 42; abuse of the, 23;
impart to us nothing but patience,
56
Music, divinity of, 16

Naldi, Naldo: 167; Ficino's love for,
4; letter to, 4
Nature: human, 62; as principles for
law, 3; of opposites, 69
Natural law, 64
Nephew of Ficino, 24
Nero, 31, 32
Nero, Pietro, as Ficino's eye, 17
Neroni, Lotterio: 168; letters to, 27,
58
Niccolini, Giovanni: 167; letter to, 60
Niccolini, Pietro, 54
Nicocreon, 32
Number, right n. of guests, 68
Nymph, human nature herself is a, 63

Octavian, 31
Oedipus, 40
One: at o. with the creator of all, 47;
he who pursues the, 26; the love of
that, 27; which is everything, 26
Opinion, popular, 33
Orators, 60, 66
Oratory represented by fine speaking,
67
Orpheus, 52

Orsini, Rinaldo, foster child of Jove, 61

Ovid, 32

Pace, secretary to the Archbishop of Florence, 64

Pain: carries an image of evil, 49; destroys nature, 48; flee from pleasure to escape from, 49; to endure, 48

Pallas, 70

Parents, 30

Patience: 17, 54, 56; lack of p. causes adversities, 55; letter about, 24; Muses impart to us nothing but, 56; conquers fate, 18; consists in suffering well, 17; in accord with the will of divine providence, 18; makes the unavoidable voluntary, 18; not difficult, 17; perfects the other virtues, 19; requires you to oppose nature, confound fate and raise yourself to the level of God, 54; teaches three things, 54; the transforming alchemy, 56; the virtue required for bearing evils, 56; transforms evils into good, 54; turns iron into gold, 56; uses good things well, 55; progress of people in, 54; three letters about, 56; virtue of, 56

Paul the Apostle: 7; chosen vessel of divine wisdom, 34

Peace to be sought only within, 18

Peasant dress, 69

Perception, acuteness of p. represents wisdom and far-sightedness of the mind, 67

Phaedrus, 9

Philosopher: profession of, 6; to act as he speaks, to speak as he thinks, 6

Philosophers: 15, 60, 66, 69; forget to ask for advice, 13; letter to, 10

Philosophy: 45, 49; Ficino's book on, 30; does not teach how to live with Princes, 30; teaches all things with one exception, 30

Phoebus, 16, 58, 65

Picture of Virtue, 66

Piety, 57

Pisa, 70

Plague, fear of the, 46

Plato, 12, 15, 31, 32, 41, 49, 64

Platonic mysteries, 51

Pleases: nothing anywhere p. except by its reflection of God, 55; God himself who p. us in things that please, 55

Pleasing: the p. blended with the serious, 45

Pleasure: afflicts us with suffering, 8; appears to carry an image of good, 49; bought with pain brings destruction, 49; flee from p. to escape from pain, 49; allurements of, 3; to abstain from, 48

Pliant, all that is p. endures unbroken, 19

Plotinus, 31

Poetry, the power of, represented by sweet singing, 67

Poets, 60, 66

Pomp, 39

Pompey, 52

Pope, 64, 71

Portrait of Virtue, 66

Power: casts us into bondage, 8, 72; most p. then most in servitude, 8; no desire for, 72

Praise, 33

Precepts: first p. given to the whole human race to be kept for all time, 64; pertaining to natural and moral law, 64; pertaining to rites and the administration of justice, 64

Pride, 39

Priest, duty of, 6

Priests: concerned with the sciences, 15; most serious of men, 10

Princes, truth does not dwell in the company of, 31

Principles: human and natural, 3; moral, 33

Proportion and harmony of Virtue, 67

Prosperity: 18; destined by fate, 63; perverse use of, 48; to prosper from, 49

Punishment, 42

Pythagoras: 10, 11, 32, 64; never any sign of anger in, 41

Qualities, heavy and light, 44

Quarquagli, Cherubino, 61, 168

Radiance of human nature, 63
Realms, ethereal, 58
Reason: to counsel and, 62; nor do or say anything for which Moon could not render good, 62
Reflection, ripen by, 22
Religion: handmaiden of truth, 43; Ficino's book on, 4, 43, 57; itself, 59; sustains the whole care of Truth, 43
Restraint, 63
Revelation to chosen disciples, 15
Riario, Cardinal Raffaele: 43, 168; letters to, 36, 37, 43, 48, 53, 69; Ficino's letter to the Pope about, 71; fulfils office with dignity, 71; installation as Cardinal, 70; as model of conduct and embodiment of the graces, 71; written to by Truth itself, 37–42
Rich houses full of gold and lies, 38
Ridicule of Ficino, 69
Rites, 64
Rocca, Pietro Guglielmo: 169; letter to, 71; as faithful Achates to the Pope, 71
Rome, 64
Rossi, Girolamo: 169; letter to, 59
Ruler of the Universe is good and without limit, 47

Salviati, Francesco: 37, 170; letters to, 24, 28, 48; as Ficino's patron, 28, 70
Salvini, Sebastiano, letter to, 17
Sassetti, Francesco: 170; letter to, 47
Saturn: 10, 45, 53, 61; signifies tardiness, 62
Saturnine element alleviated, 60
Saviour, sole s. of our country, 68
Sceptic philosophers, 38
Sciences, 15
Self: 61; for the sake of his own, 33; second, 58; write to my, 6
Senate, Venetian, 51
Seneca, 31
Senses: head alone furnished with the powers of all the, 40; serving the, 11; the servants inside, 39
Serenity the one way to the light, 12
Serious: blended with the pleasing, 45; priests the most s. of men, 10

Servant: 33, 39, 41; good, 69
Serve: no one serves truly who does not s. willingly, 36; freely, 28
Service: wages of, 32; willing, 28
Shine, He shines in all things, all things s. in Him, 29
Silence, persuasive, 52
Sirens, 42
Size represents liberality and nobility, 67
Slanderers to be driven away, 42
Slave to popular opinion, 33
Socrates: 11, 31, 64; silence an indication of his anger, 41;
Soderini, Francesco: 170; letter to, 44
Solitude should be an application of the mind, 14
Solomon, 7, 23, 49
Sophistry, letter to teachers of, 10
Sophists, 8, 12, 15
Soul: adversities pass through to the, 55; body the shadow of the, 67; mark of a great, 72; one common, 4; powers of the, 10
Speaking: fine s. to indicate oratory, 67
Speech restricted where love is abundant, 5
Splendour of Virtue, 67
Stars: book on the, 52; have decreed, 52; outside us, 63; within us, 63
State: general s. of everything, 52
Statius, 32
Stature: noble, 66; representing magnanimity, 67
Study, onerous occupation, 23
Stygian marsh, 23
Suffer: more difficult to act well than to s. well, 17; well, 17; willingly and unwillingly, 17; taught how to, 18; we always, 18; willingness to s. what you have to, 17
Suffering: ills with patience a man ultimately becomes good, 18; teaches us how to suffer, 18
Sun: 12, 23, 62; above the heavens, that is truth itself, 12; signifies God, 62; that invisible, 34
Sunlight, not infinite, 47
Superfluous, prefer to give things which are, 51
Sweetness: brings s. to all your years,

Sepe magna e laus q̃ breuis est. cxxx

Marsilius ficinus Bartolomeo scale oratorj.
Lege questiones christophori Landinj cama-
dulenses. In ijs libris maronis adyta pene-
trat. Ciceronis dialogos imitatur ad un-
guem. felicem uirum fabricam feliciss(ime).
Lege illos & tu. Scio mecum senties.
Vale. S3 quare T laudando christopho-
ro tam breuis es mãrsih. Quia habet nescio qd quod exprimere nequez.
Iterum uale.:~
Qui fauet bonis sibi fauet. cxxxij.

Marsilius ficinus Laurentio medicj Viro
magnanimo. Paps tibi. Si paci, docto
& bono sacerdoti fauebis, fauebis &
mihi. Cum in uirj boni & amici agit
res, res agitur nostra: Vale.
Que sit petitio et comedatio Justa. cxxxiij.

Marsilius ficinus Laurentio medicj Viro
magnanimo. Multi ca(l)te digniora se
petunt. Gregorius epiphanius lege dignio
e ijs q postulat. et si nobis amicissimus e,
tñ cius ueritatem magis q̃ pp amicitia
eu. tibi comedo. Nã pp utitutez ert amicus.:~

hec etç manus
scribe... ...
...ist q̃ nep̃ ...
...ua. etiam